NIGHTS IN TOWN

BY
THOMAS BURKE

Copyright © 2013 Read Books Ltd.
This book is copyright and may not be
reproduced or copied in any way without
the express permission of the publisher in writing

British Library Cataloguing-in-Publication Data
A catalogue record for this book is available from the
British Library

Thomas Burke

Thomas Burke was born in Clapham, London in 1886. His father died when he was very young, and at the age of ten he was removed to a home for middle-class boys who were "respectably descended but without adequate means to their support." Burke published his first piece of writing – a short story entitled 'The Bellamy Diamonds' – in 1901, when he was just fifteen. However, proper recognition came in 1916, with the publication of *Limehouse Nights,* a collection of melodramatic short stories set amongst the immigrant population of London's Chinatown. *Limehouse Nights* was serialized in three British periodicals, *The English Review, Colour* and *The New Witness,* and received positive attention from reviewers and a number of authors, including H. G. Wells. It also sparked something of a controversy, however, and was initially banned by libraries due to the scandalous interracial relationships it portrayed between Chinese men and white women.

It was these portrayals of London's Chinatown that Burke is best-remembered for. However, there is some degree of confusion over how much of Burke's writing was based in fact; as literary critic Anne Witchard states, most of what we know about Burke's life is based on works that "purport to be autobiographical, yet contain far more invention than truth." Whatever the truth, there is no doubt that, in his day, Burke was regarded as the foremost chronicler of London's Chinatown at the turn-of-the-century. Burke told newspaper journalists that he had "sat at the feet of Chinese philosophers who kept opium dens to learn from the lips that could frame only broken English, the secrets, good and evil, of the mysterious East," and these journalists almost uniformly took him at his word.

Burke continued to use descriptions of urban London life as a focus of his writing throughout his life. Off the back of *Limehouse Nights,* Burke published the thematically similar *Twinkletoes* in 1918, and *More Limehouse Nights* in 1921. However, he was a prolific author who tried his hand at a number of different genres. He semi-regularly published essays on the London environment, including pieces such as 'The Real East End' and 'London in My Times', and during the thirties even tried his hand at horror fiction. Indeed, in 1949, shortly after his death, Burke's short story 'The Hands of Ottermole' was voted the best mystery of all time by critics. Burke also influenced the burgeoning film industry in Hollywood; D W Griffith, for example, used the short story 'The Chink and the Child' from *Limehouse Nights* (1917) as basis for his silent movie, *Broken Blossoms* (1919), and Charlie Chaplin derived 'A Dog's Life' (1918) from the same book.

CITY DUSK

The day dies in a wrath of cloud,
  Flecking her roofs with pallid rain,
And dies its music, harsh and loud,
  Struck from the tiresome strings of pain

Her highways leap to festal bloom,
  And swallow-swift the traffic skims
O'er sudden shoals of light and gloom,
  Made lovelier where the distance dims.

Robed by her tiring-maid, the dusk,
  The town lies in a silvered bower,
As, from a miserable husk,
  The lily robes herself with flower.

And all her tangled streets are gay,
  And all her rudenesses are gone;
For, howso pitiless the day,
  The evening brings delight alone.

TO

MY MOTHER

WHO STILL ENJOYS A NIGHT IN TOWN

CONTENTS

	PAGE
NOCTURNAL	11
AN ENTERTAINMENT NIGHT (*Round the Halls*)	27
A CHINESE NIGHT (*Limehouse*)	59
A DOMESTIC NIGHT (*Clapham Common*)	75
A LONELY NIGHT (*Kingsland Road*)	85
A MUSICAL NIGHT (*The Opera, the Promenades*)	99
A JEWISH NIGHT (*Whitechapel*)	115
A HAPPY NIGHT (*Surbiton and Battersea*)	125
A WORKER'S NIGHT (*The Isle of Dogs*)	143
A CHARITABLE NIGHT (*East, West, North, South*)	167
A FRENCH NIGHT (*Old Compton Street*)	185
AN ITALIAN NIGHT (*Clerkenwell*)	197
A BASHER'S NIGHT (*Hoxton*)	209
A DOWN-STREAM NIGHT (*Blackwall*)	219

CONTENTS

AN ART NIGHT (*Chelsea*)	227
A RUSSIAN NIGHT (*Stepney*)	237
A SCANDINAVIAN NIGHT (*Shadwell*)	251
A SUNDAY NIGHT (*Anywhere*)	263
AT RANDOM	273

NOCTURNAL

EVENING

*From the Circus to The Square
There's an avenue of light;
Golden lamps are everywhere
From the Circus to The Square;
And the rose-winged hours there
Pass like lovely birds in flight.
From The Circus to The Square
There's an avenue of light.*

*London yields herself to men
With the dying of the day.
Let the twilight come, and then
London yields herself to men.
Lords of wealth or slaves of pen,
We, her lovers, all will say:
London yields herself to men
With the dying of the day.*

NIGHTS IN TOWN

NOCTURNAL

FOR the few who have an eye for the beauty of townscapes, London by night is the loveliest thing in the world. Only in the London night may the connoisseur find so many vistas of sudden beauty, because London was never made: she has "growed." Paris affords no townscapes: everything there is too perfectly arranged; its artificiality is at once apparent. In London alone he finds those fantastic groupings, those monstrous masses of light and shade and substance.

Take London from whatever point you will and she will satisfy. For the rustic the fields of corn, the craggy mountain, the blossomy lane, or the rush of water through the greenwood. But for your good Cockney the shoals of gloom, the dusky tracery of chimney-stack and gaswork, the torn waste of tiles, and the subtle tones of dawn and dark in lurking court and alley. Was there ever a lovelier piece of colour than Cannon Street Station at night? Entering by train, you see it as a huge vault of lilac shadow, pierced by innumerable pallid arclights. The roof flings itself against the sky, a mountain of glass and interlacing girders, and about it play a hundred indefinite and ever-changing tones. Each platform seems a lane through a dim forest, where the trees are of iron and steel and the leaves are sullen windows. Or where shall you find a sweeter pastoral than that field of lights that thrills the midnight sojourner in lower Piccadilly? Or where a more rapturous river-piece than that to be glimpsed from Hungerford footbridge as the Embankment lights and stones surge east and west towards Blackfriars and Chelsea? Or where a panorama like those that sweep before you from Highgate Archway or the Islington Angel?

But your good Cockney finds his joy not merely in the opulent masses of gloom and glare. For him London holds infinite delicacies. There is a short street in Walworth Road—East Street—which is as perfect as any nightscape ever conceived by any artist. At day or dark it is incomparably subtle. By day it is a lane of crazy meat and vegetable stalls and tumbling houses, whose colours chime softly with their background. By night it is a dainty riot of flame and tousled stone, the gentle dusk of the near distance deepening imperceptibly to purple, and finally to haunting chaos. And—it is a beautiful thought—there are thousands and thousands of streets in London where similar ecstasy awaits the evening wanderer. There is Edgware Road, with its clamorous by-streets, alluring at all times, but strangely so at twilight. To dash down the great road on a motor-'bus is to take a joy-ride through a fairyland of common things newly revealed, and to look back from Dollis Hill is to look back, not on Kilburn or Paddington or Marylebone, but on the Field of the Cloth of Gold.

Moreover, London wears always new beauties for the faithful—new aspects, sudden revelations. What was beautiful yesterday is gone, and a new splendour is presented. Building operations are begun here, house-breaking is in progress there, the gaunt scaffolding making its own beauty against the night sky. Always, throughout the seasons, her townscapes are there to cheer, to entrance, to satisfy. At dawn or noon or dusk she stands superb; but perhaps most superb when the day is done, and her lights, the amazing whites and yellows and golds, blossom on every hand in their tangled garden, and her lovers cluster thicker and thicker to worship at her shrine and spend a night in town.

.   .   .   .   .

Nights in town! If you are a good Cockney that phrase will sting your blood and set your heart racing back to—well, to those nights in town, gay or sad, glorious or desperate, but ever sweet to linger upon. There is no night in all the world so rich in delicate delights as the London night. You cannot have a bad night in London unless you are a bad Cockney—or a tourist; for the difference between the London night and the continental night is just the difference between making a cult of pleasure and a passion of it. The Paris night, the Berlin night, the Viennese night—how dreary and clangy and obvious! But the London night is spontaneous, always expressive of your mood. Your gaieties, your little escapades are never ready-made here. You must go out for them and stumble upon them, wondrously, in dark places, being sure that whatever you may want London will give you. She asks nothing; she gives everything. You need bring nothing but love. Only to very few of us is she the stony-hearted stepmother. We, who are all her lovers, active or passive, know that she loves each one of us. The passive lover loves her as he loves his mother, not knowing his love, not knowing if she be beautiful, not caring, but knowing that she is there, has always been there, to listen, to help, to solace. But the others, who love her consciously, love her as mistress or wife. For them she is more perfect than perfection, adorable in every mood, season, or attire. They love her in velvet, they love her in silk; she is marvellous in broadcloth, shoddy, or corduroy. But, like a woman, her deepest beauty she holds for the soft hours when the brute day is ended and all mankind sighs for rest and warmth. Then she is her very self. Beauty she has by day, but it is the cold, incomplete beauty of a woman before she has given herself. With the lyric evening she surrenders all the wealth and wonder of her person to her lover: beauty in full flower.

As a born Londoner, I cannot remember a time when London was not part of me and I part of London. Things that happen to London happen to me. Changes in London are changes in me, and changes in my affairs and circumstances have again and again changed the entire face of London. Whatever the mood or the occasion, London is behind it. I can never say that I am happy or downcast. London and I are happy, London and I are having a good time, or are lost in the deeps. Always she has fallen to my mood, caught the temper of the hour; always is waiting, the fond mother or the gracious mistress, with stretched hand, to succour and sympathize in sorrow, to rejoice in good fortune.

And always it is London by lamplight which I vision when I think of her, for it was the London of lamplight that first called to me, as a child. She hardly exists for me in any other mood or dress. It was London by night that awoke me to a sense of that terrible spirit which we call Beauty, to be possessed by which is as unsettling and as sweetly frightful as to be possessed by Love. London, of course, is always calling us, if we have ears to hear, sometimes in a soft, caressing voice, as difficult to hear as the fairies' song, sometimes in a deep, impelling chant. Open your window when you will in the gloating evening, whether you live in town, in the near suburbs, or in the far suburbs—open your window and listen. You will hear London singing to you; and if you are one of her chosen you will have no sleep that night until you have answered her. There is nothing for it but to slip out and be abroad in the grey, furtive streets, or in the streets loud with lamps and loafers, and jostle the gay men and girls, or mingle with the chaste silences.

It is the Call not only of London, but of Beauty, of Life. Beauty calls in many voices; but to me and to six million others she calls in the voice of Cockaigne, and it shall go hard with any man who hears the Call and does not answer. To every man, young or old, comes, once in his life, this Call of Beauty. At that moment he awakens to a realization of better things than himself and his foolish little life. To that vague abstraction which we call the average man it comes mostly with first love or religion, sometimes with last love. But come it does to each one of us, and it behoves us all to hearken. So many of us hear, and let it pass. The gleam pauses in our path for an instant, but we turn our backs and plod the road of materialism, and we fade and grow old and die without ever having lived. Only in the pursuit of beauty is youth retained; and beauty is no respecter of person, place, or time. Everywhere it manifests itself.

In the young man of the leisured classes this sense only awakens late in life. He is educated to consider only himself, to regard himself as, in the Broadway phrase, a serious proposition; and some time must pass before he discovers, with a pained surprise, that there are other people in the world, and that his little life matters not at all in the eternal scheme. Then, one day, something happens. He falls in love, perhaps; and under the shock of the blow he discovers that he wants something—something he has not known before, something he cannot name: God, Beauty, Prayer, call it what you will. He discovers a thousand subtle essences of life which his clumsy taste had hitherto passed. He discovers that there is a life of ideas, that principles and ideals are something more than mere fooling for dry-minded people, that thoughts are as important as things. In a word, he has heard the Call of Beauty. Just as a man may live in the same house with a girl for years, and then one day will discover that she is beautiful, that she is adorable, that he cannot lose her from his life, so we live surrounded by unregarded beauty, until we awake. So for seven years I was surrounded by the glory of London before I knew that I loved her. . . .

When I was a small child I was as other children of our set. I played their games in the street. I talked their language. I shared their ambitions. I worshipped their gods. Life was a business of Board School, breakfast, dinner, tea, struggled for and eaten casually, either at the table or at the door or other convenient spot. I should grow up. I should be, I hoped, a City clerk. I should wear stand-up collars. I might have a moustache. For Sunday I might have a frock-coat and silk hat, and, if I were very clever and got on well, a white waistcoat. I should have a house—six rooms and a garden, and I might be able to go to West End theatres sometimes, and sit in the pit instead of the gallery. And some day I might even ride in a hansom-cab, though I should have to succeed wonderfully to do that. I hoped I should succeed wonderfully, because then the other boys at the Board School would look up to me.

Thus I lived for ten years. A primrose by the river's brim was no more to me than to Peter Bell, or, since I had never seen a primrose growing, shall I say that the fried-fish shop at the corner of the High Street was but a fried-fish shop, visited once a week rapturously. But after the awakening, everything was changed. Things assumed a hitherto hidden significance. Beauty broke her blossoms everywhere about the grey streets and the sordid interiors that were my environment.

And my moment was given to me by London. The call came to me in a dirty street at night. The street was short and narrow, its ugliness softened here and there by the liquid lights of shops, the most beautiful of all standing at the corner. This was the fried-fish shop. It was a great night, because I was celebrating my seventh birthday, and I was proud and everything seemed to be sharing in my pride. Then, as I strutted, an organ, lost in strange lands about five streets away, broke into music. I had heard organs many times, and I loved them. But I had never heard an organ play " Suwanee River," in the dusk of an October night, with a fried-fish shop ministering to my nose and flinging clouds of golden glory about me, and myself seven years old. Momentarily, it struck me silly— so silly that some big boy pointed a derisive finger. It somehow ... I don't know. ... It ...

Well, as the organ choked and gurgled through the outrageous sentimentality of that song, I awoke. Something had happened to me. Through the silver evening a host of little dreams and desires came tripping down the street, beckoning and bobbing in rhythm to the old tune; and as the last of the luscious phrases trickled over the roofs I found myself half-laughing, half-crying, thrilled and tickled as never before. It made me want to die for some one. I think it was for London I wanted to die, or for the fried-fish shop and the stout lady and gentleman who kept it. I had never noticed that street before, except to remark that it wasn't half low and common. But now it had suffered a change. I could no longer sniff at it. I would as soon have said something disrespectful about Hymns Ancient and Modern.

I walked home by myself, and everything answered this wonderful new mood. I knew that life was rapture, and, as I looked back at the fried-fish shop, swimming out of the drab murk, it seemed to me that there could never be anything of such sheer lyrical loveliness outside heaven. I could have screamed for joy of it. I said softly to myself that it was Lovely, Lovely, Lovely; and I danced home, and I danced to bed, and my heart so danced that it was many hours before I slept.

From that day London has been my mistress. I knew this a few days later, when, as a birthday treat, I was taken to see the illuminations in our district—we were living near the Langham Hotel then—for the marriage of some princess or the birth of some royal baby. Whenever I am away from London—never more than ten days at a time —and think of her, she comes to me as I saw her then from a height of three-foot-five: huge black streets rent with loud traffic and ablaze with light from roof to pavement; shop-fronts full of magical things, drowned in the lemon light which served the town at that time; and crowds of wonderful people whom I had never met before and longed deeply to meet again. I wondered where they were all going, what they would do next, what they would have for supper, and why they didn't seem superlatively joyful at their good fortune in being able to ride at will in cabs and omnibuses and take their meals at restaurants. There were jolly fellows, graceful little girls, all better clad than I, enjoying the sights, and at last, like me, disappearing down side-streets to go to mysterious, distant homes.

HOMES. Yes, I think that phrase sums up my London: the City of Homes. To lie down at night to sleep among six million homes, to know that all about you, in high garret or sumptuous bedchamber, six million people are sleeping, or suffering, or loving, is to me the most impressive event of my daily life.

Have you ever, when walking home very late at night, looked down the grey suburban streets, with their hundred monotonous-faced houses, and thought that there sleep men, women, and children, free for a few hours from lust and hate and fear, all of them romantic, all of them striving, in their separate ways, to be happy, all of them passionate for their little span of life ; and then thought that that street is but one of thousands and thousands which radiate to every point, and that all the night air of one city is holding the passions of those millions of creatures? I suppose I have a trite mind, but there is, to me, something stupendous in that thought, something that makes one despair of ever saying anything illuminative about London.

Often, when I have been returning to London from the country, I have been moved almost to tears, as the train seemed to fly through clouds and clouds of homes and through torrents of windows. Along the miserable countryside it roars, and comes not too soon to the far suburbs and the first homes. Slowly, softly, the grey incertitude begins to flower with their lights, each window a little silent prayer. Nearer and nearer to town you race, and the warm windows multiply, they draw closer together, seeming to creep into one another's arms for snugness ; and, as you roll into the misty sparkle of Euston or Paddington, you experience an ineffable sense of comfort and security among those multitudinous homes. It is, I think, the essential homeliness of London that draws the Cockney's heart to her when five thousand miles away, under blazing suns or hurricanes of hail ; for your Cockney, travel and wander as he will, is at heart a purely domestic animal, and dreams ever of the lighted windows of London.

Those windows ! I wish some one with the right mind would write an essay for me on this theme. Why should a lighted window call with so subtle a message? They all have their messages—sometimes sweet, sometimes sinister, sometimes terrible, sometimes pathetic, always irresistible. They haunt me. Indeed, when a lighted window claims me, I have sometimes hung about outside, impelled almost to knock at the door, and find out what is happening behind that yellow oblong of mystery.

Some one published a few years ago a book entitled " The Soul of London," but I cannot think that any one has ever read the soul of London. London is not one place, but many places ; she has not one soul, but many souls. The people of Brondesbury are of markedly different character and clime from those of Hammersmith. They of Balham know naught of those of Walthamstow, and Bayswater is oblivious to Barking. The smell, the sound, the dress of Finsbury Park are as different from the smell, the sound, and the dress of Wandsworth Common as though one were England and the other Nicaragua. London is all things to all men. Day by day she changes, not only in external beauty, but in temperament.

As each season recurs, so one feels that London can never be more beautiful, never better express her inmost spirit. I write these lines in September, when we have mornings of pearly mist, all the city a Whistler pastel, the air bland but stung with sharp points, and the squares dressed in many-tinted garments ; and I feel that this is the month of months for the Londoner. Yet in April, when every parish, from Bloomsbury to Ilford, and from Haggerston to Cricklewood, is a dream of lilac and may, and when laburnum and jasmine are showering their petals over Shoreditch and Bermondsey Wall, when even Cherry Gardens Pier has lost its heart in a tangle of apple-blossom, and when the statue of James II is wreathed about with stars and boughs of hawthorn as fair as a young girl's arms, when Kensington Gardens, Brockwell Park, and the Tunnel Gardens of Blackwall are ablaze with colour and song, and when life riots in the sap of the trees as in the blood of the children who throng their walks, then, I say, London is herself. But I know that when November brings the profound fogs and glamorous lights, and I walk perilously in the safest streets, knowing by sound that I am accompanied, but seeing no one, scarce knowing whether I am in Oxford Street or the Barking Road, or in Stamboul, then I shall feel : "This is the real old London." The pallid pomp of the white lilac seems to be London in essence. The rich-scented winter fog seems to be London in essence. The hot, reeking dusk of July seems to be London in essence.

London, I repeat, is all things to all men. Whatsoever you may find in the uttermost corners of the earth, that you shall find in London. It is the city of the world. You may stand in Piccadilly Circus at midnight and fingerpost yourself to the country of your dreams. A penny or twopenny omnibus will land you in the heart of France, Switzerland, Italy, Germany, Russia, Palestine, China, the Malay Peninsula, Norway, Sweden, Holland, and Hooligania ; to all of which places I propose to take you, for food and drink, laughter and chatter, in the pages that follow. I shall show you London by night : not the popular melodramatic divisions of London rich and London poor, but many Londons that you never dreamed of and many curious nights.

London by night. Somehow, the pen stops there. Having written that, I feel that the book is done. I realize my impotence. My pen boggles at the task of adding another word or another hundred thousand words which shall light up those thunderous syllables. For to write about London Nights is to write a book about *Everything*. Philosophy, humanism, religion, love, and death, and delight— all these things must crowd upon one's pages. And once I am started, they will crowd—tiresomely, chaotically, tumbling out in that white heat of enthusiasm which, as a famous divine has said, makes such damned hard reading.

For the whole of my life, with brief breaks, has been spent in London, sometimes working by day and playing by night, sometimes idling by day and toiling through long midnights, either in streets, clubs, bars, and strange houses, or in the heat and fume of Fleet Street offices. But what nights they were! What things have we seen done—not at The Mermaid—but in every tiny street and alley of nocturnal London!

There were nights of delirium when the pulses hammered hot in rhythm to the old song of Carnival, when one seemed to have reached the very apex of living, to have grasped in one evening the message of this revolving world. There were nights, festive with hoof and harness bell. There were cheery nights of homeward walks from the City office at six o'clock, under those sudden Octobral dusks, when, almost at a wink, London is transformed into one long lake of light. There were nights of elusive fog and bashful lamp when one made casual acquaintance on the way home with some darling little work-girl, Ethel, or Katie, or Mabel, brown-haired or golden, and walked with her and perhaps were allowed to kiss her Goodnight at this or that crossing.

What romantic charm those little London work-girls have, with their short, tossing frocks and tumbling hair! There are no other work-girls in the world to compare with them for sheer witchery of face and character. The New York work-girl is a holy terror. The Parisian grisette has a trim figure and a doughy face. The Berlin work-girl knows more about viciousness, and looks more like a suet dumpling than any one else. But, though her figure may not be perfect, the London work-girl takes the palm by winsomeness and grace. At seven o'clock every evening you may meet her in thousands in Oxford Street, Villiers Street, Tottenham Court Road, or London Bridge, where the pavements lisp in reply to the chatter of her little light feet. The factory girl of twenty years ago has, I am glad to say, entirely disappeared. She was not a success. She screwed her hair into sausages and rolled them around her ears. She wore a straw hat tilted at an absurd angle over her nose. She snarled. Her skin was coarse, her hands brutal, and she took no care with herself. But the younger generation came along, the flapper —and behold, a change ! The factory girl or workgirl of fourteen or fifteen would surprise the ladies of the old school. She is neat. She knows enough about things to take care of herself, without being coarsened by the knowledge. And she has a zest for life and a respect for her dear little person which give her undisputed title to all that I have claimed for her. Long may she reign as one of London's beauties !

Then there were other nights of maddening pace, when music and wine, voice and laughter harnessed themselves to the chariot of youth and dashed us hither and thither. There were nights of melancholy, of anguish even, nights of failure and solitariness, when the last word seemed to be spoken, and the leaves and the lamps and all the little dear things seemed emptied of their glory. There were the nights of labour : dull nights of stress and struggle, under the hard white lights, the crashing of the presses, and the infuriating buzz of the tape machine. There were nights of . . .

It is these nights that I pretend to show you in this book, in a little series of cinematographic pictures. If you will come with me, we will slip through the foreign quarters. We will have a bloodthirsty night in the athletic saloons of Bethnal Green. We will have a bitter night in the dockside saloons. We will have a sickening night in sinister places of no name and no locality, where the proper people do not venture. We will have a glittering night in the Hoxton bars. We will have, too, a night among the sweet lights of the Cockney home, and among pleasant working-class interiors. And we will——

But let us get started.

AN ENTERTAINMENT NIGHT
ROUND THE HALLS

MUSIC-HALL BALLET

Through the sad billowing haze of grey and rose,
Stung with sharp lamps in its most velvet glooms;
Drowsy with smoke, and loud with voice and glass,
Where wine-whipped animations pass and pass—
Beauty breaks sudden blossoms all around
In happy riot of rhythm, colour, and pose.
The radiant hands, the swift, delighted limbs
Move as in pools of dream the dancer swims,
Holding our bruted sense to fragrance bound.

Lily and clover and the white May-flowers,
And lucid lane afire with honeyed blooms,
And songs that time nor tears can ever fade,
Hold not the grace for which my heart has prayed.
But in this garden of gilt loveliness,
Lapped by the muffled pulse of hectic hours,
Something in me awoke to happiness;
And through the streets of plunging hoof and horn,
I walked with Beauty to the dim-starred morn.

AN ENTERTAINMENT NIGHT

ROUND THE HALLS

OF course, every night spent in London is an entertainment night, for London has more blood and pace and devil than any city I know. Thick as the physical atmosphere is with smoke and fog, its moral atmosphere is yet charged with a sparkle as of light wine. It is more effervescent than any continental city. It is the city of cities for learning, art, wit, and—Carnival. Go where you please at nightfall and Carnival slips into the blood, lighting even Bond Street—the dreariest street in town—with a little flame of gaiety. I have assisted at carnivals and festes in various foreign parts—carnivals of students and also of the theatrically desperate apaches in the crawling underworlds. But, oh, what bilious affairs! You simply flogged yourself into it. You said, as it were: "I am in Vienna, or Berlin, or Paris, or Brussels, or Marseilles, or Trieste; therefore, I am gay. Of course I am gay." But you were not. You were only bored, and the show only became endurable after you had swallowed various absinthes, vermuths, and other rot-gut.

All the time you were—or I was—aching for Camden Town High Street, and a good old London music-hall. I cannot understand those folk who sniff at the English music-hall and belaud the Parisian shows. These latter are to me the most dismal, lifeless form of entertainment that a public ever suffered. Give me the Oxford, the Pavilion, or the Alhambra, or even a suburban Palace of Varieties. Ever since the age of eight the music-hall has been a kind of background for me. Long before that age I can remember being rushed through strange streets and tossed, breathless, into an overheated theatre roaring with colour. The show was then either the Moore and Burgess Minstrels or the Egyptian Hall, followed by that chief of all child-life entertainments —tea at a tea-shop. But at eight I was initiated into the mysteries of the Halls, for a gracious *chef d'orchestre* permitted me to sit in the orchestra of an outlying hall, by the side of a cousin who sawed the double bass.

I have loved the music-hall ever since, and I still worship that *chef d'orchestre*, and if I met him now I am sure I should bow, though I know that he was nothing but a pillow stuffed with pose. But in those days, what a man! Or no—not a man—what a demi-god! You should have seen him enter the orchestra on the call: " Mr. Francioli, please! " Your ordinary music-hall conductor ducks from below, slips into his chair, and his tap has turned on the flow of his twenty instruments before you realize that he is up. But not so Francioli. For him the old school, the old manners, laddie. He never came into the orchestra. He " entered." He would bend gracefully as he stepped from the narrow passage beneath the stage into the orchestra. He would stand upright among his boys for a little minute while he adjusted his white gloves. His evening dress would have turned George Lashwood sick with envy. The perfect shirt of the perfect shape of the hour, the tie in the correct mode, the collar of the moment, the thick, well-oiled hair, profuse and yet well in hand, the right flower in the buttonhole at just the right angle—so he would stand, with lips pursed in histrionic manner, gazing quietly before him, smiling, to casual friends, little smiles which were nothing more unbending than dignified acknowledgment. Then he would stretch a god-like arm to the rail, climb into his chair, and spend another half-minute in settling himself, turning now and then to inspect the house from floor to ceiling. At the tinkle of the stage-manager's bell the grand moment would come. His hand would sail to the desk, and he would take the baton as one might select a peach from the dessert-dish. He would look benignly upon his boys, tap, raise both resplendent hands aloft, and away he would go into the " Zampa " overture.

His attitude to the show was a study in holy detachment. He simply did not see it. He would lean back in his chair at a comfortable angle, and conduct from the score on his desk. But he never smiled at a joke, he never beamed upon a clever turn, he never even exchanged glances with the stars. He was Olympian. I think he must have met Irving as a young man, and have modelled himself on his idiosyncrasies. Certainly every pose that ever a musician or actor practised was doubled in him. I believe he must have posed in his sleep and in his bath. Indeed, my young mind used to play upon the delicate fancy that such a creature could never do anything so common as eat or drink or pursue any of the daily functions of us ordinary mortals. I shrank from conceiving him undressed. . . .

Once, I remember, he came down from his cloudy heights and stood my cousin a drink and myself a lemonade. I didn't want to drink that lemonade. I wanted to take it home and stand it under a glass shade. He himself drank what I was told was a foreign drink in a tiny glass. He lingered over it, untouched, while he discussed with us the exact phrasing of the symphony for the star man's song ; then, at the call, with a sweep of his almighty arm he carried the glass to his lips with a " To you, my boy ! " held it poised for a moment, set it down, and strode away, followed by rapt gazes from the barmaids.

A stout fellow. He took the conductor's chair with all the pomposity of a provincial borough official. He tapped for the coda with the touch of a king knighting an illustrious subject. And when he led the boys through the National Anthem, standing up in his place and facing the house, all lights up—well, there are literally no words for it. . . .

At twelve years old I grew up, and sought out my own entertainment, prowling, always alone, into strange places. I discovered halls that nobody else seemed to know, such as the Star at Bermondsey, the Queen's at Poplar, and the Cambridge in Commercial Street. I crawled around queer bars, wonderfully lighted, into dusky refreshment-houses in the Asiatic quarter, surely devised by Haroun al Raschid, and into softly lit theatres and concert-halls. At eighteen I took my pleasures less naïvely, and dined solemnly in town, and toured, solemn and critical, the western halls, enjoying everything but regarding it with pale detachment. Now, however, I am quite frank in my delight in this institution, which has so crept into the life of the highest and the lowest, the vulgar and the intellectual; and scarcely a week passes without a couple of shows.

The mechanism of the modern hall is a marvellous thing. From the small offices about Leicester Square, where the big circuits are registered, men and women and children are sent thousands and thousands of miles to sing, dance, act, or play the fool. The circuits often control thirty or forty halls in London and the provinces, each of which is under the care of a manager, who is responsible for its success. The turns are booked by the central booking manager and allocated either to this or that London hall, or to work the entire syndicate tour; and the bill of each hall, near or far, is printed and stage-times fixed weeks in advance. The local manager every Saturday night has to pay his entire staff, both of stage and house ; that is, he not only pays programme girls, chuckers-out, electricians, and so forth, but each artist, even the £200 a week man, is paid in cash at each hall he is working. When a new turn is booked for any given hall, the manager of that hall must be " in front " and watch that turn and its success or non-success with the house ; and, at the end of the week, a confidential report has to be sent to headquarters in which the manager tells the cold truth : whether the show is good, whether it "went," how much salary it is worth, and whether it is worth a re-booking.

It is, like journalism, a hard, hard life and thankless for every one concerned, from bill-topper to sweeper ; yet there is a furious colour about it, and I think no one connected with it would willingly quit. The most hard-worked of all are the electricians. First in the hall of an evening, they, with the band and the janitors, are the last to leave. Following them, at about half-past five (in the case of the two-houses halls), come programme girls, barmaids, call-boy, stage-manager, shifters, and all other stage hands.

All are philosophers, in their way, and all seem to have caught the tang of the profession and to be, sub-consciously, of the mummer persuasion. I once had a long, long talk with the chief electrician of a London hall, or, to give him the name by which he is best known, the limelight man. I climbed the straight iron ladder from the wings to his little platform, with only sufficient foothold for two people, and there I stood with him for two hours, while he waggled spots, floods, and focuses, and littered the platform with the hastily scrawled lighting-plots of the performers.

The limes man is really the most important person

in the show. Of course, the manager doesn't think so, and the stage manager doesn't think so, and the carpenter doesn't think so, and the band doesn't think so. But he is. Many of the music-hall favourites, such as La Milo and La Loie Fuller, would have no existence but for him. Skilful lighting effects and changes of colour are often all that carries a commonplace turn to popularity ; and just think of the power in that man's hands ! He could ruin any young turn he liked simply by " blacking her out "; and, if he feels good, he can help many beginners with expert advice. The young girl new to the boards, and getting her first show, has hardly the slightest idea what she shall give him in the way of lighting-plot ; very generously she leaves it to him, and he sees her show and lights it as he thinks most effective.

Long before the doors open he is moving from box to box, in wings and flies, fixing this, altering that, and arranging the other ; and cursing his assistants—usually lads of sixteen—who have to work the colours from wings, roof, circle, and side of the house. Lights are of three kinds : spot, focus, and flood. The spot is used on a dark stage, and lights only the singer's head and shoulders. The focus lights the complete figure. The flood covers the stage. Each of these is worked in conjunction with eight or nine shaded films placed before the arc light. Here is a typical lighting-plot, used by a prominent star :—

First Song. Symph.; all up stage and house. Focus for my entrance. White perches and battens for first chorus. Then black out, and gallery green focus for dance, changing to ruby at cue, and white floods at chord off.

The limelight man never sees the show. In his little cupboard, he hears nothing but the hissing of his arcs and the tinkle of the stage-manager's prompting bell at the switchboard which controls every light in the theatre, before and behind. He has to watch every movement of the artist who is on, but what he or she is doing or saying, he does not know. He is, perhaps, the only man who has never laughed at Little Tich.

John Davidson, I think, wrote a series of poems under the title of " In a Music Hall," but these were mainly philosophical, and neither he nor others seem to have appreciated the *colour* of the music-hall. It is the most delicate of all essences of pleasure, and we owe it to the free hand that is given to the limelight man. You get, perhaps, a girl in white, singing horribly or dancing idiotically, but she is dancing in white against a deep blue curtain filigreed with silver, and the whole flooded in amber light. And yet there are those who find the London music-hall dull !

The modern music-hall band, too, is a hard-working and poorly remunerated concern; and in many cases it really is a band and it does make music. It is hard at it for the whole of the evening, with no break for refreshment unless there be a sketch in the bill. There are, too, the matinées and the rehearsal every Monday at noon. The boys must be expert performers, and adaptable to any emergency. Often when a number cannot turn up, a deputy has to be called in by 'phone. The band seldom knows what the deputy will sing ; there is no opportunity for rehearsal ; and sometimes they have not even an idea of the nature of the turn until band parts are put in. This means that they must read at sight, that the conductor must follow every movement of the artist, in order to catch his spasmodic cues for band or patter, and that the boys must keep one eye on music they have never seen before, and the other on their old man's stick.

The conductor, too, works hard at rehearsals ; not, as you might think, with the stars, but, like the limelight man, with the youngsters. The stars can look after themselves; they are always sure to go. But the nervous beginner needs a lot of attention from the band, and it is pleasant to know that in most London halls he gets it ungrudgingly. A West End *chef d'orchestre* said to me some time ago: " I never mind how much trouble I take over them. If they don't go it means such a lot to the poor dears. Harry Lauder can sing anything anyhow, and he's alright. But I've often found that these girls and boys hand me out band parts which are perfectly useless for the modern music-hall; and again and again I've found that effective orchestration and a helping hand from us pulls a poor show through and gets 'em a return booking. Half the day of rehearsing is spent with the beginners."

An extraordinary improvement in the musical side of vaudeville has taken place within the last fifteen years. Go to any hall any night, and you will almost certainly hear something of Wagner, Mendelssohn, Weber, Mozart. I think, too, that the songs are infinitely better than in the old days; not only in the direction of melody but in orchestration, which is often incomparably subtle. It is, what vaudeville music should be, intensely funny, notably in the running chatter of the strings and the cunning commentary of woodwind and drums. Pathetic as its passing is, one cannot honestly regret the old school. I was looking last night at the programme of my very first hall, and received a terrible shock to my time-sense. Where are the snows of yesteryear? Where are the entertainers of 1895? Not one of their names do I recognize, and yet three of them are in heavy type. One by one they drop out, and their places are never filled. The new man, the new style of humour, comes along, and attracts its own votaries, who sniff, even as I sniff, at the performers of past times. Who is there to replace that perilously piquant *diseur* Harry Fragson? None. But Frank Tinney comes along with something fresh, and we forget the art of Fragson, and pay many golden sovereigns to Frank to amuse us in the new way.

Where, too, are the song-writers? That seems to me one of the greatest tragedies of the vaudeville world: that a man should compose a song that puts a girdle round about the globe; a song that is sung on liners, on troopships, at feasts in far-away Singapore or Mauritius; a song that inspires men in battle and helps soldiers to die; a song that, like "Tipperary," has been the slogan of an Empire; that a man should create such a thing and live and die without one in ten thousand of his singers knowing even his name. Who composed " Tipperary "? You don't know? I thought not. Who composed " Let's all go down the Strand," a song that surely should have been adopted as The Anthem of London? Who composed " Hot Time in the Old Town to-night "—the song that led the Americans to victory in Cuba and the Philippines? We know the names of hundreds of finicky little poets and novelists and pianists; but their work never shook a nation one inch, or cheered men in sickness and despair. Of the men who really captured and interpreted the national soul we know nothing and care less; and how much they get for their copyrights is a matter that even themselves do not seem to take with sufficient seriousness. Yet personally I have an infinite tenderness for these unknowns, for they have done me more good than any other triflers with art-forms. I should like to shake the composer of " La Maxixe " by the hand, and I owe many a debt of gratitude to the creator of " Red Pepper " and " Robert E. Lee." So many of these fugitive airs have been part of my life, as they are part of every Cockney's life. They are, indeed, a calendar. Events date themselves by the song that was popular at that time. When, for instance, I hear " The Jonah Man " or " Valse Bleu," my mind goes back to the days when a tired, pale office-boy worked in the City and wrote stories for the cheap papers in his evenings. When I hear " La Maxixe " I shiver with frightful joy. It recalls the hot summer of 1906, when I had money and wine and possession and love. When I hear " Beautiful Doll," I become old and sad ; I want to run away and hide myself. When I hear " Hiawatha " or " Bill Bailey," I get back the mood of that year—a mood murderously bitter. Verily, the street organ and its composers are things to be remembered in our prayers and toasts.

*.   •   •   •   •

Every London hall has its own character and its own audience. The Pavilion programme is temperamentally distinct from the Oxford bill ; the Alhambra is equally marked from the Empire ; and the Poplar Hippodrome, in patrons and performers, is widely severed from the Euston. The same turns are, of course, seen eventually at every hall, but never the same group of turns, collectively. As for the Hippodrome and the Coliseum—non-licensed houses—their show and their audience are what one would expect : a first-class show, and an audience decorous and Streathamish. I think we will not visit either, nor will we visit the hall with its world-famous promenade, about which our bishops seem to know more than I do.

Let us try the Oxford, where you are always sure of a pleasant crowd, a good all-round show, and alcoholic refreshment if you require it. There are certain residentials, if I may so term them, of the Oxford, whom you may always be sure of meeting here, and who will always delight you. Mark Sheridan, for example, is pretty certain to be there, with Wilkie Bard, Clarice Mayne, Phil Ray, Sam Mayo, Beattie and Babs, T. E. Dunville, George Formby, **and those veterans, Joe Elvin and George Chirgwin.**

There is a good overture, and the house is comfortable without being gorgeous. There is a sense of intimacy about it. The audience, too, is always on form. Audiences, by the way, have a great deal to do with the success or non-success of any particular show, quite apart from its merits. There is one famous West End hall, which I dare not name, whose audience is always " bad "—i.e. cold and inappreciative; the best of all good turns never " goes " at that house, and artists dread the week when they are booked there. I have seen turns which have sent other houses into one convulsive fit, but at this hall the audience has sat immovable and colourless while the performers wasted themselves in furious efforts to get over the footlights. At the Oxford, however, the audience is always " with you," and this atmosphere gets behind and puts the artists, in their turn, on the top of their form. The result is a sparkling evening which satisfies everybody.

It is a compact little place, as the music-hall should be. In those new caravanserai of colossal proportions and capacity, it is impossible for a man to develop that sense of good-fellowship which is inseparable from the traditions of the London hall. Intimacy is its very essence, and how can a man be intimate on a stage measuring something like seventy feet in length, a hundred feet in depth, with a proscenium over sixty feet high, facing an auditorium seating three thousand persons, and separated from them by a marbled orchestra enclosure four or five times as wide as it should be. It is pathetic to see George Mozart or George Robey trying to adapt his essentially miniature art to these vasty proportions. Physically and mentally he is dwarfed, and his effects hardly ever get beyond the orchestra. These new halls, with their circles, and upper circles, and third circles, and Louis XV Salons and Palm Courts, have been builded over the bones of old

English humour. They are good for nothing except ballet, one-act plays with large effects, and tabloid grand opera. But apparently the public like them, for the old halls are going. The Tivoli site is to bear a Y.M.C.A. home, and the merriment of the Strand will be still further frowned upon.

There is always an acrobat turn in the Oxford bill, and always a cheery cross-talk item. The old combination of knockabouts or of swell and clown has for the most part disappeared ; the Poluskis, The Terry Twins, and Dale and O'Malley are perhaps the last survivors. The modern idea is the foolish fellow and the dainty lady, who are not, I think, so attractive as the old style. Personally, I am always drawn to a hall where Dale and O'Malley are billed. " The somewhat different comedians " is their own description of themselves, and the wonder is that they should have worked so long in partnership and yet succeeded in remaining " somewhat different." But each has so welded his mood to the other that their joint humour is, as it were, a bond as spiritually indissoluble as matrimony. You cannot conceive either Mr. Dale or Mr. O'Malley working alone or with any other partner. I have heard them crack the same quips and tell the same stories for the last five years, yet they always get the same big laugh and the same large " hand." That is a delightful trait about the music-hall—the *entente* existing between the performer and audience. The favourites seem to be *en rapport* even while waiting in the wings, and the flashing of their number in the electric frame is the signal for a hand of welcome and—in the outer halls—whistles and cries. The atmosphere becomes electric with good-fellowship. It is, as Harry Lauder used to sing, " just like being at home." It must be splendid to be greeted in that manner every night of your life and —if you are working two or three halls—five times every night; to know that some one wants you, that some one whom you have never seen before loves you and is ready to pay good money away, in order to watch you play the fool or be yourself. There they are, crowds of people with whom you haven't the slightest acquaintance, all familiar with you, all longing to meet you again, and all applauding you before you have done anything but just walk on. They shout " Good Boy ! " or " Bravo, Harry ! " or George, or Ernest. It must indeed be splendid. You are all so—what is the word?— matey, isn't it? Yes, that's the note of the London hall—mateyness. You, up there, singing or dancing, have brought men and women together as nothing else, not even the club or saloon bar, can do ; and they sit before you, enjoying you and themselves and each other. Strangers have been known to speak to one another under the mellow atmosphere which you have created by singing to them of the universal things : love, food, drink, marriage, birth, death, misfortune, festival, cunning, frivolity and—oh, the thousand things that make up our daily day.

There is just one man still among us who renders these details of the Cockney's daily day in more perfect fashion than any of his peers. He is of the old school, I admit, but he is nevertheless right on the spot with his points and his psychology. His name is Harry Champion. Perhaps you have seen him and been disgusted with what you would call the vulgarity of his songs. But what you call his vulgarity, my dears, is just everyday life; and everyday life is always disgusting to the funny little Bayswaterats, who are compact of timidity and pudibonderie. The elderly adolescent has no business at the music-hall; his place is the Baptist Chapel or some other place remote from all connection with this splendid world of London, tragic with suffering and song, high endeavour and defeat. It is people of this kidney who find Harry Champion vulgar. His is the robust, Falstaffian humour of old England, which, I am glad to think, still exists in London and still pleases Londoners, in spite of efforts to Gallicize our entertainments and substitute obscenity and the salacious leer for honest fun and the frank roar of laughter. If you want to hear the joy of living interpreted in song and dance, then go to the first hall where the name of Harry Champion is billed, and hear him sing " Boiled Beef and Carrots," " Baked Sheep's Heart stuffed with Sage and Onions," " Whatcher, me Old Brown Son ! " " With me old Hambone," " William the Conqueror," " Standard Bread." If you are sad, you will feel better. If you are suicidal, you will throw the poison away, and you will not be the first man whose life has been saved by a low comedian. You may wonder why this eulogy of food in all these songs. The explanation is simple. In the old days, the music-hall was just a drinking den, and all the jolly songs were in praise of drink. Now that all modern halls are unlicensed, and are, more or less, family affairs to which Mr. Jenkinson may bring the wife and the children, and where you can get nothing stronger than non-alcoholic beers, or dry ginger, the Bacchanalian song is out of place. Next to drinking, of course, the Londoner loves eating. Mr. Harry Champion, with the insight of genius, has divined this, and therefore he sings about food, winning much applause, personal popularity, and, I hope, much money.

Watch his audience as he sings. Mark the almost hypnotic hold he has over them; not only over pit and gallery but over stalls as well, and the well-groomed loungers who have just dropped in. I defy any sane person to listen to " Whatcher, me Old Brown Son ! " without chortles of merriment, profound merriment, for you don't laugh idly at Harry Champion. His gaiety is not the superficial gaiety of the funny man who makes you laugh but does nothing else to you. He does you good. I honestly believe that his performance would beat down the frigid steel ramparts that begird the English "lady." His songs thrill and tickle you as does the gayest music of Mozart. They have not the mere lightness of merriment, but, like that music, they have the deep-plumbing gaiety of the love of life, for joy and sorrow.

But let us leave the front of the house and wander in back of a typical hall. Here is an overcharged atmosphere, feverish of railway-station. There is an entire lack of any system; everything apparently confused rush. Artists dashing out for a second house many miles away. Artists dashing in from their last hall, some fully dressed and made-up, others swearing at their dressers and dragging baskets upstairs, knowing that they have three minutes in which to dress and make-up before their call. As one rushes in with a cheery " Evening, George ! " to the stage-door keeper, he is met by the " boy "—the " boy " being usually a middle-aged ex-Army man of 45 or 50.

" Mr. Merson's on, sir."

" Righto ! "

He dashes into his dressing-room, which he shares with three others, and then it is *Vesti la giubba*. . . . The dressing-room is a long, narrow room, with a slab running the length of the wall, and four chairs. The slab is backed by a long, low mirror, and is littered with make-up tins and pots. His dresser hurls himself on the basket, as though he owed it a grudge. He tears off the lid. He dives head foremost into a foam of trousers, coats, and many-coloured shirts. He comes to the surface breathless, having retrieved a shapeless mass of stuff. He tears pieces of this stuff apart, and flings them, with apparent malice, at his chief, and, somehow, they seem to stay where he flings them. The chief shouts from a cloud of orange wig and patchwork shirt for a soda-and-milk, and from some obscure place of succour there actually appears a soda-and-milk. A hand darts from the leg of a revolving pair of trousers, grabs the glass and takes a loud swig. The boy appears at the door.

"Mr. Merson coming off, sir!"

"Right-*o*! and blast you!"

"No good blasting me, sir!"

From far away, as from another world, he hears the murmur of a large body of people, the rolling of the drum, the throbbing of the double-bass, the wail of the fiddles, sometimes the thud of the wooden-shoe dancer, and sometimes a sudden silence as the music dims away to rubbish for the big stunt of the trapeze performer.

He subsides into a chair. The dresser jams a pair of side-spring boots on his feet while he himself adjusts the wig and assaults his face with sticks of paint.

The boy appears again. He shoots his bullet head through the door, aggressively. "Mr. Benson, *please!*" This time he is really cross. Clearly he will fight Mr. Benson before long.

But Mr. Benson dashes from his chair and toddles downstairs, and is just in time to slip on as the band finishes his symphony for the fourth time. Once on, he breathes more freely, for neglect of the time-sheet is a terrible thing, and involves a fine. If your time is 8.20, it is your bounden duty to be in the wings ready to go on at 8.17; otherwise . . . trouble and blistering adjectives.

While he is on the boy is chasing round the dressing-rooms for the "next call." This happens to be a black-face comedian, who is more punctual than Mr. Benson. He is all in order, and at the call: "Mr. Benson's on, Harry!" he descends and stands in the wings, watching with cold but friendly gaze the antics of Mr. Benson, and trying to sense the temper of the house. Mr. Benson is at work. In another minute he will be at work, too. Mr. Benson is going well—he seems to have got the house. He wonders whether he will get the house—or the bird. He is about to give us something American: to sing and dance to syncopated melody. America may not have added great store to the world's music, but at least she has added to the gaiety of nations. She has given us ragtime, the voice of the negroid Bacchus, which has flogged our flagging flesh to new sensations; she has given us songs fragrant of Fifth Avenue, and with the wail of the American South; and she has given us nigger comedians. Harry doesn't much care whether he " goes " or not. They are a philosophical crowd, these Vaudevillians. If one of them gets the bird, he has the sympathy of the rest of the bill. Rotten luck. If he goes well, he has their smiles. Of course, there are certain jealousies here as in every game; but very few. You see, they never know. . . . The stars never know when their reign will end, and they, who were once bill-toppers, will be shoved in small type in obscure corners of the bill at far-distant provincial halls. That is why the halls, like journalism, is such a great game. You never know. . . . The unhappiest of the whole bill of a hall are " first call " and " last call "; nobody is there to listen to " first call "; everybody has bolted by the time " last call " is on. Only the orchestra and the electricians remain. They, like the poor, are always with them.

After the show, the orchestra usually breaks up into parties for a final drink, or sometimes fraternizes with the last call and makes a bunch for supper at Sam Isaacs'. After supper, home by the last car to Camberwell or Camden Town, seeking—and, if not too full of supper, finding—a chaste couch at about two a.m. The star, of course, does nothing so vulgar. He motors home to Streatham or St. John's Wood or Clapham Common, and plays billiards or cards until the small hours. A curious wave of temperance lately has been sweeping over the heads of the profession, and a star seldom has a drink until after the show. The days are gone when the lion comique would say: " No, laddie, I don't drink. Nothing to speak of, that is. I just have ten or twelve—just enough to make me think I'm drunk. Then I keep on until I think I'm sober. Then I *know* I'm drunk!" They are beginning, unfortunately for their audiences, to take themselves seriously. This is a pity, for the more spontaneous and inane they are, the more they are in their place on the vaudeville stage. There is more make-believe and hard work on the halls to-day, and I think they are none the better for it. As soon as art becomes self-conscious, its end is near; and that, I am afraid, is what is happening to-day. A quieter note has crept into the whole thing, a more facile technique; and if you develop technique you must develop it at the expense of every one of those more robust and essential qualities. The old entertainers captured us by deliberate unprovoked assault on our attention. But to-day they do not take us by storm. They woo us and win us slowly, by happy craft; and though your admiration is finally wrung from you, it is technique you are admiring—nothing more. All modern art—the novel, the picture, the play, the song —is dying of technique.

I have only the very slightest acquaintance with those gorgeous creatures—the £200 a week men— who top the bill to-day; only the acquaintance of an occasional drink in their rooms. But I have known, and still know, many of the rank and file, and delightful people they are. As a boy of fifteen, I remember meeting, on a seaside front, a member of a troupe then appearing called The Boy Guardsmen. He was a sweet child. Fourteen years old he was, and he gave me cigarettes, and he drank rum and stout, and was one of the most naïve and cleanly simple youths I ever met He had an angelic trust in the good of everything and everybody. He worshipped me because I bought him a book he wanted. He believed that the ladies appearing in the same bill at his hall were angels. He loved the manager of his troupe as a great-hearted gentleman. He thought his sister was the most radiant and high-souled girl that Heaven had yet sent to earth. And it was his business to sing, twice nightly, some of the smuttiest songs I have heard on any stage. Yet he knew exactly why the house laughed, and what portions of the songs it laughed at. He knew that the songs went because they were smutty, yet such was his innocence that he could not understand why smut should not be laughed at. He was a dear!

There was another family whom I still visit. Father and Mother are Comedy Acrobats and Jugglers. Night by night they appear in spangled tights, and Father resins his hands in view of the audience, and lightly tosses the handkerchief to the wings; and then bends a stout knee, and cries "Hup!" and catches Mumdear on the spring and throws her in a double somersault. There are two girls of thirteen and fifteen, and a dot of nine; and they regard Dad and Mumdear just as professional pals, never as parents. This is Dad's idea; he dislikes being a father, but he enjoys being an elder brother, and leading the kids on in mischief or jolly times.

I was having drinks one Saturday night, after the show, with Dad, in a scintillating Highbury saloon, when there was a sudden commotion in the passage. A cascade of voices; a chatter of feet; the yelping of a dog.

"What's that?" I murmured, half interested.

"Only the bother and the gawdfers," he answered.

"Eh?"

"I said it's the bother and the gawdfers. . . . Rhyming slang, silly ass. The Missus and the kids. Bother-and-strife . . . wife. Gawd-forbids . . .

kids. See? Here they come. No more mouth-shooting for us, now."

They came. Mumdear came first—very large, submerged in a feather boa and a feathered hat; salmon pink as to the bust, cream silk as to the skirt. The kids came next, two of the sweetest, merriest girls I know. Miss Fifteen simply tumbled with brown curls and smiles; she was of The Gay Glow-worms, a troupe of dancers. Miss Thirteen tripped over the dog and entered with a volley of giggles and a tempest of light stockinged legs, which spent themselves at once when she observed me. In a wink she became the demure maiden. She had long, straight hair to the waist, and the pure candour of her face gave her the air of an Italian madonna. She was of The Casino Juveniles. We had met before, so she sidled up to me and inquired how I was and what's doing. Within half a minute I was besieged by tossing hair and excited hands, and an avalanche of talk about shop, what they were doing, where they were this week, where next, future openings, and so forth; all of which was cut short by the good-humouredly gruff voice of the landlord, inquiring—

"That young lady over fourteen?"

"Well . . . er . . . she looks it, don't she?" said Dad.

"Dessay she does. But is she?"

"Well . . . tell you the truth, Ernest, she ain't. But she will be soon."

"Well, she can come back then. But she's got to go now."

"Righto! Come on, Joyce. You got the bird. Here, Maudie, take her home. Both of you. Straight home, mind. And get the supper ready. And don't forget to turn the dog out. And here—get yourselves some chocolates, little devils." He pulled out a handful of silver. "There you are—all the change I've got."

He gave Maudie four shillings, and Joyce half a crown—for chocolates; and Maudie tripped out with flustered hair and laughing ribbons, and Joyce fell over the dog, and the swing-doors caught her midwise, and there was a succession of screams fainting into the distance, and at last silence.

"Thank God they're gone, bless the little devils!" And Dad raised his dry ginger in salutation; while Mumdear allowed me to get her a port-and-lemonade. It had apparently been a stiff show.

"Funny, but . . . if you notice it . . . when one thing goes wrong everything goes. First off, Arthur wasn't there to conduct. His leader had to take first three turns, and he doesn't know us properly and kept missing the cues for changes. See, we have about six changes in our music, and when you kind of get used to doing a stunt to 'Mysterious Rag,' it sort of puts you off if the band is still doing 'Nights of Gladness.' See? Then the curtain stuck, and we was kept hanging about for a minute, and had to speed up. Then one of our ropes give, and I thought to myself: 'That's put the fair old khybosh on it, that has.' Gave me—well, you know, put me a bit nervy, like. We missed twice. Least, George says I missed, but I say he did. So one thing and another it's been a bad night. However, we went all right, so here's doing it again, sonny. Thumbs up!"

She beamed upon me a very large stage beam, as though she had got the range of the gallery and meant to reach it. But it was sincere, and though she makes three of me, she is a darling, very playful, very motherly, very strong-minded. Indeed, a Woman. She fussed with the feathers of her boa, and sat upright, as though conscious of her athletic proportions and the picture she was making against the gilded background of the saloon. She had an arm that—but I can say no more than that paraphrase of Meredith : She Had An Arm. When you remember that often four times nightly she holds her husband—no light-weight, I assure you—balanced on her right, while, with her left, she juggles with a bamboo-table and a walking-stick, you can realize that She Has An Arm, and you can understand the figure she cuts in commonplace intercourse. You are simply overwhelmed physically and morally.

"But look here, sonny, why not come home and have a bit of supper with us? That is, if there is any. But come round, and gnaw the old hambone —what? I think we got some claret and I know George's got a drop of Three-Star. Young Beryl's off to-morrow on the Northern tour with the White Bird Company, so of course we're in a devil of a muddle. George's sister's round there, packing her. But if you'll put up with the damned old upset, why, come right along."

So we drank up, and I went right along to a jolly little flat near Highbury Quadrant. As we entered the main room, I heard a high, thin voice protesting—

> But there were times, dear,
> When you made me feel so bad!

And there, flitting about the room in dainty lace petticoat, and little else, was young Beryl, superintending her aunt's feverish struggles with paint and powder-jars, frocks, petties, silk stockings, socks, and wraps, snatching these articles from a voluminous wardrobe and tossing them, haphazard, into a monumental dressing-basket, already half-full with two life-size teddy-bears.

She was a bright little maid, and, though we had not met before, we made friends at once. She had a mass of black curls, eyes dancing with elfin lights, a face permanently flushed, and limbs never in repose. She was, even in sleep—as I have seen her since—wonderfully alive, with that hectic energy that is born of spending oneself to the last ounce unceasingly ; in her case, the magnetic, self-consuming energy of talent prematurely developed. Her voice had distinctive quality, unusual in little girls of nine. When she talked, it was with perfect articulation and a sense of the value and beauty of words. Her manners were prettily wayward, but not precocious. She moved with the quiet self-possession of one who has something to do and knows just how to do it, one who took her little self seriously but not conceitedly.

On the stage she has been the delight of thousands. Her gay smile, her delicate graces, and her calm, unfaltering stage manner have touched the hearts of all sorts and conditions, from boxes to bar. Eight times a week, six evenings and two matinées, she was booked to take the stage from the rise of the curtain and leave it for scarcely more than two minutes at a time until the fall. This was by no means her first show. Before that she had been pantomime fairy, orphan child in melodrama, waif in a music-hall sketch, millionaire's pet in a Society play, a mischievous boy in a popular farce, dancer in a big ballet, and now the lead in a famous fairy play, at a salary of ten pounds a week. No wonder Dad and Mumdear, and even the elder girls, regarded her with a touch of awe and worship. But, fêted as she is, she has never been spoilt ; and she remains, in spite of her effervescent life, a genuine child. The pet of the crowd behind the scenes, the pet of the house in front, she is accustomed, every night, to salvoes of applause, to flowers left at the stage-door, and to boxes of chocolates handed over the footlights. Night after night, in dance or make-believe of life, she spends herself to exhaustion for the pleasure of the multitude ; night after night, in a tinsel-world of limelight and grease-paint, she plays at being herself.

I rather wondered what she thought of it all, and whether she enjoyed it; but, like most little girls, she was shy of confidences. Perhaps she wondered at it all, perhaps sometimes she felt very tired of it all—the noise, the dust, the glamour, and the rush. But she would not admit it. She would only admit her joy at the ten pounds a week, out of which Mumdear would be able to send her favourite cousin Billie to the seaside. So I had to leave it at that, and help with the packing; and at about a quarter to one in the morning supper was announced as ready, and we all sat down.

I forget what we ate. There was some mystery of eggs, prepared by Joyce and Maudie. There were various preserved meats, and some fruit, and some Camembert, and some very good Sauterne, to all of which you helped yourself. There was no host or hostess. You just wandered round the table, and forked what you wanted, and ate it, and then came up for more. When we had done eating, Dad brought out a bottle of excellent old brandy, and Joyce and Maudie made tea for the ladies, and Beryl sat on my knee until half-past two and talked scandal about the other members of the White Bird Company.

At three o'clock I broke up a jolly evening, and departed, Maudie and Joyce accompanying me to Highbury Corner, where I found a vagrant cab.

Perhaps, after the cleansing of the London stage, its most remarkable feature is this sudden invasion of it by the child. There has been much foolish legislation on the subject, but, though it is impossible artistically to justify the presence of children in drama, I think I would not have them away. I think they have given the stage, professionally, something that it is none the worse for.

All men, of course, are actors. In all men exists that desire to escape from themselves, to be somebody else, which is expressed, in the nursery, by their delight in "dressing up," and, in later life, by their delight in watching others pretend. But the child is the most happy actor, for to children acting is as natural as eating, and their stage work always convinces because they never consciously act —never, that is, aim at preconceived effects, but merge their personalities wholly in this or that idea and allow themselves to be driven by it. When to this common instinct is added an understanding of stage requirements and a sharp sense of the theatre, the result is pure delight. We live in a little age, and, in the absence of great figures, we are perhaps prone to worship little things, and especially to cultivate to excess the wonder-child and often the pseudo-wonder-child. But the gifted stage-children have a distinct place, for they give us no striving after false quantities, no theatricality, and their effects are in proportion to the strength of their genius. Of course, when they are submitted to the training of a third-rate manager, they become mere mechanical dolls, full of shrill speech and distorted posings that never once touch the audience. You have examples of this in any touring melodrama. These youngsters are taught to act, to model themselves on this or that adult member of the company, are made conscious of an audience, and are carefully prevented from being children. The result is a horror. The child is only an effective actor so long as it does not "act." As soon as these youngsters reach the age of fifteen or sixteen the dramatic faculty is stilled, and lies dormant throughout adolescence. They are useless on the stage, for, beginning to "find themselves," they become conscious artists, and, in the theatrical phrase, it doesn't come off. It is hardly to be expected that it should, for acting, of all the arts, most demands a knowledge of the human mind which cannot be encompassed even by genius at seventeen. That is why no child can ever play such a part as that of the little girl in Hauptmann's "Hannele." Intuition could never cover it. Nor should children ever be set to play it. The child of melodrama is an impossibility and an ugliness. Children on the stage must be childish, and nothing else. They must not be immature men and women. Superficially, of course, as I have said, every child of talent becomes world-weary and sophisticated; the bright surface of the mind is dulled with things half-perceived. But this, the result of moving in an atmosphere of hectic brilliance, devoid of spiritual nourishment, is not fundamental: it is but a phase. Old-fashioned as the idea may be, it is still true that artificial excitement is useful, indeed necessary, to the artist; and conditions of life that would spoil or utterly destroy the common person are, to him, entirely innocuous, since he lives on and by his own self. And, though some stage children may become prematurely wise, in the depths of their souls, they must preserve, fresh and lovely, the child-spirit, the secret glory shared by all children. If they lose that, they have no justification of any kind.

There was a little girl on the London stage some few years ago whom I have always remembered with joy. I first saw her accidentally at a Lyceum pantomime, into which I strolled after a dull evening in Fleet Street.

The theatre was drowned in a velvet gloom. Here and there sharp lamps stung the dusks. There was a babble of voices. The lights of the orchestra gleamed subtly. The pit was a mist of lilac, which shifted and ever shifted. A chimera of fetid faces swam above the gallery rail. Wave after wave of lifeless heads rolled on either side of me.

Then there was a quick bell; the orchestra blared the chord on, and I sat up. Something seemed about to happen. Back at the bar was a clamour of glass and popping cork, and bashful cries of "Order, please!" The curtain rushed back on a dark, blank stage. One perceived, dimly, a high sombre draping, very far up-stage. There was silence. Next moment, from between the folds, stole a wee slip of a child in white, who stood, poised like a startled fawn. Three pale spot-limes swam uncertainly from roof and wings, drifted a moment, then picked her up, focusing her gleaming hair and alabaster arms. I looked at the programme.

It was Marjorie Carpenter.

The conductor tapped. A tense silence ; and then our ears were drenched in the ballet music of Délibes. Over the footlights it surged, and, racing down-stage, little Marjorie Carpenter flung herself into it, caressing and caressed by it, shaking, as it seemed, little showers of sound from her delighted limbs. On that high, vast stage, amid the crashing speed of that music and the spattering fire of the side-drums, she seemed so frail, so lost, so alone that—oh ! one almost ached for her.

But then she danced : and if she were alone at first, she was not now alone. She seemed at a step to people the stage with little companies of dream.

I say she danced, and I must leave it at that. She gave us more than dance ; she gave us the spirit of Childhood, bubbling with delight, so fresh, so contagious that I could have wept for joy of it. It was a thing of sheer lyrical loveliness, the lovelier, perhaps, because of its very waywardness and disregard of values. Here was no thing of trick and limelight. It was Blake's " Infant Joy " materialized. She was a poem.

In the heated theatre, where the opiate air rolled like a fog, we sat entranced before her—the child, elfish and gay and hungry for the beauty of life ; the child, lit by a glamorous light. Far below the surface this light burns, and seldom is its presence revealed, save by those children who live very close to Nature : gipsy and forest children. But every child possesses it, whether bred in the whispering

wood or among sweetstuff shops and the Highbury
'buses; and I, for one, recognized it immediately
this lovely child carried it over the footlights of
the Lyceum Theatre.

Hither and thither she drifted like a white snow-
flake, but all the time . . . dancing; and one had
a sense of dumb amazement that so frail a child,
her fair arms and legs as slender as a flower-stem,
should so fill that stage and hold the rapt attention
of a theatreful of people. Here was evidence of
something stronger than mere mastery of ballet
technique. Perfect her dancing was. There was
no touch of that automatic movement so noticeable
in most child dancers. When she went thus or so,
or flitted from side to side of the stage, she clearly
knew just why she did it, why she went up-stage
instead of down. But she had more than mere
technical perfection: she had personality, that
strange, intangible something so rare in the
danseuse, that wanders over the footlights. The
turn of a foot, the swift side look, the awakening
smile, the nice lifting of an eyebrow—these things
were spontaneous. No amount of rehearsal or
managerial thought could have produced effects so
brilliantly true to the moment.

I am not exaggerating. I am speaking quite
literally when I say that, for me, at that time,
Marjorie Carpenter and her dancing were the
loveliest things in London. She danced as no child
has ever danced before or since, though, of course,
it would never do to say so. It was the most fragile,
most evanescent genius that London had seen; and
nobody cared, nobody recognized it. It attracted
no more attention than the work of any other child-
actress. Yet you never saw such gazelle-like
swiftness and grace.

When she had completed one dance, a new back-
cloth fell, and she danced again and yet again.
I forget what she danced, but it spoke to me of

a thousand forgotten things of childhood. I know that I touched finger-tips with something more generously pure and happy than, I had met for years. Through the hush of lights the sylvan music stole, and Marjorie Carpenter stole with it, and every step of her whispered of April and May.

    The curtain fell. I was jerked back to common things. But I was in no mood for them. The house applauded. It thought it was applauding Marjorie Carpenter for her skill as a dancer. It was really worshipping something greater—that elusive quality which she had momentarily snatched from nothing and presented to them : the eternal charm and mystery of Childhood.

A CHINESE NIGHT
LIMEHOUSE

AT LIMEHOUSE

Yellow man, yellow man, where have you been?
Down the Pacific, where wonders are seen.
Up the Pacific, so glamorous and gay,
Where night is of blue, and of silver the day.

Yellow man, yellow man, what did you there?
I loved twenty maids who were loving and fair.
Their cheeks were of velvet, their kisses were fire,
I looked at them boldly and had my desire.

Yellow man, yellow man, what do you know?
That living is lovely wherever I go;
And lovelier, I say, since when soft winds have passed
The tides will race over my bosom at last.

Yellow man, yellow man, why do you sigh?
For flowers that are sweet, and for flowers that die.
For days in fair waters and nights in strange lands,
For faces forgotten and little lost hands.

A CHINESE NIGHT

LIMEHOUSE

IT was eight o'clock. We had dined in Soho, and conversed amiably with Italian waiters and French wine-men. There were now many slack hours before us, and nothing wherewith to tighten them. We stood in the low-lit gaiety of Old Compton Street, and wondered. We were tired of halls and revues ; the theatres had started work ; there was nothing left but to sit in beer-cellars and listen to dreary bands playing ragtimes and bilious waltzes.

Now it is a good tip when tired of the West, and, as the phrase goes, at a loose end, to go East, young man, go East. You will spot a winner every time, if it is entertainment you seek, by mounting the first East-bound omnibus that passes. For the East is eternally fresh, because it is alive. The West, like all things of fashion, is but a corpse electrified. They are so tired, these lily-clad ladies and white-fronted gentlemen, of their bloodless, wine-whipped frivolities. They want to enjoy themselves very badly, but they do not know how to do it. They know that enjoyment only means eating the same dinner at a different restaurant, and afterwards meeting the same tired people, or seeing the same show, the same songs, jests, dances at different houses. But Eastward . . . there, large and full, blossoms Life—a rather repellent Life, perhaps, for Life is always that. Hatred, filth, love, battle, and death—all elemental things are here, undisguised ; and if elemental things repel you, my lamb, then you have no business to be on this planet. Night, in the particular spots of the East to which these pages take you, shows you Life in the raw, stripped of its silken wrappings ; and it is of passionate interest to those for whom humanity is the only Book. In the West pleasure is a business ; in the East it is recreation. In the East it may be a thinner, poorer body, but it is alive. The people are sick, perhaps, with toil ; but below that sickness there is a lust for enjoyment that lights up every little moment of their evening, as I shall show you later, when we come to Bethnal Green, Hoxton, and the athletic saloons. You may listen to Glazounoff's " L'Automne Bacchanale " at the Palace Theatre, danced by Pavlova, but I should not look in Shaftesbury Avenue or Piccadilly for its true spirit. Rather, I should go to Kingsland Road, Tunnel Gardens, Jamaica Road ; to the trafficked highways, rent with naphthas, that rush about East India Dock. There, when the lamps are lighted, and bead the night with tears, and the sweet girls go by, and throw their little laughter to the boys—there you have your true Bacchanales.

So, leaving the fixed grin of decay in Coventry Street, we mounted a motor-'bus, and dashed gaily through streets of rose and silver—it was October— and dropped off by the Poplar Hippodrome, whose harsh signs lit the night to sudden beauty.

To turn from East India Dock Road to West India Dock Road is to turn, contradictorily, from West to East, from a fury of lights and noise and faces into a stillness almost chaste. At least, chaste is the first word you think of. In a few seconds you feel that it is the wrong epithet. Something . . . something there is in this dusky, throttled byway that seems to be crawling into your blood. The road seems to slink before you ; and you know that, once in, you can only get out by retracing your steps or crossing into the lost Isle of Dogs. Against the wrath of October cloud, little low shops peer at you. In the sharp shadows their lights fall like swords across your path. The shuttered gloom of the eastern side shows strangely menacing. Each whispering house seems an abode of dread things. Each window seems filled with frightful eyes. Each corner, half-lit by a timid gas-jet, seems to harbour unholy features. A black man, with Oriental features, brushes against you. You collide with a creeping yellow man. He says something—it might be Chinese or Japanese or Philippinese jargon. A huge Hindoo shuffles, cat-like, against the shops. A fried-fish bar, its windows covered with Scandinavian phrases, flings a burst of melodious light for which you are grateful.

No ; chaste was certainly not the right word. Say, rather, furtive, sinister. You are in Limehouse. The peacefulness seems to be that attendant upon underhand designs, and the twilight is that of people who love it because their deeds are evil.

But now we come to Pennyfields, to the thunderous shadows of the great Dock, and to that low-lit Causeway that carries such subtle tales of flowered islands, white towns, green bays, and sunlight like wine. At the mouth of Pennyfields is a cluster of Chinks. You may see at once that they dislike you.

But my friend Sam Tai Ling will give us better welcome, I think ; so we slip into the Causeway, with its lousy shop-fronts decorated with Chinese signs, among them the Sign of the Foreign Drug Open Lamp. At every doorway stand groups of the gallant fellows, eyeing appreciatively such white girls as pass that way. You taste the curious flavour of the place—its mixture of camaraderie and brutality, of cruelty and pity and tears ; of precocious children and wrecked men—and you smell its perfume, the week before last. But here is the home of Tai Ling, one of the most genial souls to be met in a world of cynicism and dyspepsia ;

a lovable character, radiating sweetness and a tolerably naughty goodness in this narrow street. Not immoral, for to be immoral you must first subscribe to some conventional morality. Tai Ling does not. You cannot do wrong until you have first done right. Tai Ling has not. He is just non-moral; and right and wrong are words he does not understand. He is in love with life and song and wine and the beauty of women. The world to him is a pause on a journey, where one may take one's idle pleasure while others strew the path with mirth and roses. He knows only two divisions of people: the gay and the stupid. He never turns aside from pleasure, or resists an invitation to the feast. In fact, by our standards a complete rogue, yet the most joyous I have known. Were you to visit him and make his acquaintance, you would thank me for the introduction to so charming a character. I never knew a man with so seductive a smile. Many a time it has driven the virtuously indignant heart out of me. An Oriental smile, you know, is not an affair of a swift moment. It has a birth and a beginning. It awakens, hesitates, grows, and at last from the sad chrysalis emerges the butterfly. A Chinese smile at the full is one of the subtlest expressions of which the human face is capable.

Mr. Sam Tai Ling keeps a restaurant, and, some years ago, when my ways were cast about West India Dock Road, I knew him well. He was an old man then; he is an old man now: the same age, I fancy. Supper with him is something to remember—I use the phrase carefully. You will find, after supper, that soda-mints and potass-water are more than grateful and comforting.

When we entered he came forward at once, and such was his Celestial courtesy that, although we had recently dined, to refuse supper was impossible. He supped with us himself in the little upper room, lit by gas, and decorated with bead curtains and English Christmas-number supplements. A few oily seamen were manipulating the chop-sticks and thrusting food to their mouths with a noise that, on a clear night, I should think, could be heard as far as Shadwell. When honourable guests were seated, honourable guests were served by Mr. Tai Ling. There were noodle, shark's fins, chop suey, and very much fish and duck, and lychee fruits. The first dish consisted of something that resembled a Cornish pasty—chopped fish and onion and strange meats mixed together and heavily spiced, encased in a light flour-paste. Then followed a plate of noodle, some bitter lemon, and finally a pot of China tea prepared on the table : real China tea, remember, all-same Shan-tung ; not the backwash of the name which is served in Piccadilly tea-shops. The tea is carefully prepared by one who evidently loves his work, and is served in little cups, without milk or sugar, but flavoured with chrysanthemum buds.

As our meal progressed, the café began to fill ; and the air bubbled with the rush of labial talk from the Celestial company. We were the only white things there. All the company was yellow, with one or two tan-skinned girls.

But we were out for amusement, so, after the table hospitality, Sam took us into the Causeway. Out of the coloured darkness of Pennyfields came the muffled wail of reed instruments, the heart-cry of the Orient ; noise of traffic ; bits of honeyed talk. On every side were following feet : the firm, clear step of the sailor ; the loud, bullying boots of the tough ; the joyful steps that trickle from " The Green Man " ; and, through all this chorus, most insistently, the stealthy, stuttering steps of the satyr. For your Chink takes his pleasure where he finds it ; not, perhaps, the pleasure that you would approve, for probably you are not of that gracious temperament that accords pity and the soft hand to the habits of your fellows. Yet so many are the victims of the flesh, and for so little while are we here, that one can but smile and be kind. Besides, these yellow birds come from an Eastern country, where they do not read English law or bother about such trifles as the age of consent.

Every window, as always, was closely shuttered, but between the joints shot jets of slim light, and sometimes you could catch the chanting of a little sweet song last sung in Rangoon or Swatow. One of these songs was once translated for me. I should take great delight in printing it here, but, alas! this, too, comes from a land where purity crusades are unknown. I dare not conjecture what Bayswater would do to me if I reproduced it.

We passed through Pennyfields, through clusters of gladly coloured men. Vaguely we remembered leaving Henrietta Street, London, and dining in Old Compton Street, Paris, a few hours ago. And now —was this Paris or London or Tuan-tsen or Taiping? Pin-points of light pricked the mist in every direction. A tom-tom moaned somewhere in the far-away.

It was now half-past ten. The public-house at the extreme end was becoming more obvious and raucous. But, at a sudden black door, Sam stopped. Like a figure of a shadowgraph he slid through its opening, and we followed. Stairs led straight from the street to a basement chamber—candle-lit, with two exits. I had been there before, but to my companions it was new. We were in luck. A Dai Nippon had berthed a few hours previously, and here was its crew, flinging their wages fast over the fan-tan tables, or letting it go at Chausa-Bazee or Pachassee.

It was a well-kept establishment where agreeable fellows might play a game or so, take a shot of opium, or find other varieties of Oriental delight. The far glooms were struck by low-toned lanterns. Couches lay about the walls; strange men decorated them and three young girls in socks, idiotically drunk. Small tables were everywhere, each table obscured in a fog of yellow faces and greasy hair. The huge scorbutic proprietor, Ho Ling, swam noiselessly from table to table. A lank figure in brown shirting, its fingers curled about the stem of a spent pipe, sprawled in another corner. The atmosphere churned. The dirt of years, tobacco of many growings, opium, betel-nut, bhang, and moist flesh allied themselves in one grand assault on the nostrils. Perhaps you wonder how they manage to keep these places clean. That may be answered in two words: they don't.

On a table beneath one of the lanterns squatted a musician with a reed, blinking upon the company like a sly cat, and making his melody of six repeated notes.

Suddenly, at one of the tables was a slight commotion. A wee slip of a fellow had apparently done well at fan-tan, for he slid from his corner, and essayed a song—I fancy it was meant to be "Robert E. Lee"—in his seaman's pidgin. At least, his gestures were those of a ragtime comedian, and the tune bore some faint resemblance. Or is it that the ragtime kings have gone to the antiquities of the Orient for their melodies? But he had not gone far before Ho Ling, with the dignity of a mandarin, removed him. And the smell being a little too strong for us, we followed, and strolled to the Asiatics' Home.

The smell—yes. There is nothing in the world like the smell of a Chinatown in a Western city. It is a grand battle between a variety of odours, but opium prevails. The mouth of West India Dock Road is foul with it. For you might as well take away a navvy's half-pint of beer as deprive a Chink of his shot of dope and his gambling-table. Opium is forbidden under the L.C.C. regulations, and therefore the Chink sleeps at a licensed lodging-house and goes elsewhere for his fun.

Every other house in this quarter is a seamen's lodging-house. These hotels have no lifts, and no electric light, and no wine-lists. You pay threepence a night, and you get the accommodation you pay for. But then, they are not for silk-clad ossifications such as you and me. They are for the lusty coloured lads who work the world with steam and sail : men whose lives lie literally in their great hands, who go down to the sea in ships and sometimes have questionable business in great waters.

These India Docks are like no other docks in the world. About their gates you find the scum of the world's worst countries ; all the peoples of the delirious Pacific of whom you have read and dreamed—Arab, Hindoo, Malayan, Chink, Jap, South Sea Islander—a mere catalogue of the names is a romance. Here are pace and high adventure ; the tang of the East ; fusion of blood and race and creed. A degenerate dross it is, but, do you know, I cannot say that I don't prefer it to the wellspun gold that is flung from the Empire on boatrace nights. Place these fellows against our blunt backgrounds, under the awful mystery of the City's night, and they present the finest spectacle that London affords.

You may see them in their glory at the Asiatics' Home, to which we now came. A delightful place, this home for destitute Orientals ; for it has a veranda and a compound, stone beds and caged cubicles, no baths and a billiard-table ; and extraordinary precautions are taken against indulgence of the wicked tastes of its guests. Grouped about the giant stove are Asiatics of every country, in wonderful toilet creations. A mild-eyed Hindoo, lacking a turban, has appropriated a bath-towel. A Malay appears in white cotton trousers, frockcoat, brown boots, and straw hat ; and a stranded Burmese cuts no end of a figure in under-vest, steward's jacket, yellow trousers, and squash hat.

All carry a knife or a krees, and all are quite pleasant people, who will accept your Salaam and your cigarette. Rules and regulations for impossibly good conduct hang on the walls in Hindustani, Japanese, Swahili, Urdu, and Malayan. All food is prepared and cooked by themselves, and the slaughter of an animal for the table must be witnessed and prayed upon by those of their own faith. Out in the compound is a skittle-alley, where the boys stroll and play ; and costumes, people, and setting have all the appearance of the *ensemble* of a cheap revue.

I suppose one dare not write on Limehouse without mentioning opium-rooms. Well, if one must, one must, though I have nothing of the expected to tell you. I have known Limehouse for many years, and have smiled many times at the articles that appear perennially on the wickedness of the place. Its name evokes evil tradition in the public mind. There are ingenuous people who regard it as dangerous. I have already mentioned its sinister atmosphere ; but there is an end of it. There is nothing substantial. These are the people who will tell you of the lurking perils of certain quarters of London—how that there are streets down which, even in broad daylight, the very police do not venture unaccompanied. You may believe that, if you choose ; it is simply a tale for the soft-minded with a turn for the melodramatic. There is no such thing as a dangerous street in London. I have loafed and wandered in every part of London, slums, foreign quarters, underground, and docksides, and if you must have adventure in London, then you will have to make your own. The two fiercest streets of the metropolis—Dorset Street and Hoxton Street—are as safe for the wayfarer as Oxford Street ; for women, safer. And the manners of Limehouse are certainly a lesson to Streatham Hill.

But we are talking of opium. We left Mr. Tai

Ling on the steps of the Asiatics' Home, and from there we wandered to High Street, Poplar, to the house of a gracious gentleman from Pi-chi-li, not for opium but for a chat with him. For my companions had not smoked before, and I did not want two helpless invalids on my hands at midnight. Those amazingly thrilling and amazingly ludicrous stories of East End opium-rooms are mainly, I may say, the work of journalistic specials. A journalistic special is a man who writes thrillingly on old-fashioned topics on which he is ill-informed. The moment he knows something about his subject he is not allowed to write; he ceases to be a special. Also, of course, if a man, on sociological investigation, puts an initial pipe of opium on top of a brandy or so—well, one can understand that even the interior of the Bayswater omnibus may be a haunt of terror and wonder. Taking a jolt of " chandu " in a Limehouse room is about as exciting as taking a mixed vermuth at the Leicester Lounge.

The gracious gentleman received us affably. Through a curtained recess was the small common room, where yellow and black men reclined, in a purple dusk, beaded with the lights of little lamps. The odour was sickly, the air dry. The gentleman wondered whether we would have a room. No, we wouldn't; but I bought cigarettes, and we went upstairs to the little dirty bedrooms. The bed is but a mattress with a pillow. There, if you are a dope-fiend, you may have your pipe and lamp, very cosy, and you may lock the door, and the room is yours until you have finished. One has read, in periodicals, of the well-to-do people from the western end, who hire rooms here and come down, from time to time, for an orgy. That is another story for the nursery. White people do visit the rooms, of course, but they are chiefly the white seamen of the locality; and, in case you may ever feel tempted to visit any of the establishments displaying the Sign of the Open Lamp, I may tell you that your first experiment will result in violent nausea, something akin to the effect of the cigar you smoked when you were twelve, but heightened to the nth power. Opium does nasty things to the yellow man ; it does nastier things to the white man. Not only does it wreck the body, but it engenders and inflames those curious vices to which allusion has been made elsewhere. If you do not believe me, then you may accept the wisdom of an unknown Formosan, who, three hundred years ago, published a tract, telling of the effects of the Open Lamp on the white man. They are, in a word, parallel with the effects of whisky on the Asiatic. Listen :—

> The opium is boiled in a copper pan. The pipe is in appearance like a short club. Depraved young men, without any fixed occupation, meet together by night and smoke ; and it soon becomes a habit. Fruit and sweetmeats are provided for the sailors, and no charge is made for the first time, in order to tempt them, After a while they cannot stay away, and will forfeit all their property so as to buy the drug. Soon they find themselves beyond cure. If they omit smoking for a day, their faces become shrivelled, their lips stand open, and they seem ready to die. Another smoke restores vitality, but in three years they all die.

So now you know. The philanthropic foreigner published his warning in 1622. In 1915 . . . well, walk down Pennyfields and exercise your nose, and calculate how much opium is being smoked in London to-day.

Nobody troubles very much about Chinatown, except the authorities, and their interference is but perfunctory. The yellow men, after all, are, as Prologue to " Pagliacci " observes, but men like you, for joy or sorrow, the same broad heaven above them, the same wide world before them. They are but men like you, though the sanitary officials may doubt it. They *will* sleep six and seven in one dirty bed, and no law of London can change their ways. Anyway, they are peaceful, agreeable people, who ask nothing but to be allowed to go about their business and to be happy in their own way. They are shy birds, and detest being looked at, or talked to, or photographed, or written about. They don't want white men in their restaurants, or nosing about their places. They carry this love of secrecy to strange lengths. Not so long ago a press photographer set out boldly to get pictures of Chinatown. He marched to the mouth of Limehouse Causeway, through which, in the customary light of grey and rose, many amiable creatures were gliding, levelled his nice new Kodak, and got—an excellent picture of the Causeway after the earthquake. The entire street in his plate was deserted.

Certain impressionable people—Cook's tourists and Civil Servants—return from the East mumbling vague catchwords—mystic, elusive, subtle, haunting, alluring. These London Chinese are neither subtle nor mystic. They are mostly materialist and straightforward; and, once you can gain their confidence, you will find yourself wonderfully at home. But it has to be gained, for, as I have said, they are shy, and were you to try to join a game of cards on a short acquaintance . . . well, it would be easier to drop in for a cigarette with King George. To get into a Grosvenor Square mansion on a ball night is a comparatively easy matter: swank and an evening suit will do it; nothing very exclusive about those people. But the people of Limehouse, and, indeed, of any slum or foreign quarter, are exclusive; and to get into a Poplar dope-house on bargain night demands the exercise of more Oriental ingenuity than most of us possess.

Only at the mid-January festival do they forget themselves and come out of their shells. Then things happen. The West India Dock Road is whipped to life. The windows shake with flowers, the roofs with flags. Lanterns are looped from house to house, and the slow frenzy of Oriental carnival begins. In the morning there is solemn procession, with joss-sticks, to the cemetery, where prayers are held over the graves of departed compatriots, and lamentations are carried out in native fashion, with sweet cakes, whisky, and song and gesture. In the evening—ah !—dancing in the halls with the white girls. Glamorous January evening . . . yellow men with much money to spend . . . beribboned girls, gay, flaunting, and fond of curious kisses . . . lighted lanterns swinging lithely on their strings . . . noise, bustle, and laughter of the cafés . . . all these things light this little bit of London with an alluring Eastern flame.

There was a time, years ago, when the East End was the East End—a land apart, with laws and customs of its own, cut off from civilization, and having no common ground with Piccadilly. But the motor-'bus has changed all that. It has so linked things and places that all individual character has been swamped in a universal chaos, and there is now neither East nor West. All lost nooks of London have been dug out and forced into the traffic line, and boundaries are things which exist to-day only in the mind of the borough councillor. Hyde Park stretches to Shadwell, Hampstead to Albert Docks. Soho is *vieux jeu*. Little Italy is exploded. The Russian and Jewish quarters are growing stale and commercial, and the London Docks are a region whose chief features are Cockney warehouse clerks. This corner of Limehouse alone remains defiantly its Oriental self, no part of London ; and I trust that it may never become popular, for then there will be no spot to which one may escape from the banalities of the daily day.

But as we stood in the little bedroom of the gentleman from Pi-chi-li the clock above Millwall Docks shot twelve crashing notes along the night. The gentleman thrust a moon face through the dusky doorway to inquire if I had changed my mind.

Would myself and honourable companions smoke, after all? We declined, but he assured me that we should meet again at Tai-Ling's café, and perhaps hospitality . . .

So we tumbled down the crazy stairs, through the room from which the Chinks were fast melting, and into the midnight glitter of the endless East India Dock Road. We passed through streets of dark melancholy, through labyrinthine passages where the gas-jets spluttered asthmatically, under weeping railway arches, and at last were free of the quarter where the cold fatalism of the East combats the wistful dubiety of the West. But the atmosphere, physical and moral, remained with us. Not that the yellow men are to blame for this atmosphere. The evil of the place is rather that of Londoners, and the bitter nightmare spirit of the place is rather of them than of Asia. I said that there was little wickedness in Chinatown, but one wickedness there is, which is never spoken of in published articles; opium seems the only point that strangers can fasten on. Even if this wickedness were known, I doubt if it would be mentioned. It concerns . . . But I had better not.

We looked back at Barking Road, where it dips and rises with a sweep as lovely as a flying bird's, and on the bashful little streets, whose lights chime on the darkness like the rounding of a verse. Strange streets they are, where beauty is unknown and love but a grisly phantom; streets peopled, at this hour, with loose-lipped and uncomely girls —mostly the fruit of a yellow-and-white union— and with other things not good to be talked of. I was philosophizing to my friend about these things, and he was rhapsodizing to me about the stretch of lamplights, when a late 'bus for the Bank swept along. We took a flying mount that shook the reek of Limehouse from our clothes and its nastiness from our minds, and twenty minutes later we were taking a final coffee at the "Monico."

A DOMESTIC NIGHT
CLAPHAM COMMON

THE LAMPLIT HOUR

*Dusk—and the lights of home
  Smile through the rain:
A thousand smiles for those that come
  Homeward again.*

*What though the night be drear
  With gloom and cold,
So that there be one voice to hear,
  One hand to hold?*

*Here, by the winter fire,
  Life is our own.
Here, out of murk and mire,
  Here is our throne.*

*Then let the wild world throng
  To pomp and power;
And let us fill with love and song
  The lamplit hour.*

A DOMESTIC NIGHT

CLAPHAM COMMON

AT six o'clock every evening London Bridge vomits its stream of tired workers, hurrying home, most of them living at Clapham Common or similar places with a different name. Some of them walk home along those straggling streets which, after many years, reach the near suburbs; some of them go by car or 'bus. All are weary. All are gay. They are Going Home.

I think it was Mr. Mark Sheridan who was singing, some few years back, that " All the girls are lover-ly by the seaside ! " I do not know the poet responsible for this sentiment, but I should like to take him to any of the London bridges and let him watch the crowd coming home at six o'clock. He was all wrong, anyway. The girls are not lovely by the seaside. If there is one place where the sweetest girl is decidedly plain and ill-kempt it is at the seaside. His song should read, " All the girls are lover-ly up in London ! " And they are, whether they be chorus-girls, typists, shop-girls, Reuter's messenger-girls, modistes, or factory girls. Do you know those delightful London children, the tailors' collectors, who "fetch it and bring it home"? Their job is to take out the work from the big tailoring establishments to the dozens and dozens of home workers, and to collect it from them at the appointed time. You may easily recognize them by the large black-lining bundles which they carry so deftly under either arm. Mostly they are dear little girls of about fourteen, in short frocks, and mostly they are pretty. They have a casual manner, and they smile very winningly. Often their little feet tramp twelve and fourteen miles a day delivering and collecting; often they are sworn at by the foreman for being late; often they are very unhappy, and hardly ever do they get more than seven and sixpence a week. But they always smile : a little timidly, you know, because they are so young and London is so full of perils ; yea, though they work harder than any other sweated labourer—they smile.

And over the bridges they come at nightfall, if they are not doing overtime, chattering and smiling, each with a Dorothy-bag, or imitation leather dispatch-case, each with a paper novelette, and so to the clear spaces of Clapham Common, now glittering with the lights of home, and holding in its midst a precious jewel—the sparkled windows of the Windmill Inn.

At home, tea is ready set for them and their brothers. Brothers are probably in warehouses or offices, somewhere in the brutal City; for every member of the suburban family earns something; they all contribute their little bit to help " keep the home going." Tea is set in the kitchen, or living-room, and Mother sits there by the fire, awaiting the return of her brood, and reading, for the forty-fourth time, *East Lynne*. Acacia Grove is a narrow street of small houses, but each house is pridefully held by its owners, and fierce competition, in the matter of front gardens, is waged during spring and summer. Now it is a regiment of soft lights, each carrying its message of cheer and promises of tea, arm-chair, and slippered ease. The fragrance of the meal is already on the air, and through the darling twilight comes the muffin-man and the cheery tinkle of his bell—one of the last of a once great army of itinerant feeders of London. Gaslight and firelight leap on the spread table, glinting against cups and saucers and spoons, and lighting, with sudden spurts, the outer gloom. A sweet warmth fills the room—the restful homeliness imparted by a careful, but not too careful, woman. The wall-paper is flaring, but very clean. The pictures are flaring, but framed with honest love. The dresser holds, not only crockery but also items of decoration : some carved candlesticks, some photographs in gilt frames, an ornament with a nodding head, kept there because it always amuses young Emmie's baby when she calls. Everywhere pride of home is apparent. . . .

When the lady hears a familiar step, she lays *East Lynne* aside, pokes up the fire, places a plate in the fender, and a kipper over the griddle, where it sizzles merrily; for it is wasteful to use the gas grill when you have a fire going. Then the boys come clumping in, or the girls come tripping in, and Mother attends them while she listens to recitals of the day's doings in the City. Sometimes the youngsters are allowed to postpone their tea until the big ones come home; and then they take a Scramble Tea on the rug before the fire. You take a Scramble Tea by turning saucers and plates upside down, and placing the butter in the sugar-basin, the sugar on the bread-board, and the bread, so far as possible, in the sugar-basin, and the milk in the slop-basin. Taken in this way, your food acquires a new and piquant flavour, and stimulates a flagging appetite. Or they lounge against the table, and help themselves to sly dips in the jam with the handle of a teaspoon, or make predatory assaults on the sugar-basin.

After tea, the bright boys wash, clean their boots, and change into their "second-best" attire, and stroll forth, either to a picture palace or to the second house of the Balham Hippodrome; perchance, if the gods be favourable, to an assignation on South Side Clapham Common; sometimes to saunter, in company with others, up and down that parade until they "click" with one of the "birds." The girls are out on much the same programme. They, too, promenade until they "click" with some one, and are escorted to picture palace or hall or chocolate shop. Usually, it is a picture palace, for, in Acacia Grove, mothers are very strict as to the hours at which their young daughters shall be in. Half-past ten is the general rule, with an extension on certain auspicious occasions.

It is a great game, this "clicking"; with very nice rules. However seasoned the player may be, there are always, in certain districts, pitfalls for the unwary. The Clapham manner is sharply distinct from the Blackheath manner, as the Kilburn manner is distinct from that of Leyton. On Clapham Common, the monkeys' parade is South Side; and the game is started by strolling from "The Plough" to Nightingale Lane. As the boys pass the likely girls they glance, and, if not rebuffed, offer wide smiles. But they do not stop. At the second meeting, however, they smile again and touch hands in passing, or cry over the shoulder some current witticism, as: "'Snice night, Ethel!" or "I should shay sho!"

And Ethel and Lucy will swing round, challengingly, with scraping feet, and cry, "Oooh!" The boys linger at the corner, looking back, and the girls, too, look back. Ethel asks Lucy, "Shall we?" and Lucy says, "Ooh—I d'no," and by that time the boys have drawn level with them. They say, "Isn't it cold?" or "Awf'ly warm 'sevening!" And then, "Where you off to in such a hurry?"

"Who—me?"

"Yes—you. Saucy!"

"Ooh—I d'no!"

"Well—shall we stroll 'cross the Common?"

"I don' mind."

Then boys and girls move forward together for the bosky glades of the Common. They have "clicked." They have "got off."

In the light evenings the children sometimes take Mother for a 'bus ride to Kingston or Mitcham, or Uncle George may drop in and talk to them about the garden. While the elders talk gardens, the kiddies play in the passage at sliding down the banisters. Having regard to its value in soothing the nerves and stimulating the liver, and to the fact that it is an indoor pastime within the reach of high and low, I never understand why banister-sliding has not become more popular. I should imagine that it would be an uproariously successful innovation at any smart country house, during the long evenings, and the first hostess who has the courage to introduce it will undoubtedly reap her reward. . . .

There are, of course, other domesticities around Clapham Common on a slightly higher scale; for there are roads and roads of uniform houses at rents of £60 and £70 per annum, and here, too, sweetness and (pardon the word) Englishness spread their lambent lustre.

Here they do not come home to tea; they come home to dinner. Dinner is usually the simple affair that you get at Simpson's: a little soup followed by a joint and vegetables, and a sweet of some sort. Beer is usually drunk, though they do rise to wine on occasion. Here, too, they have a real dining-room, very small, but still . . . a dining-room. They keep a maid, trim and smiling. And after dinner you go into the drawing-room. The drawing-room is a snug little concern, decorated in a commonplace way, but usually a corner where you can be at ease. The pictures are mostly of the culture of yesterday—Watts, Rossetti, a Whistler or so; perhaps, courageously, a Monet reproduction. The occasional tables bear slim volumes of slim verse, and a novel from Mudie's. There is one of those ubiquitous fumed-oak bookcases. They go in a little for statuettes, of a kind. There is no attempt at heavy lavishness, nor is there any attempt at breaking away from tradition. The piano is open. The music on the stand is "Little Grey Home in the West"; it is smothering Tchaikowsky's "Chant sans Paroles." There are several volumes of music—suspiciously new—Chopin's Nocturnes, Mozart's Sonaten, Schubert's Songs.

After dinner, the children climb all over you, and upset your coffee, and burn themselves on your cigarette. Then Mother asks the rumple-haired baby, eight years old, to recite to the guest, and she declines. So Mother goes to the piano, and insists that she shall sing. To this she consents, so long as she may turn her back on her audience. So she stands, her little legs looking so pathetic in socks, by her mother, and sings, very prettily, "Sweet and Low" and that delicate thing of Thomas Dekker's—"Golden Slumbers"—with its lovely seventeenth-century melody, full of the graceful sad-gaiety of past things, and of a pathos the more piercing because at first unsuspected; beauty and sorrow crystallized in a few simple chords.

Then baby goes in care of the maid to bed, and Mother and Father and Helen, who is twelve years old, go to the pictures at the Palladium near Balham Station. There, for sixpence, they have an entertainment which is quite satisfying to their modest temperaments and one, withal, which is quite suitable to Miss Twelve Years Old; for Father and Mother are Proper People, and would not like to take their treasure to the sullying atmosphere of even a suburban music-hall.

So they spend a couple of hours with the pictures, listening to an orchestra of a piano, a violin, and a 'cello, which plays even indifferent music really well. And they roar over the facial extravagances of Ford Sterling and his friends Fatty and Mabel; they applaud, and Miss Twelve Years Old secretly admires the airy adventures of the debonair Max

Linder—she thinks he is a dear, only she daren't tell Mother and Father so, or they would be startled. And then there is Mr. C. Chaplin—always there is Mr. C. Chaplin. Personally, I loathe the cinematograph. It is, I think, the most tedious, the most banal form of entertainment that was ever flung at a foolish public. The Punch and Judy show is sweetness and light by comparison. It is the mechanical nature of the affair that so depresses me. It may be clever; I have no doubt it is. But I would rather see the worst music-hall show that was ever put up than the best picture-play that was ever filmed. The darkness, the silence, the buzz of the machine, and the insignificant processions of shadows on a sheet are about the last thing I should ever describe by the word Entertainment. I would as soon sit for two hours in a Baptist Chapel. Still, Mr. C. Chaplin has made it endurable.

After the pictures, they go home, and Miss Twelve goes to bed, while Mother and Father sit up awhile. Father has a nightcap, perhaps, and Mother gives him a little music. She doesn't pretend to play, she will tell her guests; she just amuses herself. Often they have a friend or two in for dinner and a little music, or music and a little dinner. Or sometimes they visit other friends in an exchange of hospitalities, or book seats for a theatre, or for the Coliseum, and perhaps dine in town at Gatti's or Maxim's, and feel very gay. Mother seizes the opportunity to air her evening frock, and father dresses, too, and they have a taxi to town and a taxi home.

Then, one by one, the lights in their Avenue disappear; the warm windows close their tired eyes; and in the soft silence of the London night they ascend, hand in hand, to their comfortable little bedroom; and it is all very sweet and sacramental. . . .

A LONELY NIGHT
KINGSLAND ROAD

A LONELY NIGHT

In the tinted dayspring of a London alley,
  Where the dappled moonlight cools the sunburnt lane,
Deep in the flare and the coloured noise of suburbs,
  Long have I sought you in shade and shine and rain!
Through dusky byways, rent with dancing naphthas,
  Through the trafficked highways, where streets and streets collide,
Through the evil twilight, the night's ghast silence,
  Long have I wandered, and wondered where you hide.

Young lip to young lip does another meet you?
  Has a lonely traveller, when day was stark and long,
Toiling ever slower to the grey road's ending,
  Reached a sudden summer of sun and flower and song?
Has he seen in you the world's one yearning,
  All the season's message, all the heavens' play?
Has he read in you the riddle of our living?
  Have you to another been the dark's one ray?

Well, if one has held you, and, holding you, beheld you
  Shining down upon him like a single star;
If Love to Love leans, even as the June sky,
  Laughing down to earth, leans strangely close and far;
Has he seen the moonlight mirrored in the bloomy,
  Softly-breathing gloom of your dear dark hair;
And seeing it, has worshipped, and cried again for heaven!
  Then am I joyful for a fire-kissed prayer!

A LONELY NIGHT

KINGSLAND ROAD

KINGSLAND ROAD is one of the few districts of London of which I can say, definitely, that I loathe it. I hate to say this about any part of London, but Kingsland Road is Memories . . . nothing sentimental, but Memories of hardship, the bitterest of Memories. It is a bleak patch in my life; even now the sight of its yellow-starred length, as cruelly straight as a sword, sends a shudder of chill foreboding down my back. It is, like Barnsbury, one of the lost places of London, and I have met many people who do not believe in it. " Oh yes," they say, " I knew that 'buses went there; but I never knew there really was such a place."

Many miles I have tramped and retramped on its pavements, filled with a brooding bitterness which is no part of seventeen. Those were the days of my youth, and, looking back, I realize that something, indeed, a great deal, was missing. Youth, of course, in the abstract, is regarded as a kingship, a time of dreams, potentialities, with new things waiting for discovery at every corner. Poets talk of it as some kind of magic, something that knows no barriers, that whistles through the world's dull streets a charmed tune that sets lame limbs pulsing afresh. Nothing of the kind. Its only claim is that it is the starting-point. Only once do we make a friend—our first. Only once do we succeed —and that is when we take our first prize at school.

All others are but empty echoes of tunes that only once were played.

There are fatuous folk who, having become successful and lost their digestions, look back on their far youth, and talk, saying that their early days, despite miseries and hardships, were really, now they regard them dispassionately, the happiest of their lives. That is a lie. And everybody, even he who says it, secretly knows it to be a lie. Youth is not glorious; it is shamefaced. It is a time of self-searching and self-exacerbation. It is a horrible experience which everybody is glad to forget, and which nobody ever wants to repeat. It knows no zest. It is a time of spiritual unrest, a chafing of the soul. Youth is cruel, troubled, sensitive to futilities. Only childhood and middle-age can be light-hearted about life: childhood because it doesn't understand, middle-age because it does.

And a youth of poverty is, literally, hell. There is a canting phrase in England to the effect that poverty is nothing to be ashamed of. Yet if there is one country in the world where poverty is a thing to be superlatively ashamed of, that country is England. There never was an Englishman who wasn't ashamed of being poor. I myself had a youth of hardship and battle : a youth in which I invaded the delectable countries of Literature and Music, and lived sometimes ecstatically on a plane many degrees above everyday life, and—was hungry. Now, looking back, when I have, at any rate, enough to live upon and can procure anything I want within reason ; though I am no longer enthusiastic about Art or Music or Letters, and have lost the sharp palate I had for these things ; yet, looking back, I know that those were utterly miserable days, and that right now I am having the happiest time of my life. For, though I don't very much want books and opera and etchings and wines and liqueurs—still, if I want them I can have them at any moment. And that sense of security is worth more than a thousand of the temperamental ecstasies and agonies that are the appanage of hard-up youth.

At that time, fired by a small journalistic success, I insulted the senior partner of the City firm which employed me at a wicked wage, and took my departure. Things went well, for a time, and then went ill. There were feverish paradings of Fleet Street, when I turned out vivid paragraphs for the London Letter of a Northern daily, receiving half a crown apiece. They were wonderful paragraphs. Things seemed to happen in London every day unknown to other newspapers; and in the service of that journal I was, by the look of it, like Sir Boyle Roche's bird, in five places at once. But that stopped, and for some time I drifted, in a sort of mental and physical stupor, all about highways and byways. I saw naked life in big chunks. I dined in Elagabalian luxury at Lockhart's on a small ditto and two thick 'uns, and a marine. I took midnight walks under moons which—pardon the decadent adjectives—were pallid and passionate. I am sure they were at that time: all moons were. Then, the lightness of my stomach would rise to the head, so that I walked on air, and brilliance played from me like sparks from a cat's back. I could have written wonderful stuff then—had I the mind. I wandered and wandered; and that is about all I remember. Bits of it come back to me at times, though. . . .

I remember, finally, sloughing through Bishopsgate into Norton Folgate, when I was down to fifteen-and-sixpence. In Norton Folgate I found a timid cocoa-room, and, careless of the future, I entered and gorged. Sausages . . . mashed . . . bread . . . tomatoes . . . pints of hot tea. . . . Too, I found sage wisdom in the counter-boy. He had been through it. We put the matter into committee, and it was discussed from every possible point of view. I learnt that I could get a room for next to nothing round about there, and that there was nothing like studying the "Sits. Vacant" in the papers at the Library; or, if there was anything like it, it was trusting to your luck. No sense in getting the bleeding pip. As he was eighteen and I was seventeen, I took his counsel to heart, and, fired with a repletion of sausage and potato, I stalked lodgings through the forests of Kingsland Road and Cambridge Road. In the greasy, strewn highway, where once the Autonomie Club had its home, I struck Cudgett Street—a narrow, pale cul-de-sac, containing fifty dilapidated cottages; and in the window of the first a soiled card: "One Room to Let."

The doorstep, flush with the pavement, was crumbling. The door had narrowly escaped annihilation by fire; but the curtains in the front-room window were nearly white. Two bare-armed ladies, with skirts hiked up most indelicately behind them, were sloshing down their respective doorsteps, and each wall was ragged with five or six frayed heads thrust from upper windows for the silken dalliance of conversation. However, it was sanctuary. It looked cheap. I knocked.

A lady in frayed alpaca, carrying a house-flannel, came to hearken. "Oh, yerss. Come in. Half a jiff till I finished this bottom stair. Now then—whoa!—don't touch that banister; it's a bit loose. Ver narsely furnished you'll find it is. There. Half-a-crown a week. Dirt cheap, too. Why, Mrs. Over-the-Road charges four for hers. But I can't. I ain't got the cheek."

I tripped over the cocoanut mat. The dulled windows were draped with a strip of gauze. The "narse furnicher" wasn't there. There was a chest of drawers whose previous owner had apparently been in the habit of tumbling into bed by candlelight and leaving it to splutter its decline and shed its pale blood where it would. The ceiling was picked out with fly-spots. It smelt—how shall I give it to you? The outgoing tenant had obviously used the hearth as a spittoon. He had obviously supped nightly on stout and fish-and-chips. He had obviously smoked the local Cavendish. He had obviously had an acute objection to draughts of any kind. The landlady had obviously " done up " the room once a week. ... Now perhaps you get that odour.

But the lady at my side, seeing hesitation, began a kind of pæan on the room. She sang it in its complete beauty. She dissected it, and made a panegyric on the furniture in comparison with that of Mrs. Over-the-Road. She struck the lyre and awoke a louder and loftier strain on the splendour of its proportions and symmetry—" heaps of room here to swing a cat "—and her rapture and inspiration swelled as she turned herself to the smattering price charged for it. On this theme she chanted long and lovingly and a hundred coloured, senescent imageries leaped from the song.

Of course, I had to take it. And towards late afternoon, when the grey cloak of twilight was beginning to be torn by the gas lamps, I had pulled the whole place to pieces and found out what made it work. I had stood it on its head. I had reversed it, and armlocked it, and committed all manner of assaults on it. I had found twenty old cigarette ends under the carpet, and entomological wonders in the woodwork of the window. Fired by my example, the good lady came up to help, and when I returned from a stroll she had garnished it. Two chairs, on which in my innocence I sat, were draped with antimacassars. Some portraits of drab people, stiffly posing, had been placed on the mantelshelf, and some dusty wool mats, set off with wax flowers, were lighting the chest of drawers to sudden beauty.

In my then mood the false luxury touched me curiously.

There I was and there I stayed in slow, mortifying idleness. *You* get stranded in Kingsland Road for a fortnight ... I wish you would. It would teach you so many things. For it is a district of cold, muddy squalor that it is ashamed to own itself. It is a place of narrow streets, dwarfed houses, backed by chimneys that growl their way to the free sky, and day and night belch forth surly smoke and stink of hops. The poverty of Poplar is abject, and, to that extent, picturesque in its frankness; there is no painful note of uncomely misery about it. But the poverty of Kingsland is the diseased poverty of bead flowers in the front room and sticky furniture on the hire system.

My first night was the same as every other. My window looked out on a church tower which still further preyed on the wan light of the street, and, as I lay in bed, its swart height, pierced by the lit clock face, gloated stiffly over me. From back of beyond a furry voice came dolefully—

Goo bay to sum-*mer*, goo bay, goo baaaaay!

That song has thrilled and chilled me ever since. Next door an Easy Payments piano was being tortured by wicked fingers that sought after the wild grace of Weber's "Invitation to the Valse." From the street the usual London night sounds floated up until well after midnight. There was the dull, pessimistic tramp of the constable, and the long rumble of the Southwark-bound omnibus. Sometimes a stray motor-car would hoot and jangle in the distance, swelling to a clatter as it passed, and falling away in a pathetic *diminuendo*. A traction-engine grumbled its way along, shaking foundations and setting bed and ornaments a-trembling. Then came the blustering excitement of chucking-out at the "Galloping Horses." Half a dozen wanted to fight ; half a dozen others wanted to kiss ; everybody wanted to live in amity and be jollyolpal. A woman's voice cried for her husband, and abused a certain Long Charlie ; and Long Charlie demanded with piteous reiteration : " Why don't I wanter fight? Eh? Tell me that. Why don't I wanter fight? Did you 'ear what he called me? Did you 'ear? He called me a—a—what was it he called me? "

Then came police, disbandment, and dark peace, as the strayed revellers melted into the night. Sometimes there would sound the faint tinkle of a belated hansom, chiming solitarily, as though weary of frivolity. And then a final stillness of which the constable's step seemed but a part.

It was a period of chill poverty that shamed to recognize itself. I was miserably, unutterably lonely. I developed a temper of acid. I looked on the world, and saw all things bitter and wicked. The passing of a rich carriage exasperated me to fury : I understood in those moments the spirit that impels men to throw bombs at millionaires and royalties. Among the furious wilds of Kingsland, Hackney, and Homerton I spent my rage. There seemed to be no escape, no outlet, no future. Sometimes I sat in that forlorn little room ; sometimes I went to bed ; sometimes I wandered and made queer acquaintance at street corners ; sometimes I even scanned that tragic column of the *Daily Telegraph*—Situations Vacant. Money went dribbling away. At " Dirty Dick's " you can get a quartern of port for threepence, and gin is practically given away. Drink is a curse, I know, but there are innumerable times when it has saved a man from going under. . . . I wish temperance fiends would recognize this.

After a time, all effort and anxiety ceased. I became listless. I neither wondered nor anticipated. I wandered about the Christmas streets, amid radiant shops. The black slums and passages were little gorges of flame and warmth, and in Morning Lane, where the stalls roared with jollity, I could even snatch some of their spirit and feel, momentarily, one of them. The raucous mile of Cambridge Road I covered many times, strolling from lit window to lit window, from ragged smears of lights to ragged chunks of dark. The multitudes of "Useful Presents," "Pretty Gifts," "Remarkable Value," "Seasonable Offerings" did not tantalize me; they simply were part of another world. I saw things as one from Mars.

That was a ghastly Christmas. Through the whole afternoon I tramped—from Hackney to Homerton, thence to Clapton, to Stoke Newington, to Tottenham, and back. Emptiness was everywhere: no people, little traffic. Roofs and roads were hard with a light frost, and in the sudden twilight the gleaming windows of a hundred houses shone out jeeringly. Sounds of festivity disturbed the brooding quiet of the town. Each side street was a corridor of warm blinds. Harmoniums, pianos, concertinas, mouth organs, gramophones, tin trumpets, and voices uncertainly controlled, poured forth their strains, mingling and clashing. The whole thing seemed got up expressly for my disturbance. In one street I paused, and looked through an unshaded window into a little interior. Tea was in progress. Father and Mother were at table, Father feeding the baby with cake dipped in tea, Mother fussily busy with the teapot, while two bigger youngsters, with paper head-dresses from the crackers, were sprawling on the rug, engaged in the exciting sport of toast-making. It made me sick. A little later the snow unexpectedly came down, and the moon came out and flung long passages of light over the white world, and forced me home to my room.

Next day, I had no food at all, and in the evening I sprawled on the bed. Then things happened.

The opposite room on the same landing had been let to a girl who worked, so I understood from my hostess, at the cork factory close at hand. She came home every evening at about six, and the little wretch invariably had a hot meal with her tea. It was carried up from below. It was carried past my door. I could not object to this, but I could and did object to the odour remaining with me. Have you ever smelt Irish stew after being sixteen hours without food? I say I objected. What I said was : " Can't you keep that damn stink out of my room?" Landlady said she was sorry; didn't know it annoyed me ; but you couldn't keep food from smelling, could you?

So I slammed the door. A little later came a timid tap. I was still lying on the bed, picturing for myself an end in the manner of a youth named Chatterton, but I slithered off to answer the knock. Before I could do so, the door was pushed softly open, and Miss Cork Factory pushed a soft head through it.

" Say, don't mind me, do you? But here, I know all about you. I been watching you, and the old girl's told me, too. She given you notice? Listen. I got a good old stew going in here. More'n enough for two. Come on ! "

What would you have done? I was seventeen ; and she, I imagine, was about twenty. But a girl of twenty is three times older than a boy of seventeen. She commanded. She mothered. I felt infinitely childlike and absurd. I thought of refusing ; but that seemed an idiotic attempt at dignity which would only amuse this very mature young person. To accept seemed to throw away entirely one's masculinity. Somehow, I . . . But she stepped right into the room then, instinctively patting her hair and smoothing herself, and she took me by the arm.

"Look here, now. Don't you go on this silly way; else you'll be a case for the morchery. Noner your nonsense, now. You come right along in." She flitted back, pulling me with her, to the lit doorway of her room, a yellow oblong of warmth and fragrance. "Niff it?" she jerked in allusion to the stew. I nodded; and then I was inside and the door shut.

She chucked me into a rickety chair by the dancing fire, and chattered cheerily while she played hostess, and I sat pale and tried to recover dignity in sulky silence.

She played for a moment or so over a large vegetable dish which stood in the fender, and then uprose, with flaming face and straying hair, and set a large plate of real hot stuff before me on the small table. "*There* you are, me old University chum!" served as her invitation to the feast. She shot knife, fork, and spoon across the table with a neat shove-ha'p'ny stroke. Bread followed with the same polite service, and then she settled herself, squarely but very prettily, before her own plate, mocking me with twinkling eyes over her raised spoon.

Her grace was terse but adequate: "Well—here's may God help us as we deserve!" I dipped my spoon, lifted it with shaking hand, my heart bursting to tell the little dear girl what I thought about her, my lips refusing to do anything of the sort; refusing, indeed, to do anything at all; for having got the spoon that far, I tried to swallow the good stuff that was in it, and—well . . . I . . . I burst into tears. Yes, I did.

"What the devil——" she jerked. "Now what the devil's the matter with—— Oh, I know. I see."

"I can't help it," I hiccuped. "It's the st-st-st-stew! It's so goo-goo-good!"

"There, that's all right, kid. I know. I been like that. You have a stretch of rotten luck, and you don't get nothing for perhaps a day, and you feel fit to faint, and then at last you get it, and when you got it, can't touch it. Feel all choky, like, don't you? I know. You'll be all right in a minute. Get some more into you!"

I did. And I was all right. I sat by her fire for the rest of the evening, and smoked her cigarettes—twelve for a penny. And we talked; rather good talk, I fancy. As the food warmed me, so I came out of my shell. And gradually the superior motherliness of my hostess disappeared; I was no longer abject under her gaze; I no longer felt like a sheepish schoolboy. I saw her as what she really was—a pale, rather fragile, very girlish girl. We talked torrentially. We broke into one another's sentences without apology. We talked simultaneously. We hurled autobiography at each other. . . .

That was my last week in Kingsland Road; for luck turned, and I found work—of a sort. I left on the Saturday. I parted from her at Cudgett Street corner. I never asked her name; she never asked mine. She just shook hands, and remarked, airily, "Well, so long, kid. Good luck."

A MUSICAL NIGHT
THE OPERA, THE PROMENADES

AT THE PIANO

Cane chairs, a sleek piano, table and bed in a room
  Lifted happily high from the loud street's fermentation;
Tobacco and chime of voices wreathing out of the gloom,
  Out of the lilied dusk at the firelight's invitation.
Then, in the muffled hour, one, strange and gracious and sad,
Moves from the phantom hearth, and, with infinite delicacies,
Looses his lissome hands along the murmurous keys.

Valse, mazurka, and nocturne, prelude and polonaise
  Clamour and wander and wail on the opiate air,
Piercing our hearts with echo of passionate days,
  Peopling a top front lodging with shapes of care.
And as our souls, uncovered, would shamefully hide away,
The radiant hands light up the enchanted gloom
With the ture flame of life from the shadowless tomb.

A MUSICAL NIGHT

THE OPERA, THE PROMENADES

FOR a few months of the year London is the richest of all cities in the matter of music ; but it is only for a few months. From the end of August to the end of October we have Sir Henry Wood's Promenade Concerts. From the end of May to mid-July we have the Grand Season at Covent Garden. Interspersed between these, at intervals all too rare, we have individual concerts at the Queen's, Steinway, and Æolian Halls ; sometimes an Autumn Season of opera or Russian ballet ; and the Saturday and Sunday concerts, the former at the Albert and Queen's Halls, and the latter, under the auspices of the Sunday League, at pretty well every theatre and music-hall in London and the suburbs.

There are, however, long spells of emptiness when nothing or little is doing in musical London, and that little hardly ever at night, though Sir Thomas Beecham, the greatest philanthropist of his time, is doing splendid work in feeding the hungry music-lover.

I should like, just here, to enter a protest against the practice prevalent among our best soloists of giving their concerts in the afternoons. Does it not occur to MM. Pachmann, Paderewski, Backhaus, Mischa Elman, Hambourg, and others that there are thousands of music-lovers in London who are never free at afternoons, and cannot turn their little world upside down in order to snatch an afternoon even for something so compelling as their recitals? Continually London gives you these empty evenings. You do not want theatre or vaudeville; you want music. And it is not to be had at any price; though when it is to be had it is very well worth having. No artist of any kind in music—singer, pianist, violinist, conductor—considers himself as established until he has appeared in London and received its award of merit; and whatever good things may be going in other continental cities we know that, with the least possible waste of time, those good things will be submitted to us for our sealing judgment. There is only one other city in the world which has so firm a grip on the music of the hour, and that is Buenos Ayres.

Let the superior persons, like Mr. Oscar Hammerstein, who says that London is not musical, because it sniffs at Schonberg, and doesn't get excited over the dead meat of Rossini, Auber, and Bellini, pay a visit any night to Queen's Hall during the Promenade Season. Where are the empty seats? In the five-shilling tier. Where is the hall packed to suffocation? In the shilling promenade. In the promenade there are seats for about one hundred, and room for about seven hundred. That means that six hundred Londoners stand, close-packed, with hardly room for a change of posture and in an atmosphere overcharged with heat and sound, for two hours and a half, listening, not to the inanities of Sullivan or Offenbach or Arditi, but to Weber, Palestrina, Debussy, Tchaikowsky, Wieniawski, Chopin, Mozart, Handel, and even the starch-stiff Bach.

Personally, I prefer the sugar and spice of Italian Opera. I know it is an execrable taste, but as I am a most commonplace person I cannot help myself. I have loved it since childhood, when the dull pages of my Violin Tutor were lit by crystalline fragments of Cherubini and Donizetti, and when the house in which I lived was chattering day and night Italianate melody. One of my earliest recollections is of hearing, as a tiny thing in petticoats, the tedious noises of the professional musician, and the E A D G of the fiddle was the accompaniment to all my games. From noon until seven in the evening I played amid the squeak of the fiddle, the chant of the 'cello, the solemn throb of the double bass, and the querulous wail of flute and piccolo; and always the music was the music of Italy, for these elders worked in operatic orchestras. So I learned to love it, and especially do I still love the moderns—Leoncavallo, Wolf-Ferrari, Mascagni, Puccini—for it was in "La Bohème" that I heard both Caruso and grand opera for the first time; and whenever I now hear "Che gelida manina," even badly sung, I always want to sit down and have a good cry. It reminds me of a pale office-boy of fifteen, who had to hoard his pence for a fortnight and wait weary hours at the gallery door of Covent Garden to hear Caruso, Scotti, Melba, and Journet as the Bohemians. What nights! I remember very clearly that first visit. I had heard other singers, English singers, the best of whom are seldom better than the third-rate Italians, but Caruso . . . What is he? He is not a singer. He is not a voice. He is a miracle. There will not be another Caruso for two or three hundred years; perhaps not then. We had been so accustomed to the spurious, manufactured voices of people like de Reszke and Tamagno and Maurel, that when the genuine article was placed before us we hardly recognized it. Here was something lovelier than anything that had yet been heard; yet we must needs stop to carp because it was not quite proper. All traditions were smashed, all laws violated, all rules ignored. Jean de Reszke would strain and strain, until his audience suffered with him, in order to produce an effect which this new singer of the South achieved with his hands in his pockets, as he strolled round the stage.

The Opera in London is really more of a pageant than a musical function. The front of the house frequently claims more attention than the stage. On Caruso and Melba nights it blazes. Tiers and tiers of boxes race round in a semicircle. If you are early, you see them as black gaping mouths. But very soon they are filled. The stalls begin to leap with light, for everybody who is not anybody, but would like to be somebody, drags out everything she possesses in the way of personal adornment, and sticks it on her person, so that all the world may wonder. At each box is a bunch of lights, and, with the arrival of the silks and jewellery, they are whipped to a thousand scintillations.

The blaze of dancing light becomes painful; the house, especially upstairs, is spitefully hot. Then the orchestra begin to tumble in; their gracefully gleaming lights are adjusted, and the monotonous A surges over the house—the fiddles whine it, the golden horns softly blare it, and the wood-wind plays with it.

But now there is a stir, a sudden outburst of clapping. Campanini is up. Slowly the lights dissolve into themselves. There is a subdued rustle as we settle ourselves. A few peremptory *Sh-sh-sh!* from the ardent galleryites.

Campanini taps. His baton rises . . . and suddenly the band mumbles those few swift bars that send the curtain rushing up on the garret scene. Only a few bars . . . yet so marvellous is Puccini's feeling for atmosphere that with them he has given us all the bleak squalor of his story. You feel a chill at your heart as you hear them, and before the curtain rises you know that it must rise on something miserable and outcast. The stage is in semi-darkness. The garret is low-pitched, with a sloping roof ending abruptly in a window looking over Paris. There is a stove, a table, two chairs, and a bed. Nothing more. Two people are on. One stands at the window, looking, with a light air of challenge, at Paris. Down stage, almost on the footlights, is an easel, at which an artist sits. The artist is Scotti, the baritone, as Marcello. The orchestra shudders with a few chords. The man at the window turns. He is a dumpy little man in black, wearing a golden wig. What a figure it is ! What a make-up ! What a tousled-haired, down-at-heel, out-at-elbows Clerkenwell exile ! The yellow wig, the whited-out moustache, the broken collar. . . . But a few more brusque bars are tossed from Campanini's baton, and the funny little man throws off, cursorily, over his shoulder, a short passage explaining how cold he is. The house thrills. That short passage, throbbing with tears and laughter, has rushed, like a stream of molten gold, to the utmost reaches of the auditorium, and not an ear that has not jumped for joy of it. For he is Rudolfo, the poet ; in private life, Enrico Caruso, Knight of the Order of San Giovanni, Member of the Victorian Order, Cavalier of the Order of Santa Maria, and many other things. . . .

As the opera proceeds, so does the marvel grow. You think he can have nothing more to give than he has just given ; the next moment he deceives you. Towards the end of the first Act, Melba enters. You hear her voice, fragile and firm as fluted china, before she enters. Then comes the wonderful love-duet—" Che gelida manina " for Caruso and " Mi chiamano Mimi " for Melba. Gold swathed in velvet is his voice. Like all true geniuses, he is prodigal of his powers ; he flings his lyrical fury over the house. He gives all, yet somehow conveys that thrilling suggestion of great things in reserve. Again and again he recaptures his first fine careless rapture. His voice dances forth like a little girl on a sunlit road, wayward, captivating, never fatigued, leaping where others stumble, tripping many miles, with fresh laughter and bright quick blood. There never were such warmth and profusion and display. Not only is it a voice of incomparable magnificence: it has that intangible quality that smites you with its own mood: just the something that marks the difference between an artist and a genius. There are those who sniff at him. "No artist," they say; "look what he sings." They would like him better if he were not popular; if he concerned himself, not with Puccini and Leoncavallo, but with those pretentiously subtle triflers, Debussy and his followers. Some people can never accept beauty unless it be remote. But true beauty is never remote. The art which demands transcendentalism for its appreciation stamps itself at once as inferior. True art, like love, asks nothing, and gives everything. The simplest people can understand and enjoy Puccini and Caruso and Melba, because the simplest people are artists. And clearly, if beauty cannot speak to us in our own language, and still retain its dignity, it is not beauty at all.

Caruso speaks to us of the little things we know, but he speaks with a lyric ecstasy. Ecstasy is a horrible word; it sounds like something to do with algebra; but it is the one word for this voice. The passion of him has at times almost frightened me. I remember hearing him at the first performance of "Madame Butterfly," and he hurt us. He worked up the love-duet with Butterfly at the close of the first act in such fashion that our hands were wrung, we were perspiring, and I at least was near to fainting. Such fury, such volume of liquid sound could not go on, we felt. But it did. He carried a terrific crescendo passage as lightly as a schoolgirl singing a lullaby, and ended on a tremendous note which he sustained for sixty seconds. As the curtain fell we dropped back in our seats, limp, dishevelled, and pale. It was we who were exhausted. Caruso trotted on, bright, alert, smiling, and not the slightest trace of fatigue did he show.

It seems to have been a superb stroke of fortune for us that Caruso should have come along contemporaneously with Puccini. Puccini has never definitely written an opera for his friend; yet, to hear him sing them, you might think that every one had been specially made for him alone. Their temperaments are marvellously matched. Each is Italian and Southern to the bone. Whatever Caruso may be singing, whether it be Mozart or Gounod or Massenet or Weber, he is really singing Italy. Whatever setting Puccini may take for his operas, be it Japan, or Paris, or the American West, his music is never anything but Italian.

And I would not have it otherwise. It may offend some artistic consciences that Butterfly, the Japanese courtesan, should sob out her lament in music which is purely Italian in character and colour; but what a piece of melody it is!

Puccini's is a still small voice; very pleading, very conscious of itself and of the pathos of our little span of living; but the wistfulness of its appeal is almost heartbreaking. He can never, I suppose, stand among the great composers; dwarfed he must always be against Mozart or Weber, or even Verdi. But he has done what all wise men must do: he has discovered the one thing he can perform well, and he is performing it very well indeed. His genius is slim and miniature, but he handles it as an artist. There is no man living who can achieve such effects with so slender material. There is no man living who can so give you, in a few bars, the soul of the little street-girl; no man living who can so give you the flavour of a mood, or make you smell so sharply the atmosphere of a public street, a garret, a ball-room, or a prairie. And he always succeeds because he is always sincere. A bigger man might put his tongue in his cheek and sit down to produce something like "La Bohème," and fail miserably, simply because he didn't mean it.

When Puccini has something to say, though it may be nothing profound or illuminating, he says it; and he can say the trite thing more freshly, with more delicacy, and in more haunting tones, than any other musician. His vocabulary is as marvellous as his facility in orchestration and in the development of a theme. He gets himself into tangles from which there seems no possible escape, only to extricate himself with the airiest of touches. Never does his fertility of melodic invention fail him. He is as prodigal in this respect as Caruso in his moments. Where others achieve a beautiful phrase, and rest on it, Puccini never idles; he has others and others, and he crowds them upon you until the ear is surfeited with sweetness, and you can but sit and marvel.

There it is. Sniff at it as you will, it is a great art that captures you against your reason, and when Puccini and Caruso join forces, they can shake the soul out of the most rabid of musical purists. What they do to commonplace people like myself is untellable. I have tried to hint at it in these few remarks, but really I have told you nothing . . . nothing.

. . . . .

I am not over-fond of the Promenade Concerts. You have, of course, everything of the best—the finest music of the world, the finest English orchestra, and a neat little concert-hall; but somehow there is that about it that suggests Education. I have a feeling that Sir Henry is taking me by the hand, training me up in the way I should, musically, go. And I hate being trained. I don't want things explained to me. The programme looks rather like " Music without Tears " or " First Steps for the Little Ones." I know perfectly well what Wagner meant by the " Tannhäuser " overture, and what Beethoven wants to say to me in the Ninth Symphony. I don't want these things pointed out to me, and sandwiched between information as to when the composer was born, how long he lived, and how many hundred works he wrote. However, all that apart, the Promenades are an institution which we should cherish. For a shilling you can lean against the wall of the area, and smoke, and take your fill of the best in music. If there is anything that doesn't interest you, you can visit the bar until it is concluded. The audience on the Promenade is as interesting as the programme. All types are to be found here—the serious and hard-up student, the musically inclined working-man, probably a member of some musical society in his suburb, the young clerk, the middle-aged man, and a few people who KNOW.

The orchestra is well set, and its pendant crimson lamps and fernery make a solemn picture in the soft light. The vocalists and soloists are not, usually, of outstanding merit, but they sing and play agreeably, and, even if they attempt more than their powers justify them in doing, they never distress you. Sir Henry Wood's entrance on the opening night of any season is an impressive affair. As each known member of the orchestra comes in, he receives an ovation; but ovation is a poor descriptive for Sir Henry's reception. There is no doubt that he has done more for music in England than any other man, and his audiences know this; they regard him almost as a friend.

He is an artist in the matter of programmes. He builds them as a chef builds up an elaborate banquet, by the blending of many flavours and essences, each item a subtle, unmarked progression on its predecessor. He is very fond of his Russians, and his readings of Tchaikowsky seem to me the most beautiful work he does. I do not love Tchaikowsky, but he draws me by, I suppose, the attraction of repulsion. The muse who guides the dreamings of the Russian artist is a sombre and heavy-lidded lady, but most sombre, I think, when she moves in the brain of the musician. Then she wears the glooms and sables of the hypochondriac. She does not "nerve us with incessant affirmations." Rather, she enervates us with incessant dubitations. It is more than a relief to leave the crowded Promenade, after a Tchaikowsky symphony, to stroll in the dusky glitter of Langham Place, and return to listen to the clear, cool tones of Mozart, as sparkling and as gracious as a May morning! Next to Tchaikowsky, Sir Henry gives us much of Wagner and Beethoven and Mendelssohn. I can never understand why Mendelssohn is played nowadays. His music always seems to me to be so provincial and gentlemanly and underbred as to remind one of a county ball. I am sure he always composed in a frock-coat, silk hat, and lavender gloves. When he is being played, many of us have to rush away and saunter in the foyer.

Usually the programme contains some examples of modern French music (a delicate horror by Ravel, perhaps) and of the early Italians. You will get something sweet and suave and restful by Palestrina or Handel, and conclude, perhaps, with a tempest of Berlioz.

During the season of the Promenades, there are also excellent concerts going on in the lost districts of London. There is, to begin with, the Grand Opera season at the Old Vic. in Waterloo Road, where you can get a box for one-and-sixpence, and a seat in the gallery for twopence. The orchestra is good, and the singers are satisfactory. The operas include "Daughter of the Regiment," and run through Verdi and some of Wagner to Mascagni and Charpentier. The audience is mostly drawn from the surrounding streets, the New Cut and Lower Marsh. It wears its working clothes, and it smokes cut Cavendish; but there is not a whisper from the first bar of the overture to the curtain. The chorus is drawn from the local clubs, and a very live and intelligent chorus it is. Then there are the Saturday evening concerts at the People's Palace in Whitechapel, at the Surrey Masonic Hall, in Camberwell, at Cambridge House, and at Vincent Square. In each case the programme is distinctly classical. It is only popular in the sense that the prices are small and the performers' services are honorary. Many a time have I attended one of these concerts, because I knew I should hear there some old, but obscure, classic that I should never be likely to hear at any of the West End concert-halls.

These West End halls are unhappily situated. The dismal Bond Street holds one, another stands cheek by jowl with Marlborough Police Court, and the other two are stuck deep in the melancholic greyness of Wigmore Street. All are absurdly inaccessible. However, when it is a case of Paderewski or Hambourg or Backhaus or Ysayt, people will make pilgrimages to the end of the earth . . . or to Wigmore Street. It was at the Bechstein, on a stifling June evening, that I first heard that mischievous angel, Vladimir de Pachmann.

We had dined solidly, with old English ale, at " The Cock," in Fleet Street. Perhaps tomato soup, mutton cutlets, quarts of bitter, apple and blackberry tart and cream, macaroni cheese, coffee, and kümmel are hardly in the right key for an evening with Chopin. But I am not one of those who take their pleasures sadly. If I am to appreciate delicate art, I must be physically well prepared. It may be picturesque to sit through a Bayreuth Festival on three dates and a nut, but monkey-tricks of that kind are really a slight on one's host. However, I felt very fat, physically, and very Maeterlinckian, spiritually, as we clambered into a cab and swung up the great bleak space of Kingsway.

At the entrance to the Steinway we ran against a bunch of critics, and adjourned to the little place at the opposite corner, so that one of the critics might learn from us what he ought to say about the concert. We had just time to slip into our seats, and then Pachmann, sleek and bullet-headed, minced on to the platform. I said that I felt fat, physically, and Maeterlinckian or Burne-Jonesy, or anything else that suggests the twilight mood, spiritually. But the moment Pachmann came on he drove the mood clean out of us. Obviously, *he* wasn't feeling Maeterlinckian or Chopinesque. He was feeling very full of Pachmann, one could see. Nothing die-away or poetic about him. He was fat physically, and he looked fat spiritually. One conceived him much more readily nodding over the fire with the old port, than playing Chopin in a bleak concert-hall, laden with solemn purples and drabs, stark and ungarnished save for a few cold flowers and ferns.

However, there he was; and after he had played games and cracked jokes, of which nobody knew the secrets but himself, with the piano-stool, his hair, and his handkerchief, he set to work. He flourished a few scales; looked up; giggled; said something to the front row; looked off and nodded; rubbed his fingers; gently patted his ashen cheek; then stretched both hands to the keys.

He played first a group of Preludes. What is there to say about him? Nothing. Surely never, since Chopin went from us, has Chopin been so played. The memory of my Fleet Street dinner vanished. The hall vanished. All surroundings vanished. Vladimir, the antic, took us by the hand and led us forth into a new country: a country, like nothing that we have seen or dreamed of, and therefore a country of which not the vaguest image can be created. It was a country, or, perhaps, a street of pale shadows . . . and that is all I know. Its name is Pachmann-land.

Before he was through the first short prelude, he had us in his snare. One by one the details of the room faded, and nothing was left but a cloud of lilac in which were Pachmann and the sleek, gleaming piano. As he played, change succeeded change. The piano was labelled Chappell, but it might just as well have been labelled Bill Bailey. Under Pachmann, the wooden structure took life, as it were, and became a living thing, breathing, murmuring, clamouring, shrieking. Soon there was neither Chappell, nor Pachmann, nor Chopin; only a black creature—Piano. One shivered, and felt curiously afraid.

Then, suddenly, there was a crash of chords— and silence. That crash had shattered everything, and, looking up, we saw nothing but the grinning Pachmann. One half-remembered that he had been grinning and gesturing and grimacing with ape-like imbecility all the time, yet, somehow, one had not noticed it. He bobbed up and down, and grinned, and applauded himself. But there was something uncanny, mysterious. We looked at one another uneasily, afraid to exchange glances. Nobody spoke. Nobody wanted to speak. A few smiled shy, secret smiles, half-afraid of themselves. For some moments nobody even applauded. Something had been with us. Something strange and sad and exquisitely fragile had gone from us.

Pachmann looked at us, noted our dumb wonder, and—giggled like an idiot.

A JEWISH NIGHT
WHITECHAPEL

LONDON ROSES

*When the young year woos all the world to flower
With gold and silver of sun and shower,
   The girls troop out with an elfin clamour,
   Delicate bundles of lace and light.
And London is laughter and youth and playtime,
Fair as the million-blossomed may-time:
   All her ways are afire with glamour,
   With dainty damosels pink and white.*

*The weariest streets new joys discover;
The sweet glad girl and the lyric lover
   Sing their hearts to the moment's flying,
   Never a thought to time or tears.
O frivolous frocks! O fragrant faces,
Scattering blooms in the gloomy places!
   Shatter and scatter our sombre sighing,
   And lead us back to the golden years!*

A JEWISH NIGHT

WHITECHAPEL

WHITECHAPEL exists under false pretences. It has no right to its name, for the word Whitechapel arouses grim fears in the minds of those who know it not. Its reputation is as theatrically artificial as that of the New York Bowery. Its poverty and its tradition of lawlessness are sedulously fostered by itself for the benefit of the simple-minded slummer.

To-day it is, next to St. John's Wood, the most drably respectable quarter of the town. This is explained by the fact that it is the Ghetto : the home of the severely moral Jew. There is no disorder in Whitechapel. There is no pillage or rapine or bashing. The colony leads its own pleasant life, among its own people, interfering with none and desiring intercourse with none. It has its own manners and customs and its own simple and very beautiful ceremonies. The Jews in London are much scattered. They live in various quarters, according to the land of their birth. Thus, the French Jews are in Soho, the German Jews in Great Charlotte Street, the Italian Jews in Clerkenwell, while those of Whitechapel are either Russian Jews or Jews who have, for three generations, been settled in London. The wealthy Jew, who fancies himself socially, the fat, immoral stockbroker and the City philanderer, has deserted the surroundings of his humbler compatriots for the refinements of Highbury, Maida Vale, and Bayswater.

The Whitechapel Ghetto begins at Aldgate,

branches off at that point where Commercial Street curls its nasty length to Shoreditch, and embraces the greater part of Commercial Road East, sprawling on either side. Here at every turn you will meet the Jew of the comic papers. You will see expressive fingers, much jewelled, flying in unison with the rich Yiddish tongue. You will see beards and silk hats which are surely those which decorated the Hebrew in Eugène Sue's romance. And you will find a spirit of brotherhood keener than any other race in the world can show. It is something akin to the force that inspired that splendid fraternity that once existed in London, and is now no more: I mean the Costers. If a Jew is in trouble or in any kind of distress, a most beautiful thing happens: his friends rally round him.

The atmosphere of the Ghetto is a singular mixture. It is half-ironic gaiety and half-melancholy. But it has not the depressing sadness of the Russian Quarter. Its temper is more akin to that of the Irish colony that has settled around Southwark and Bermondsey. There is sadness, but no misery. There is gloom, but no despair. There is hilarity, but no frivolity. There is a note of delight, with sombre undertones. There is nothing of the rapture of living, but rather the pride of accepted destiny. In the hotels and cafés this is most marked. At the Aldgate Hotel, you may sit in the brasserie and listen to the Russian Trio discoursing wistful music, while the packed tables reek with smoke and Yiddish talk; but there is a companionable, almost domestic touch about the place which is so lacking about the Western lounges. Young Isaacs is there, flashing with diamonds and hair-oil, and Rebecca is with him, and the large, admiring parents of both of them sit with them and drink beer or eat sandwiches. And Isaacs makes love to his Rebecca in full sight of all. They lounge in their chairs, arms enclasped, sometimes kissing, sometimes patting one another. And the parents look on, and roll their curly heads and say, with subtle significance, " Oi-oi-oi ! " many times.

Out in the street there is the same homely, yearning atmosphere. It is the homeliness of a people without a home, without a country. They are exiles who have flung together, as well as may be, the few remnants of their possessions, adding to them little touches that may re-create the colour of their land, and have settled down to make the best of things. Their feasts and festivals are full of this yearning. The Feast of Maccabeus, which is celebrated near our Christmas-time, is delightfully domestic. It is preceded, eight days before, by the Feast of the Lights. In each house a candle is lit—one candle on the first day, two on the second, three on the third, and so on until the eighth day, which is that dedicated to Maccabeus. Then there are feastings, and throughout the rich evenings the boys walk with the girls or salute the latter as they lounge at the corners with that suggestion in their faces of lazy strength and smouldering fire. A children's service is held in the synagogues, and cakes and sweets are distributed. The dark, vivid beauty of these children shows marvellously against the greys of Whitechapel. Every Saturday of the year the streets are filled with them, for then all shops are shut, all work suspended, and the little ones are in those best frocks and velvet suits in which even the poorest parents are so proud to clothe their offspring. They love colour ; and ribbons of many hues are lavished on the frocks and tunics. One of my London moments was when I first saw, in Whitechapel High Street, a little Jewess, with masses of jet-black hair, dressed in vermilion and white. I wonder, by the way, why it is that the children of the genteel quarters of London, such as Kensington Gardens, have no hair, or at any rate, only skimpy little twigs of it, while the children of the

East are loaded with curls and tresses of an almost tropical luxuriance, and are many times more beautiful. Does that terrifying process called Good Breeding kill all beauty? Does careful feeding and tending poison the roots of loveliness? I wonder.... Anyway, the Jews, beautiful alike in face and richness of tresses, stand to the front in two of the greatest callings of the world—art and fighting. Examine the heroes of the prize-ring; at least two-thirds of them are Jews. Examine the world's greatest musicians and singers, and the same may be said.

On Sundays, of course, only the rags of everyday are seen, for then the work of the week begins again. At about the time of our Easter the Feast of the Passover is celebrated. Then, if you walk down Middlesex Street any Sunday morning you will notice an activity even more feverish than that which it mostly presents. Jews of every nationality flock to it; and for the week preceding this Feast the stall-holders do tremendous business, not, as is customary, with the Gentiles, but among their own people. The Feast of the Passover is one of the oldest and quaintest religious ceremonies of the oldest religion in the world. Fasting and feasting intermingle with observances. Spring-cleaning is general at this season, for all things must be *kosher-al-pesach*, or clean and pure. At the cafés you will find a special kosher bar, whereon are wines and spirits in brand new decanters, glasses freshly bought and cleansed, and a virgin cloth surmounting the whole. The domestic and hardware shops are busy, for the home must be replenished with chaste vessels—pots and pans and all utensils are bought with reckless disregard of expense. Milk may not be bought from the milkman's cans. Each house fetches its own from the shops, in new, clean jugs, which are, of course, *kosher*; and nothing is eaten but unleavened bread.

When the fast is over, begins the feast, and the cafés and the family dining-rooms are full. Down a side street stand straggling armies of ragged, unkempt Jews—men, women, and children. These are the destitutes. For them the season brings no rejoicing. Therefore their compatriots come forward, and at the office of the Jewish Board of Guardians they assemble to distribute supplies of grocery, vegetables, meat, fish, eggs, and so forth. Country or sex matters not; all Jews must rejoice, and, when necessary, must be supplied with the means of rejoicing. So here are gathered all the wandering Jews without substance. Later, after the fine feed which is provided for them, there are services in the synagogue. The men and women, in strict isolation, are a drama in themselves. Men with long beards and sad, shifty faces; men with grey beards, keen eyes, and intellectual profile; men with curly hair and Italian features; and women with dark, shining hair and flashing eyes—men, women, and children of every country and clime, rich and poor, are gathered there to worship after the forms of the saddest of all faiths.

The Ghetto is full of life every evening, for then the workshops and factories and warehouses are closed, and the handsome youth of Whitechapel is free to amuse itself. Most of the girls work at the millinery establishments, and most of the boys at the wholesale drapery houses. The High Street is one of the most picturesque main streets of London. The little low butchers' shops, fronted by raucous stalls, the gabled houses, and the flat-faced hotels, are some of the loveliest bits of eighteenth-century domestic architecture remaining in London. And the crowd! It sweeps you from your feet; it catches you up, drags you, drops you, jostles you; and you don't mind in the least. They are all so gay, and they look upon you with such haunting glances that it is impossible to be cross with them.

If you leave the London Docks, and crawl up the dismal serenity of Cable Street, the High Street seems to snatch you. You catch the mood of the moment; you dance with the hour. There is noise and the flare of naphtha. There are opulent glooms. The regiment of lame stalls is packed so closely, shoulder to shoulder, that if one gave an inch the whole line would fall. Meat, greengrocery, Brummagem jewellery for the rich beauty of Rhoda, shell-fish, confectionery, old magazines, pirated music, haberdashery, "throw-out" (or Sudden Death) cigars—all these glories are waiting to seize your pennies. Slippery slices of fish sprawl dolefully on the slabs. The complexion of the meatshops, under the yellow light, is rich and strange. But there is very little shouting; the shopkeepers make no attempt to entice you. There are the goods : have 'em if you like; if not, leave 'em.

If you are hungry, and really want something to eat, I suggest your going to one of the restaurants or hotels, and trying their table d'hôte. They run usually to six or seven courses, two of which will satisfy any reasonable hunger. Yet I have seen frail young girls tackle the complete menu, and come up fresh and smiling at the end. Of course, women are, as a rule, much heavier eaters than men, but these delicate, pallid girls of the Ghetto set you marvelling. I have occasionally joined a party, and delightful table companions they were. For they can talk; they have, if not humour, at any rate a very mordant wit, as all melancholy peoples have; and they languish in the most delicately captivating way.

On my first experience, we started the meal with Solomon Gundy—pickled herring. Then followed a thick soup, in which were little threads of a paste made from eggs and flour and little balls of unleavened dough. Then came a kind of pea-soup, and here a little lady of the party ordered unfermented Muscat wine. The good Jew may not touch shell-fish or any fish without scales, so we were next served with fried soles and fried plaice, of which Rachel took both, following, apparently, the custom of the country. Although the menu consists of seven courses, each item contains two, and sometimes three or four, dishes; and the correct diner tastes every one. Roast veal, served in the form of stew, followed, and then came roast fowl and tongue. There were also salads, and sauerkraut, and then a pease-pudding, and then almond-pudding, and then staffen, and then . . . I loosened a button, and gazed upon Rachel in wonder. She was still eating bread.

It is well to be careful, before visiting any of the Ghetto cafés, to acquaint yourself with rules and ceremonies. Otherwise you may unintentionally give offence and make yourself several kinds of idiot. I have never at any period of my London life been favoured with a guiding hand. Wherever I went, whatever I did, I was alone. That is really the only way to see things, and certainly the only way to learn things. If I wanted to penetrate the inmost mysteries of Hoxton, I went to Hoxton, and blundered into private places and to any holy of holies that looked interesting. Sometimes nothing happened. Sometimes I got what I asked for. When at seventeen I wanted to find out if the Empire Promenade was really anything like the Empire Promenade, I went to the Empire Promenade. Of course, I made mistakes and muddled through. I made mistakes in the Ghetto. I was the bright boy who went to a shabby little café in Osborn Street, and asked for smoked beef, roll and butter, and coffee. The expression on that waiter's face haunts me whenever I feel bad and small. He did not order me out of the restaurant. He did not assault me. He looked at me, and I grieved to see his dear grey eyes . . . so sad. He said: " Pardon, but this is a kosher café. I am not a Jew myself, but how can I serve what you order? Tell me—how can I do it? What?"

I said: "I beg your pardon, too. I don't understand. Tell me more."

He said: "Would you marry your aunt? No. Neither may a Jewish restaurant serve milk, or its derivatives, such as, so to speak, butter, cheese, and so forth, on the same table with flesh. You ask for meat and bread and butter. You must have bread with your meat. If you have coffee, sir, you will have it BLACK."

I said: "It is my fault. No offence intended. I didn't know. Once again, I have made an ass of myself. Had I better not go?"

He said, swiftly: "No, don't go, sir. Oh, don't go. Listen: have the smoked beef, with a roll. Follow with prunes or kugel. And if you want a drink *with* your meal, instead of afterwards, have tea-and-lemon in place of black coffee."

And so, out of that brutal mistake, I made yet another London friend, of whom I have, roughly, about two thousand five hundred scattered over the four-mile radius.

A HAPPY NIGHT
SURBITON AND BATTERSEA

A SUBURBAN NIGHT

Oh, sweetly sad and sadly sweet,
  That rain-pearled night at Highbury!
The picture-theatre, off the street,
That housed us from the lisping sleet,
  Is a white grave of dreams for me.

Though smile and talk were all our part,
Sorrow lay prone upon your heart
That never again our lips might meet,
And never so softly fall the sleet
  In gay-lamped, lyric Highbury.
Love made your lily face to shine,
But oh, your cheek was salt to mine.
  As we walked home from Highbury.

O starry street of shop and show,
And was it thus long years ago?
Was the full tale but waste and woe,
And Love but doom in Highbury,
My dusty, dreaming Highbury?

A HAPPY NIGHT

SURBITON AND BATTERSEA

WHEN I received the invitation to the whist-drive at Surbiton my first thought was, " Not likely ! " I had visions of a boring evening : I knew Surbiton. I knew its elegances and petty refinements. I knew its pathetic apings of Curzon Street and Grosvenor Square. I knew its extremely dull smartness of speech and behaviour. I foresaw that I should enjoy myself as much as I did at the Y.M.C.A. concert where everybody sang refined songs and stopped the star from going on because he was about to sing the " Hymn to Venus," which was regarded as " a little amorous." The self-conscious waywardness, the deliberate Bohemianism of Surbiton, I said to myself, is not for me. I shall either overplay it or underplay it. Certainly I shall give offence if I am my normal self. For the Bohemianism of Surbiton, I continued, has very strict rules which nobody in Bohemia ever heard of, and you cannot be a Surbiton Bohemian until you have mastered those rules and learned how gracefully to transgress them. If I throw bread pellets at the girls, they will call me unmannerly. If I don't they will call me stiff. You may have noticed that those pseudo-intellectuals who like to think themselves Bohemian are always terrified when they are brought up against anything that really is unconventional. On the other hand, your true Bohemian is disgusted if anybody describes him by that word; if there is one word that he detests more than Belgravia, it is Bohemia. No, I shall certainly not go.

Surbiton . . . Surbiton. I repeated the name aloud, tasting its flavour. It has always had to me something brackish, something that fills my mind with grey pain and makes me yearn for my old toys. It is curious how the places and streets of London assume a character from one's own moods. All the big roads have a very sharp character of their own. If all other indications were lacking, one might know at once whether the place were Edgware Road or Old Ford Road, simply by the sounds and by the sweep of it. Pull down every house and shop, and still Oxford Street could never pass itself off as Barking Road. But they have, too, a message for you. I still believe that a black dog is waiting to maul me in Stepney Causeway. I still dance with delight down Holborn. Peckham Road still speaks to me of love. And Maida Vale always means music for me, music all the way. I had my first fright in Stepney Causeway. I first walked down Holborn when I had had a streak of luck. I first knew Peckham Road when first I loved. And I first made acquaintance with Maida Vale and its daintily naughty flats at the idiotic age of seventeen, when I was writing verses for composers at five shillings a time. They all lived in Maida Vale, and I spent many evenings in the music-rooms of those worn-out or budding composers and singers who, with the Jews, have made this district their own; so that Maida Vale smells always to me of violets and apple-blossom: it speaks April and May. The deep blue of its night skies is spangled with dancing stars. The very sweep and sway of the road to Kilburn and Cricklewood is an ecstasy, and the windows of the many mansions seem to shine from heaven, so aloof are they.

Surbiton, I repeated. I shall certainly not go. I know it too well. Surbiton is one of those comfortable, solid places, and I loathe comfortable places. I always go to Hastings and avoid St. Leonards. I always go to Margate and fly from Eastbourne. I always go to Southend and give Knocke-sur-Mer a miss. I like Clacton. I detest Cromer. I love Camden Town. I hate Surbiton. Surbiton is very much like Hampstead, except that, while Hampstead is horrible for 362 days of the year, there are three days in the year when it is inhabitable. On Bank Holidays the simple-minded minor poet like myself can live in it. I was there one August Bank Holiday, and, flushed and fatigued with the full-blooded frolic, I had turned aside to "cool dahn" in Heath Street, when I ran against some highly respectable and intelligent friends.

"What !" they said. "You here to-day? Ah ! observing, I suppose ? Getting copy ? Or perhaps as a literary man you come here for Keats . . . Coleridge . . . and all that ? "

"No," I answered. "I come here for boat-swings. I come here to throw sticks at coconuts. I come here to buy ticklers to tickle the girls with. I come here for halfpenny skips. I come here for donkey rides. I do not come for Keats. I do not care a damn for Coleridge. I do not come to gloat about Turner or Constable or anybody else who lived at Hampstead a hundred years ago. I come here to enjoy myself—for roundabouts, cockles and whelks, steam-organs—which, after all, are the same thing as Keats or Coleridge. They're Life."

Wherefore I felt determined that I could not and would not go to a whist-drive at Surbiton, when I could get the real thing in Upper Street, Islington.

Then Georgie called for me at the office, and we went out to lunch. Georgie had sold a picture. He had five pounds in his pocket. We went to Maxim's and had lunch. Georgie insisted on sparkling

Moselle, and we had two bottles, and three rounds of Cointreau triple sec. By that time it was too late to think of going back to work, so I took Georgie to tea at a literary club, and we talked. I then discovered in a panic that it was half-past six. The whist-drive was at eight, and I had yet to dine and get down to Surbiton. Georgie, by that subtle magnetism which he possesses, had drawn a bunch of the boys about him, and had induced them to make a night of it with him; so we went to Simpson's to eat, and I left them at the table, very merry, and departed to Waterloo. Somewhere, between lunch and dinner, I had unconsciously decided, you see, that I would go to Surbiton. I can't remember just when the change in my attitude took place; but there it was. I went to Surbiton, feeling quite good and almost in love with Surbiton.

The whist-drive was to be held in the local hall, and when I arrived cabs and motors were forming a queue. Each cab vomited some dainty arrangement in lace or black cloth. Everybody was "dressed." (I think I said that it was Surbiton.) Everybody was on best behaviour. Remembering the gang at Simpson's, I felt rather a scab, but a glance in the mirror of the dressing-room reassured me. I recollected some beautiful words of Mr. Mark Sheridan's, "If I'm not clever, thank God, I'm clean." The other fellows in the dressing-room were things of beauty. Their public-school accent, with its vile mispronunciation of the English tongue, would have carried them into the inner circles of any European chancellery. I never heard anything so supernally affecting. I have heard many of our greatest actors and singers, but I have never heard so much music put into simple words, as, "I say, you fellers!"

Everybody was decent. Everybody, you felt sure, could be trusted to do the decent thing, to do whatever was "done," and to leave undone those things that were not "done," and, generally, to be a very decent sort. Their features were clean and firm; they were well-tended. Their minds were clean. They talked clean; and, if they did not display any marked signs of intelligence or imagination, if they had not the largeness of personality for the noble and big things of life, you felt that at least they had not the bent for doing anything dirty. Altogether, a nice set, as insipid people mostly are : what are known in certain circles as Gentlemen.

The girls. . . . Well, they, too, were a decent sort. Not so decent as the boys, of course, because they were girls. They scanned one another a little too closely. They were too obviously anxious to please. They were too obviously out for the evening. Those who were of the at-home type simpered. They talked in italics. The outdoor type walked like horses. They looked unpleasant, too. I wonder why "Madge" or "Felice" or "Ermyntrude," or some other writer of toilet columns in the ladies' papers, doesn't tell her outdoor girl readers how hideous they look in evening frocks. Why don't they urge them not to uncover themselves? For the outdoor girl has large hands and large arms, both of a beefy red. She has a face and neck tanned by sun and wind, and her ensemble, in a frock cut to the very edge of decency, shows you red hands and forearms, with a sharp dividing line where the white upper arm begins, and a raw face and neck, with the same definite line marking the beginning of white bosom and shoulders. The effect is ridiculous. It is also repulsive. I think they ought to know about it.

The hall was tastefully decorated with white flowers and palms. There was a supper-room, which looked good. The prizes, arranged on a table by the platform, were elegant, well chosen, and of some value. I started at a table with an elderly matron, a very self-conscious Fabian girl, and a rather bored-looking man of middle age, who seemed to be bursting to talk—which is the deadliest of sins at a Surbiton whist-drive. The whist that I play is the very worst whist that has ever been seen. I told my partner so, and she said, " Oh, really ! " and asked me if I had had any tennis yet. Then some one begged us to be seated, and, with much arrangement of silks and laces and wraps, we sat down and began to play whist. As I moved from table to table I made no fresh partners. They were differently dressed, but otherwise there was no distinction. They were a very decent sort. . . .

After many hours we stopped playing whist, and broke up for chewing and chatting. The bored-looking man of middle age picked me up, and we took two stray girls in tow for wine and sandwiches. The manners at the supper-crush were elegance itself. The girls smoked cigarettes just a little too defiantly, but they were quite well-bred about it. A lot of well-bred witticisms floated around, with cool laughter and pretty smiles. A knot of girls with two boys talked somewhat decryingly of Shaw and Strindberg; and one caught stray straws of talk about Masefield, Beecham opera, Scriabine, Marinetti, Augustus John. Two girls were giving a concert at the Steinway next week. Others were aiming at the Academy. Another had had a story accepted by the *English Review*. They were a very decent sort.

The bored man plucked at my arm and suggested that we get rid of the girls, and go across to " The Railway " and have one. We did. In the lounge of " The Railway " he told me the one about the lady and the taxi. It was very good, but extremely ill-bred. He was a prominent local doctor, so I told him the one about the medical man on the panel, and about the Bishop who put gin in his whisky. Then he told me another . . . and another. He remembered the old days at the

London. . . . He said he had had to go to this show because his boy and girl were there. Cards bored him to death, but he liked to be matey with the youngsters. Suppose we had just one more?

We had just one more. From across the way came, very sweet and faint, the sound of laughter and young voices. Some one had started a piano, and the Ballade in A Minor was wandering over Surbiton. I looked into my brandy-glass, and, as I am very young, I rather wanted to cry. I don't know why. It was just the mood . . . the soft night, Surbiton, young boys and girls, Chopin, Martell. . . . I said I had to catch an immediate train to Waterloo, and I drank up and bolted.

.   .   .   .   .

The other Saturday morning I met a friend at the Bedford Street Bodega. He said, "Laddie, doing anything to-night?" I said, "No; what's on?"

He said: "Like to help your old uncle?"

I said: "Stand on me."

"Well, it's a little charity show. A Social at Battersea Town Hall. Some local club or tennis-party or some jolly old thing of that sort. All receipts to the local hospital. All the gang are going to do something—kind of informal, you know. I'm the Star. Yes, laddie, I have at last a shop, for one night only. My fee—seven-and-sixpence and tram-fares. All other services gratuitous. No platform. No auditorium. Just a little old sit-round, drinking limp coffee and eating anæmic pastry, and listening. Come?"

I said I would, and we adventured along the dreary Wandsworth Road, down the evil-smelling Lavender Hill, into the strenuous endeavour of Clapham Junction. It was gay with lights and shoppers and parading monkeys. Above us hung a pallid, frosty sky. No stars; no moon; but down in the streets, warmth and cheer and companionship. We called at the blazing, bustling "Falcon," which is much more like a railway-junction than the station itself, and did ourselves a little bit of good, as my professional friend put it. Then we mounted to the gas-lit room where the fun was to take place. We wandered down long, stark passages, seeking our door. We heard voices, but we saw no door.

"Harold," said some one, "sometimes wish you wasn't quite such a fool."

"What's the matter now, Freddie?" asked A Voice.

"Why, you know very well it's ten to eight, and you ain't even pulled the piano out."

"Gaw! Lucky you reminded me. Come on, old chew-the-fat, give us a hand with the musical-box."

There were noises "off," from which it seemed that some one had put something on top of something else. There were noises of some one hitting a piece of wood with another piece of wood.

Then "Damn!" cried A Voice. "Steady on my feet, can't yeh? Bit more to the right. Whoa! Up your end a bit. 'At's it. When was she tuned last? Give us a scale."

Some one flourished, and then a bright door opened, and two young men in shirt-sleeves with tousled brows, appeared.

"Laddie," cried my friend, dramatically, "is this the apartment for the Young People's Society In Connection With The Falcon Road Miss——?"

"That's us!" cried, I imagine, Freddie.

"Then I am Victor Maulever."

"Oh, step inside, won't you. Bit early, I'm 'fraid. Mr. Diplock ain't here yet. But come in. We got a fire going, and it's sort of turning chilly out, eh?"

We stepped in, and Freddie introduced us.

"Harold—this is Mr. Maulever, the actor. Mr. Maulever, may I introduce our sec't'ry, Mr. Worple—Mr. Harold Worple, I should say."

Mr. Worple came forward and shook hands. "'Scuse my shirt-sleeves, won't you, sir?"

"Certainly, laddie, cer-tain-ly," said Victor, with that *empressement* which has earned him so many drinks in Maiden Lane. "Cer-tain-ly. And how are you?"

"Nicely, thanks," said Harold. "How's 'self?"

"So-so, just so-so. Now just tell me about your little affair, so I can get 'em fixed good and plenty before I start. What d'you think'll go best; you know 'em better than I do? Shakespeare—what? Bransby Williams? 'Dream of Eugene Aram'? 'Kissing Cup's Race'? Imitations of Robey, Formby, Chirgwin—what?"

Harold pondered a moment. Then he had an inspiration. "Sort 'em up if I was you, sir. Sort 'em up. Then ev'body'll get something they like, see?"

We entered the clubroom where the Social was to be held—a large, lofty room, genial, clean, and well-lighted. The floor was bare, but a red rug before the leaping fire gave a touch of cosiness. Small tables were scattered everywhere; draughts here, dominoes there, chess elsewhere, cards in other places. Chairs were distributed with a studied air of casual disorder. Newspapers littered a side-bench. The grand piano, by Cadenza of The Emporium, stood diagonally across the left centre, and on it lay the violin-case of Freddie, who told us, with modesty, that he "scraped nows and thens." Along the length of the farther wall stood a large, white-robed table, heaped with coffee-urns, sandwiches, buns, cakes, biscuits, bananas, and other delicacies. All these arrangements were the joint work of Freddie and Harold.

At five minutes to eight the company arrived.

At first it trickled in by stray couples, but later it swelled to a generous flood, each couple nodding in acknowledgment of the deprecatory greetings of the stewards: "Here we are again, what-oh?" and, in more professional tones: "Gentlemen's Room to the Right, Ladies' Room to the Left!"

Victor and myself stood by the fire, Victor receiving bashful but definitely admiring glances from the girls, for he is of the old school, and looks more like Sir Henry Irving even than Mr. H. B. Irving, except that he does not limp. For the first few minutes the atmosphere was cold. The boys obviously wanted to talk to Victor, but they seemed all too shy; so I gave Victor the tip, and with his exquisite courtesy he moved over to a group of the boys and the girls and, with a bow, asked a girl with a baby face, that burnt delightfully red under his attention, if he might take a seat on that settee. In just a minute and a half the thaw set in, and he had the company about him bubbling with laughter and excited comment. As other groups came in from the dressing-rooms they made at once for the centre of attraction, and soon Victor was the centre of a crowd that buzzed about him like bees about a flower, seeking the honey of laughter. I doubt if he was ever so much on the "spot" before. I could see him revelling in it. I could see him telling Rule's about it. But in the middle of his best story, Freddie bustled up.

"Oh, 'scuse me, sir, but I forgot to tell you before. I said sort 'em up, but . . . you might just be careful, 'cos the Vicar's dropping in during the evening. I'll give you the word when he's here, so's you'll be sure to hand 'em something quiet. It's all right until he comes. Just give 'em anything you like."

And Victor waved a faded hand, and said, "Righto, laddie, righto. I get you," and turned again to the blushing little girl, who certainly seemed now to be Quite The Lady in her manner of receiving his attentions. Under his expansive mood everybody soon knew everybody else, and all traces of stiffness vanished. The company was a little mixed, and it was inevitable that there should be demarcations of border, breed, and birth. Some were shop-assistants, some were mechanics, some were clerks, some were even Civil Servants; and as all were Christians they were naturally hesitant about loving one another. But Victor broke down all barriers by his large humanity and universal appeal.

Suddenly, there was a hammering on the floor, and a voice called, "Attention, please!" And then—"Duet for violin and piano: Miss Olive Craven and Mr. Fred Parslow."

We broke into little groups, and settled ourselves. Then came a crash of chords from the piano, and a prolonged reiteration of the A while Freddie tuned. They set to work. I heard the opening bars, and I held my breath in dismay. They were going to play a Tchaikowsky Concerto. But the dismay was premature. They *played*; both of them. I do not know whether Freddie was engaged to Olive, but there was a marvellous sympathy uniting them; and, though little technical flaws appeared here and there, the beauty of the work was brought right out. Freddie and Olive were musicians. It was a delicious quarter of an hour. They got a big handful of applause, and then Freddie asked: "Ready, sir?" and Victor said he was, and Freddie said, "What is it?" and conveyed the answer to the portly old fellow who seemed to be president. After a minute or so, during which the girls chattered and giggled and compared ribbons and flounces, he called again for silence, and a tremendous outburst of clapping and stamping followed his announcement: "Mr. Victor Maulever, the famous West End actor, will recite 'Who'll have a Blood Orange?'"

Victor made good with his first three sentences. In the language of his profession, he got 'em with both hands. They rose at him. He had 'em stung to death. He did what he liked with 'em. The girls giggled and kicked little feet. They shamelessly broke into his periods with "*Isn't* he IT?" and he had to wait while the laughs went round.

When he had finished he got such a hand as I'm sure he never had in the whole of his stage career. They wouldn't let him sit down. They would give him no rest; he must go straight on and give more. So he gave them two more, including his impressions of George Robey, G. P. Huntley, Joe Elvin, R. G. Knowles, and Wilkie Bard singing "Little Grey Home in the West."

Then the President appealed to the audience to let poor Mr. Maulever have a rest and a little refreshment; and at once the girls rushed to the table and fought with one another for sandwiches and coffee and cakes with which they might minister to the exhausted Thespian. The boys did not get savage about this; they seemed to share in the fun, and when new girl-arrivals came in, they were solemnly introduced to the star. "Oh, Mr. Maulever, may I introduce my friend, Miss Redgrove?" Miss Redgrove smiled becomingly, and Victor rose, bowed, extended his graceful hand, and said: "Delighted, Miss Redgrove!" and Miss Redgrove said: "Pleased to meet you!" And in reply to Victor's inquiry: "I hope you're well?" she said that she mustn't grumble.

A few of the girls wore evening frocks; others, with more limited means, contented themselves with Sunday frocks or delicately coloured robes that had been manœuvred into something that showed enough white neck and bosom to be at once alluring and decorous. There was nothing of the plain or the dowdy. They were all out for enjoyment, and they meant to make the best of everything, themselves included. Frills and fluffiness were the order. They were all darlings.

A gentle raillery was the note of intercourse between girls and boys. One of the little girls, a typist, I gathered, in a mercantile office, whispered to her boy that Victor was A Love, and added that she always did like men best when they were old and had grey hair. They were so . . . kind of . . . if he knew what she meant. She said she would most likely fall in love with a grey-haired man, and her boy said: "Yes, of course you *would*." Whereupon she told him not to be so sarcastic.

The attitude of gentlemen to ladies was also delightful. Some of the gentlemen were guilty of bad manners, in the Surbiton sense of the word. That is to say, they did not all do what was "done," and they very frequently did things that were not "done" by Good People. But everything they did was inspired by a consideration for the comfort of others. They committed *gaucheries*, but the fount thereof was kindliness.

The conversation was varied. Some talked frocks, some music, some picture-palaces, some odds-and-ends. Those who affected theatres stuck firmly to Victor, and lured him on to talk about the idols of the stage. The dear boy *might* have told them things . . . he might have disillusioned their golden heads about certain actor-managers of whom he has had intimate experience; but he didn't, and I rather liked him for it. While more recitations and more music went round, he told them heroic stories about their heroes. He told them strange stories and beautiful stories and funny stories; but never, never disparaging stories. One saw their faces glow with wonder. Then the time came for him to work again. He certainly earned that seven-and-six. This time the Vicar was there, so he handed them "The Dream of Eugene Aram."

Again he got 'em. The girls shivered and moved nearer to their boys. He got his horror in voice and face and gesture and pauses. There was perfect silence while he did it. There was perfect silence for some seconds afterwards. Then came a rain of clapping, and the Vicar walked across to him and shook him by the hand, showering warm compliments upon him, and trusting that he would be kind enough to come again.

Then, while we drank coffee and handed cakes to the girls, the reverend gentleman stood on the rug before the fire and gave us an informal address. It was all very bright and homely, and the merry twinkle in the old man's eye when he saw the cluster of girls about Victor told us that he was very much alive to this world.

At half-past ten the meeting broke up, with a final effort by Victor in two of Albert Chevalier's songs. The girls pelted to the dressing-rooms and returned, robed for the street and radiant, and all anxious to shake hands and bid farewell to the Star. They literally danced round him, and fought to shake hands with him, and the boys fought with them. Then, when all had saluted him, each boy appropriated a girl. Those who were known tucked arms in arms and marched off. Those who were strangers approached deferentially, and said: "You got a friend, miss? If not . . . m'I see you home?" and were at once elected.

Victor and the Vicar and the President and myself remained behind till the last, while Freddie and Harold "cleared up the mess," as they said. Then Victor winked at the two boys, and lured them to the passage. "Well, boys," he said, jingling his three half-crowns which had just been paid him, "what about it? A short one at 'The Falcon'—what?"

They really blushed. The honour was too much. "Oh—really—well—very kind of you, Mr. Maulever,

I'm sure." They stammered through their hot
smiles, but they came along, and after the short one
at "The Falcon" they lingered a moment. They
appeared nervous. It seemed that they had something on their minds. Harold looked at Freddie
and Freddie looked at Harold, and Freddie said
emphatically, "You." So Harold, very rapidly,
turned and said—

"I was going t'say, Mr. Maulever—I mean, would
you—ah—might I ask if you and your friend'd have
another—with *us*?" He was obviously glad to get
it over.

Victor smiled. "Well, laddie, it's a cold night.
Dammit, we *will* have another."

So we did. As a matter of fact, we had three
others; and in the loud passage of "The Falcon"
we parted with the lads, who wrung Victor's hand,
and said he'd given them a delightful evening, and
they hoped he'd recite for their next Social, adding
that he was a real sport.

I saw Victor to his 'bus, and as he leaped aboard
he said he had enjoyed himself. He turned half-way
up the stairs to cry his customary valediction.

"*Si longtemps*, old kiddo. Cling good and tight
to the water-wagon!"

A WORKER'S NIGHT

THE ISLE OF DOGS

THE WORK CHILD

I

Fair flakes of wilding rose
  Entwine for Seventeen,
With lovely leaves of violet
That dares not live till fields forget
The grey that drest their green with snows,
  And grow from grey to green.

And when the wreath is twining,
  Oh, prithee, have a care!
Weave in no bloom of subtle smell;
The simple ones she loves too well.
Let violets on her neck lie shining,
  Wild rose in her hair.

And bring her rose-winged fancies,
  From shadowy shoals of dream,
To clothe her in the wistful hour,
When girlhood steals from bud to flower.
Bring her the tunes of elfin dances,
  Bring her the faery Gleam!

II

At the world's gate she stands,
  Silent and very still;
And lone as that one star that lights
The delicate dusk of April nights
Oh, let love bind her holy hands,
  And fetter her from ill!

Her tumbled tresses cling
  Adown her like a veil.
And cheek and curls as sweetly chime
As verses with a rounding rhyme.
Surely there is not anything
  So valiant and so frail.

In faith and without fear,
  She brings to a rude throng,
At war with beauty and with truth,
The wonder of her blossomy youth.
And faith shall wither to a sneer,
  And need shall silence song.

III

Her soul is a soft flame,
  Set in a world of grey.
Help her, O Life, to keep its shrine
That her white window's vigilant sign
May pierce the tangled mists of shame,
  Where we have lost our way!

So linger at this day,
  My little maid serene!
Or, since the dancing feet must go,
Take Childhood with you still, and so
Live in a year-worn world, but stay
  For ever Seventeen!

A WORKER'S NIGHT

THE ISLE OF DOGS

I AM not of those who share the prevailing opinions of the Isle of Dogs : I do not see it as a haunt of greyness and distress. To the informed mind it is full and passionate. Every one of its streets is a sharp-flavoured adventure. Where others find insipidity, I find salt and fire. Its shapes and sounds and silences and colours have allured me from first acquaintance. For here, remember, are the Millwall Docks, and here, too, is Cubitt Town. . . . Of course, like all adorable things, it has faults. I am ready to confess that the cheap mind, which finds Beauty only in that loathly quality called Refinement, will suffer many pains by a sojourn in its byways. It will fill them with ashen despair. In the old jolly days it was filthy ; it was full of perils, smelly, insanitary, crumbling ; but at least one could live in it. To-day it has been taken in hand by those remote Authorities who make life miserable for us. It is reasonably clean ; it is secure ; the tumbling cottages have been razed, and artisans' dwellings have arisen in their stead. Its highways—Glengall Road, East Ferry Road, Manchester Road—are but rows of uniform cottages, with pathetically small front gardens and frowzy " backs," which, throughout the week, flap dismally with the most intimate items of their households' underwear. Its horizon is a few grotto-like dust-shoots, decorated with old bottles and condensed-milk tins.

It is, I admit, the ugly step-child of parishes; but, then, I love all ugly step-children. It is *gauche* and ridiculous. It sprawls. It is permanently overhung with mist. It has all the virtues of the London County Council, and it is very nearly uninhabitable. Very nearly uninhabitable . . . but not quite.

For here are many thousands of homes, and where a thousand homes are gathered together there shall you find prayer and beauty. Yes, my genteel lambs of Kensington, in this region of ashpits and waterways and broken ships and dry canals are girls and garlands and all the old lovely things that help the human heart to float and flow along its winding courses. If you inform the palate of the mind by flavours, then life in Queen's Gate must be a round of labour and lassitude, and, from the rich faces that pass you in the Isle of Dogs, you know that it must always be the time of roses there. Stand by the crazy bridge at the gates of West India Dock, at six o'clock, when, through the lilac dusks, comes that flock of chattering magpies—the little work-girls—and see if I am not right.

And the colour. . . . There is nothing in the world like it for depth and glamour. I know no evenings so tender as those that gather about the Island: at once heartsome and subdued. The colour of street and sky and water, sprinkled with a million timid stars, is an ecstasy. You cannot name it. You see it first as blue, then as purple, then lilac, rose, silver. The clouds that flank the high-shouldered buildings and chimneys share in these subtle changes, and shift and shift from definite hues to some haunting scheme that was never seen in any colourman's catalogue.

On the night when I took Georgie round the Island a hard, clear frost was abroad. The skies glittered with steady stars. The streets seemed strangely wide and frank, clear-cut, and definite. A fat-faced moon lighted them. The waters were

THE ISLE OF DOGS

swift and limpid, flecked with bold light. The gay public-house at the Dock gates shone sharp, like a cut gem. Georgie had never toured the Island before, and he enjoyed it thoroughly. As we stood on the shuddering bridge the clear night spread such a stillness over the place that you could almost hear a goods train shunt; and we stood there watching the berthing of a big P. & O. for many pensive minutes.

By the way, you ought to know Georgie; he is a London character. Perhaps you do, for he has thousands of acquaintances. He knows all that there is to know about London—or, at least, the real London, by which phrase I exclude the foreign quarters and the Isle of Dogs. These he does not regard as part of London. His acquaintance among waiters alone is a matter for wonder. At odd times you may meet him in a bar with a stranger, an impressive-looking personage who, you conjecture, is an attaché of a foreign Embassy. But no; you do him an injustice; he is greater than that. Georgie introduces you with a histrionic flourish—

"This is Mr. Burke—young Tommy Burke. This is Carlo, of Romano's." Or, "This is young Tommy. This is Frank from the Cornhill Chop House," or Henry from Simpson's, or Enrico from Frascati's, or Jules from Maxim's.

I believe that Georgie knows more about food and feeding than any man in London. I don't mean that he could seriously compete with Lieutenant-Colonel Newnham Davis. He couldn't draw up a little dinner for you at the Ritz or Claridge's or Dieudonné's. But, then, here again he shows his prejudices; for he doesn't regard a dinner at the Ritz or Claridge's as anything to do with eating. His is the quieter sphere; but he has made it his own. There is something uncanny about his knowledge in this direction. He knows where you can get a meal at two o'clock in the morning, and he can tell you exactly what you will get. He can tell you in an instant what is the prime dish at any obscure little eating-house and the precise moment at which it is on the table. He knows the best house for cabbage, and the house to be avoided if you are thinking of potatoes. He knows where to go for sausage and mashed, and he can reel off a number of places which must be avoided when their haricot mutton is on. He knows when the boiled beef is most *à la mode* at Wilkinson's, when the pudding at the " Cheshire Cheese " is just so, and when the undercut at Simpson's is most to be desired. You meet him, say, on Tuesday, and, in course of conversation, you wonder where to lunch. "Tuesday," he will murmur, "Tuesday. What d'you fancy? It's fowl-and-bacon day at 'The Mitre.' That's always good. Or it's stewed-steak day at 'The Old Bull,' near the Bank; beautiful steak; done to a turn at one-fifteen. Or it's curry day at the Oriental place in Holborn, if you like curries. Or it's chop toad-in-the-hole day at Salter's; ready at two o'clock. The one in Strand's the best. But don't go sharp at two. Wait till about two-twenty. The batter ain't quite what it should be at two sharp; but just after that it's perfect. Perfect, my boy!"

We crossed the bridge to a running accompaniment from Georgie about the times he had had in the old days before I was born or thought of—he is always flinging this in my face. Motor-'buses were roaring through the long, empty streets, carrying loads of labourers from the docks to their northern homes, or work-girls from the northern factories to their homes in the Island. The little, softly lighted toy and sweetstuff shops gleamed upon us out of the greyness, and the tins of hot saveloys and baked apples, which the hawkers were offering, smelt appetizing. From tiny stalls outside the sweetstuff shops you may still purchase those luscious delicacies of your childhood which seem to have disappeared from every other quarter of London. I mean the toffee-apple about which, if you remember, Vesta Victoria used to sing so alluringly.

    I have two friends residing here—one at Folly Wall and one in Havana Street. I decided that we would call on the latter, so Georgie stopped at ",The Regent," and took in a bottle of Red Seal for my friend and a little drop of port for the missus— " just by way," as he explained, " of being matey." My friend, a gateman at one of the dock stations, had just got home, and was sitting down to his tea. There is no doubt that the housewives of the Island know how to prepare their old men's tea. In nearly every house in this district you will find, at about six or seven o'clock, in the living-room of the establishment, a good old hot stew going, or tripe and onions, or fish and potatoes, or a meat-pudding ; and this, washed down with a pint of tea, is good enough hunting for any human. Old Johnnie comes from the docks in his dirty working clothes ; but before ever he ventures to sit down to table he goes into the scullery, strips, and has what he calls a " slosh down," afterwards reappearing in a clean print shirt and serge trousers. Then, in this comfortable attire, he attacks whatever the missus has got for him, and studies the evening paper, to ascertain, firstly, what the political (i.e. labour) situation is, and, secondly, what's good for tomorrow's big race ; for Johnnie, quite innocently, likes to have a shilling on all the classics—the Lincoln, the Cambridgeshire, the Caesarewitch, the Gold Cup, City and Sub., the Oaks and the Derby, and so on.

    After his meal he shaves and puts on a collar. Sometimes he will take the missus to the pictures, or, if it is Saturday, he will go marketing with her in Poplar, or in the summer for a moonlight sail on the Thames steamers. Other nights he attends his slate club, or his union, or drops in at one or other of the cheery bars on the Island, to meet his pals and talk shop. The Isle of Dogs, I may tell you, is a happy hunting-ground for all those unhappy creatures who can find no congenial society in their own circles: I mean superior Socialists, Christian workers, Oxford and Cambridge settlement workers, and the immature intellectuals. There are literally dozens and dozens of churches and chapels on the Island, and dozens of halls and meeting-places where lectures are given. The former do not capture Johnnie, but the latter do, and he will often wash and brush up of an evening to hear some young boy from Oxford deliver a thoroughly uninformed exposition of Karl Marx or Nietzsche. The Island is particularly happy in being so frequently patronized by those half-baked ladies and gentlemen, the Fabians, who have all the vices of the middle classes, and—what is more terrible—all the virtues of the middle classes.

The majority of Socialists, if you observe, are young people of the well-to-do middle classes. They embrace the blue-serge god, not from any conviction, not from any sense of comradeship with their overworked and underpaid fellows, but because Socialism gives them an excuse for escape from their petty home life and pettier etiquettes. As Socialists they can have a good time, they can go where they choose, do as they choose, and come home at what hour they choose without fearing the wrath of that curious figure whom they name The Pater. They have merely to explain that they are Socialists, and their set say, " Oh . . . Socialists . . . yes, of course." Socialism opens to them the golden gates of that Paradise, Bohemia. The freedom of the city is thus presented to them; and they have found it so convenient and so inexpensive that they have adopted Socialism in their thousands. But observe them in the company of the horny-handed, the roughshod, and the ill-spoken; they are either ill at ease or frankly patronizing. They are Bohemians among aristocrats and aristocrats among Bohemians.

Johnnie is just beginning to be noted at their meetings as a debater of some importance. In fact, after the lecture, he will rise and deliver questions so shrewd and penetrating that the young folk of Sidcup and Blackheath and Hampstead have found it a saving to their personal dignity to give him a seat on the platform, where, of course, he is not only rendered harmless to them but is an encouragement to other sons of the soil in the audience.

It is in the region of the Island that most of the battles take place between organized labour and the apostles of free labour. Let there be any industrial trouble of any kind, and down upon the district swoop dozens of fussy futilitarians, to argue, exhort, bully, and agitate generally. Fabians, Social Democrats, Clarionettes, Syndicalists, Extremists, Arbitrators, Union leaders, Christian Care Committees—gaily they trip along and take charge of the hapless workers, until the poor fellows or girls are hustled this way and that, driven, coerced, commanded, and counter-commanded till, in desperation, they take refuge, one and all, in the nearest bar. Then the Fabians, the Social Democrats, the Clarionettes, the Syndicalists, the Extremists, the Arbitrators, and the Union leaders return to Blackheath and Sidcup and Bedford Park, crying that it is useless to attempt to help the poor; they won't be helped: they are hopeless dipsomaniacs.

Here were organized those Unemployed marches which made our streets so cheery a few years ago. I once joined Johnnie on a tramp with one of these regiments, and it was the most spiritless march I have ever been in. The men didn't want to march. It was the Social Service darlings who wanted to form them into a pretty procession, and lead them all round London as actual proof of the Good that was being done among the Right People. We started at nine o'clock on a typically London morning. The day was neither cold nor warm, neither light nor dark. The sky was an even stretch of watery grey, and the faces that passed us were not kindly. Mostly they suggested impaired digestions or guilty consciences. We had a guard of honour of about ten hefty constables, and for us, as for the great ones of the town, the traffic was held up that we might pass. Among the crowd our appointed petitioners, with labelled collecting-boxes, worked with subdued zeal, and above the rumble of the 'buses and the honk-honk of motors and the frivolous tinkle of hansoms rose their harsh, insistent rattle. Now and again a gust of wind would send a dozen separate swirls of dust into our eyes. People stared at us much as one stares at an Edgware Road penny-museum show. We were not men. We were a procession of the Unemployed : An Event. We were a jolly lot. Most of us stared at the ground or the next man's back ; only a few gazed defiantly around. None talked. Possibly a few were thinking, and if any of them were imaginative, that slow shuffle might have suggested a funeral march of hopes and fears. There was a stillness about it that was unpleasant ; a certain sickness in the air. I think the crowd must have wondered what we were going to do next. You may punch an Englishman's nose, and heal the affront with apologies and a drink. You may call him a liar, and smooth over the incident by the same means. You may take bread out of his mouth, and still he may be pacified. But when you touch his home and the bread of the missus and the kids, you are touching something sacred and thereby inviting disaster ; and I think the crowd was anticipating some concerted assault. As a matter of fact, we were the tamest lot of protesters you ever saw. I don't think any of us realized that he had anything sacred.

As we reached Piccadilly Circus the watery grey suddenly split, and through the ragged hole the sun began to peer : a pale sun that might have been out all night. It streamed weakly upon us, showing up our dismal clothes, glancing off the polished rails of the motor-'buses and the sleek surfaces of the hansoms. But it gave us no heart. Our escorts deigned us an occasional glance, but they had a soft job ; we were not gnashing our teeth or singing the " Marseillaise " or " The Red Flag." People stared . . . and stared. The long black snake of our procession threaded disconsolately into Knightsbridge. Hardly a word or a sign of interest escaped us. On the whole four hours' march there was but one laugh. That came from a fellow on the near side, who thought he'd found a cigar by the kerb, and fell and hurt his knee in the effort to secure his treasure—a discoloured chip of wood. Curiously enough, we didn't laugh. It was he who saw the fine comedy of the incident.

We debouched into Church Street, so to Notting Hill, and up the wretched Bayswater Road to Oxford Street. The sun was then—at one o'clock—shining with a rich splendour. The roadway blazed. Under the shop-blinds, which drooped forward like heavy lids over the tired eyes of the windows, little crowds from Streatham and Kentish Town were shopping. They stared at us. Through the frippery of this market-place we reached the homelier atmosphere of Holborn. The rattle of our boxes had grown apace, and we made small bets among ourselves as to what the total takings would be. I was thankful when the march or solemn walk was ended. For days afterwards my ears rang with the incessant clat-clat-clatter of those boxes, and for days afterwards I was haunted by those faces that stared at us, and then turned to stare at us, and then called other faces to stare at us. Nobody in the whole march troubled us. Nobody cursed us; nobody had a kind word for us. They just gave us their pennies, because we had been " got up " for that procession by those dear, hard-working friends of theirs. On our return, and after the very thin *croûte-au-pot* that was served out to us, we were addressed on the subject of our discontents. I forget what they were, if, indeed, I ever knew, for I had joined the march only as Johnnie's guest.

Whether Johnnie really knows or cares anything about economics I cannot say. I only know that I don't like him in that part. I like him best sitting round his open kitchen-range, piled with coke, or sitting in the four-ale bar of " The Griffin." For what he does know a tremendous lot about is human nature; only he does not know that he knows it. His knowledge drops out of him, casually, in side remarks. At his post on the docks he observes not only white human nature but black and yellow and brown, and he knows how to deal with it all. He can calm a squabble among Asiatics of varying colour and creed, when everybody else is helpless; not by strength of arm or position or character, but simply because he appreciates the subtle differences of human natures, and because he understands the needs and troubles of the occasion.

"Yes," he has said to me sometimes, on my asking whether he didn't find his night-watch rather lonely—" yes, I suppose some chaps would find it lonely. But not me. If you're a philosopher, you ain't ever lonely. Another thing—there's too much to do, old son. Night-watchman at a docks ain't the same thing as night-watchman at the road-up. Notterbitterfit. Thieves, my boy. Wouldn't think they'd venture into a place the size of ours, perhaps? Don't they, though? And, my word, if I catch 'em at it! Not big burglars, of course,

THE ISLE OF DOGS

but the small pilfering lot. Get in during the day, they do, and hide behind bales and in odd corners. Then they come out when it's dark and nose around, and their little fingers, in spite of their Catechism, start right away at picking and stealing. . . . Funny lot, these jolly Lascars. If I was manager of a music-hall and I wanted a real good star turn—something fresh—I'd stand at my gate and bag the crew of a Dai Nippon, just as they come off, and then bung 'em on just as they are, and let 'em sing and dance just as they do when they've drawn their pay. That'd be a turn, old son.. I bet that'd be a goer. Something your West End public ain't ever seen ; something that'd knock spots off 'em and make their little fleshes creep. Of course it looks fiercer'n it really is. All that there chanting and chucking knives about is only, as you might say, ceremonial. But if they happen to come off at two o'clock of a foggy winter morning—my word, it don't do to be caught bending then ! But lucky for me I know most of 'em. And they know me. And even if they're away for three months on end, next time they're back at West India they bring some little ' love gift ' for the bloke at the gate—that's me. Often I've had to patch 'em up at odd times, after they've had a thick night with the boys and have to join their boats. Sometimes one of 'em tumbles into the dock half an hour before she sails, with a smashed lip and that kind of air about him that tells you he can see a dock jam full of shipping and is trying to sort 'em out and find his little show. Of course, as a watchman and a man, I kind of sympathize. We've all done it one time or another. I remember one night . . ."

And when Johnnie remembers, that is the time to drink up and have another, for once he starts yarning he is not easily stopped. Wonderful anecdotes he has to relate, too ; not perhaps brilliant stories, or even stories with a point of any kind, but stories brimful of atmosphere, stories salt of the sea or scented with exotic bloom. They begin, perhaps, "Once, off Rangoon," or "I remember, a big night in Honolulu," or Mauritius, or Malabar, or Trinidad. Before the warning voice cries, "Time, gentermen!" you have circled the globe a dozen times under the spell of Johnnie's rememberings.

You may catch him any night of the week, and find him ready to yarn, save on Saturdays. Saturday night is always dedicated to the missus and to shopping in Poplar or Blackwall. Shopping on Saturday nights in these districts is no mere domestic function : it is a festival, an event. Johnnie washes and puts on his second-best suit, and then he and the missus depart from the Island, he bearing a large straw marketing bag, she carrying a string-bag and one of those natty stout-paper bags given away by greengrocers and milliners. As soon as the 'bus has tossed them into Salmon Lane, off Commercial Road, they begin to revel.

Salmon Lane on a Saturday night is very much like any other shopping centre in the more humane quarters of London. Shops and stalls blaze and roar with endeavour. The shops, by reason of their more respectable standing, affect to despise stalls, but when it comes to competition it is usually stalls first and shops hanging round the gate. The place reeks of naphtha, human flesh, bad language, and good-nature. Newly-killed rabbits, with their interiors shamelessly displayed, suspend themselves around the stalls, while their proprietors work joyfully with a chopper and a lean-bladed knife. Your earnest shopper is never abroad before nine o'clock in the evening, and many of them have to await the still riper hours when Bill shall have yielded up his wages. Old ladies of the locality are here in plenty, doubtfully fingering the pieces of meat which smother the slabs of the butchers' shops. Little Elsie is here, too, buying for a family of motherless brothers and sisters with the few shillings which Dad has doled out. Who knows so well as Little Elsie the exact spending value of twopence-halfpenny? Observe her as she lays in her Sunday gorge. Two penn'orth of " pieces " from the butcher's to begin with (for twopence you get a bagful of oddments of meat, trimmings from various joints, good nourishing bones, bits of suet, and, if the assistant thinks you have nice eyes, he will throw in some skirt). Then to the large greengrocer's shop for a penn'orth of " specks " (spotted or otherwise damaged fruit, and vegetables of every kind). Of this three penn'orth the most valuable item is the bones, for these, with a bit of carrot and potato and onion, will make a pot of soup sufficient in itself to feed the kiddies for two days. Then, at the baker's, you get a market basket full of stale bread for twopence, and, seeing it's for Sunday, you spend another penny and get five stale cakes. At the grocer's, two ounces of tea, two ounces of margarine, and a penn'orth of scraps from the bacon counter for Dad's breakfast. And there you have a refection for the gods.

Observe also the pale young man who lodges in some remote garret by Limehouse Hole. He has but a room, and his landlady declines the responsibility of "doing" for him. He must, therefore, do his own shopping, and he does it about as badly as it can be done. His demeanour suggests a babe among wolves, innocence menaced by the wiles of Babylon ; and sometimes motherly old dears audibly express pity at his helplessness, which flusters him still more, so that he leaves his change on the counter.

The road is a black gorge, rent with dancing flame. The public-house lamps flare with a jovial welcome for the jaded shopper, and every moment its doors flap open, and fling their fire of joy on the already overcharged air. Between the stalls parade the youth and beauty, making appointments for the second house at the Poplar Hippodrome, or assignations for Sunday evening.

As the stalls clear out the stock so grows the vociferousness of their proprietors, and soon the ear becomes deadened by the striving rush of sound. Every stall and shop has its wide-mouthed laureate, singing its present glories and adding lustre to its latest triumphs.

" I'll take any price yeh like, price yeh like ! Comerlong, comerlong, Ma ! This is the shop that does the biz. Buy-buy-buy-uy ! "

" Walk up ladies, don't be shy. Look at these legs. Look at 'em. Don't keep looking at 'em, though. Buy 'em. Buy 'em. Sooner you buy 'em sooner I can get 'ome and 'ave my little bath. Come along, ladies ; it's a dirty night, but thank God I got good lodgings, and I hope you got the same. Buy-buy-buy ! "

" 'Ere's yer lovely bernanas. Fourer penny. Pick 'em out where yeh like ! "

In one ear a butcher yells a madrigal concerning his little shoulders. In the other a fruit merchant demands to know whether, in all your nacheral, you ever see anything like his melons. Then a yard or so behind you an organ and cornet take up their stand and add " Tipperary " to the swelling symphony. But human ears can receive so much, and only so much, sound ; and clapping your hands over your ears, you seek the chaste seclusion, for a few minutes, of the saloon of " The Black Boy," or one of the many fried-fish bars of the Lane.

Still later in the evening the noise increases, for then the stalls are anxious to clear out their stock at any old price. The wise wife—and Johnnie's missus is one—waits until this hour before making her large purchases. For now excellent joints and rabbits and other trifles are put up for auction. The laureates are wonderful fellows, many of them, I imagine, decayed music-hall men. A good man in this line makes a very decent thing out of it. The usual remuneration is about eight or ten shillings for the night and whatever beer they want. And if you are shouting for nearly six hours in the heavy-laden air of Salmon Lane, you want plenty of beer and you earn all you get. They have a spontaneous wit about them that only the Cockney possesses. Try to take a rise out of one of them, and you will be sadly plucked. Theirs is Falstaffian humour—large and clustering : no fine strokes, but huge, rich-coloured sweeps. It is useless to attempt subtleties in the roar of a Saturday night. What you have to aim at is the obvious—but with a twist ; something that will go home at once : something that can be yelled or, if the spirit moves you, sung. It is, in a word, the humour of the Crowd.

At about eleven o'clock, the laureate, duly refreshed, will mount on the outside counter, where he can easily reach the rows of joints. Around him gathers the crowd of housewives, ready for the auction. He takes the first—a hefty leg of mutton.

" Nah then! " he cries challengingly, " nah then! Just stop shooting yer marth at the *OO*lans for a bit, and look at this 'ere bit o' meat. *Meat* was what I said," with a withering glance at the rival establishment across the Lane, where another laureate is addressing another crowd. " Meat, mother, meat. If yer don't want Meat, then it ain't no use comin' 'ere. If yer wants a cut orf an animal what come from Orstralia or Noo Zealand, then it ain't no use comin' 'ere. Over the road's where they got them. They got joints over there what come from the Anty-Podeys, and they ain't paid their boat-passage yet. No, my gels, this what I got 'ere is Meat. None of your carvings orf a cow what looks like a fiddle-case on trestles. You—sir—just cast yer eye over that. Carry that 'ome to the missus, and she'll let yeh stay out till a quarter to ten, and yeh'll never find a button orf yer weskit long as yeh live. That's the sort 'o meat to turn the kiddies into sojers and sailors. Nah then—what say to six-and-a-arf?"

He fondles the joint much as one would a babe in long clothes, dandling it, patting it, stroking it, exhibiting it, while the price comes steadily down from six-and-a-half to six, five, four-and-a-half, and finally is knocked down at four. Often a prime-looking joint will go as low as twopence a pound, and the smaller stuff is practically given away when half-past twelve is striking.

It is the same with the other shops—greengrocery, fish, and fruit. All is, so far as possible, cleared out before closing time, and only enough is held in reserve to supply that large army of Sunday morning shoppers who are unable to shop on Saturday night owing to Bill's festivities.

.   .   .   .   .

That is one worker's night. But there are others. There are those workers whose nights are not domestic, and who live in the common lodging-houses and shelters which are to be found in every district in London. There are two off Mayfair. There are any number round Belgravia. Seven Dials, of course, is full of them, for there lodge the Covent Garden porters and other early birds. In these houses you will find members of all-night trades that you have probably never thought of before. I met in a Blackwall Salvation Army Shelter a man who looks out from a high tower, somewhere down the Thames, all night. He starts at ten o'clock at night, and comes off at six, when he goes home to his lodging-house to bed. I have never yet been able to glean from him whose tower it is he looks out from, or what he looks out for. Then there are those exciting people, the scavengers, who clean our streets while we sleep, with hose-pipe and cart-brush; the printers, who run off our newspapers; the sewer-men, who do dirty work underground; railwaymen, night-porters, and gentlemen whose occupation is not mentioned among the discreet.

The Salvation Army Shelters are very popular among the lodging-house patrons, for you get good value there for very little money, and, by paying weekly, instead of nightly, you get reductions and a better-appointed dormitory. I know many street hawkers who have lived for years at one Shelter, and would not think of using a common lodging-house. The most popular quarter for this latter class of house is Duval Street, Spitalfields. At one time the reputation of this street was most noisome; indeed, it was officially known as the worst street in London. It holds a record for suicides, and, I imagine, for murders. It was associated in some way with that elusive personality, Jack the Ripper; and the shadow of that association has hung over it for ever, blighting it in every possible way. To-day it is but a very narrow, dirty, ill-lit street of common lodging-houses within the meaning of the Act, and, though it is by no means so gay and devilish as it is supposed to have been of old, they do say that the police still descend first on Duval Street in cases of local murder where the culprit has, as the newspapers say, made good his escape. I do not recommend it as a pleasure-jaunt for ladies or for the funny and fastidious folk of Bayswater. They would suffer terribly, I fear. The talk of the people would lash them like whips; the laughter would sear like hot irons. The noises bursting through the gratings from the underground cellars would be like a chastisement on the naked flesh, and shame and smarting and fear would grip them. The glances of the men would sting like scorpions. The glances of the women would bite like fangs. For these reasons, while I do not recommend it, I think a visit would do them good; it would purify their spotty little minds with pity and terror. For I think Duval Street stands easily first as one of the affrighting streets of London. There is not the least danger or disorder; but the tradition has given it an atmosphere of these things. Here are gathered all the most unhappy wrecks of London — victims and apostles of vice and crime. The tramps doss here: men who have walked from the marches of Wales or from the Tweed border, begging their food by the way. Their clothes hang from them. Their flesh is often caked with dirt. They do not smell sweet. Their manners are crude: I think they must all have studied Guides to Good Society. They spit when and where they will. Some of them writhe in a manner so suggestive as to give you the itch. This writhe is known as the Spitalfields Crawl. There is a story of a constable who was on night duty near the doors of one of the doss establishments, when a local doctor passed him. "Say," said the doctor, with a chuckle, "you're standing rather close, aren't you? Want to take something away with you?" "Not exactly that, sir; but it's lonely round here for the night stretch, and, somehow, it's kind of company if I can feel the little beggars dropping on my helmet."

In this street you are on the very edge of the civilized world. All are outcasts, even among their own kind. All are ready to die, and too sick even to go to the trouble of doing it. They have no hope, and, therefore, they have no fear. They are just down and out. All the ugly misery of all the ages is collected here in essence, and from it the atmosphere is charged; an atmosphere more horrible than any that I know: worse than that of Chinatown, worse than that of Shadwell. These are merely insidious and menacing, but Duval Street is painful.

It was here that I had the nearest approach to an adventure that I have ever had in London. I was sitting in the common kitchen of one of the houses which was conspicuously labelled on its outer whitewashed lamp—

> GOOD BEDS
>
> FOR MEN ONLY
>
> FOURPENCE

The notice, however, was but the usual farcical compliance with a law which nobody regards and which nobody executes. Women were there in plenty—mostly old, unkempt women, wearing but a bodice and skirt and boots. The kitchen was a bare, blue-washed apartment, the floor sanded, with a long wooden table and two or three wooden forms. A generous fire roared up a wide chimney. The air was thick with fumes of pipes that had been replenished with " old soldiers " from West End gutters. Suddenly a girl came in with an old man. I looked at her with some interest because she was young, with copper-coloured hair that strayed about her face with all the profusion of an autumn sunset. She was the only youthful thing in the place, bar myself. I looked at her with rather excited interest because she was very drunk. She called the old man Dad. A few of the men greeted him. One or two nodded to the girl. " 'Lo, Luba. Bin on the randy? " The women looked at her, not curiously, or with compassion or disgust, but cursorily. I fancied, from certain incipient movements, that she was about to be violently bilious ; but she wasn't. We were sitting in silence when she came in. The silence continued. Nobody moved, nobody offered to make way. Dad swore at a huge scrofulous tramp, and kneed him a little aside from the fire. The tramp slipped from the edge of the form, but made no rebuke. Dad sat down and left Luba to herself. She swayed perilously for a moment, and then flopped weakly to the form on which I sat. The man I was with leaned across me.

" 'Ad a rough time in the box, Luba ? "

Luba nodded feebly. Her mouth sagged open ; her eyes drooped ; her head rolled.

" I 'eard abaht it," he went on. " Hunky Bottles see a *Star* wi' your pickcher in. And the old man's questions. Put you through it, din' 'e ? "

Again Luba nodded. The next moment she seemed to repent the nod, for she flared up and snapped : " Oh, shut up, for Christ's sake, cancher ? Give any one the fair pip, you do. Ain't I answered enough damsilly questions from ev'body without you ? Oo's got a fag ? "

I had, so I gave her one. She fumbled with it, trying to light it with a match held about three inches from it. Finally, I lit it for her, and she seemed to see me for the first time. She looked at me, at once shiftily and sharply. Her eyes narrowed. Suspicion leaped into her face, and she seemed to shrink into herself like a tortoise into its shell. " Oo's 'e ? " she demanded of my mate.

" 'E's all right. Oner the boys. Chuck knows 'im."

Then the match burnt her fingers, and she swore weak explosive oaths, filthier than any I have heard from a bookmaker. She lisped, and there was a suggestion in her accent of East Prussia or Western Russia. Her face was permanently reddened by alcohol. The skin was coarse, almost scaly, and her whole person sagged abominably. She wore no corsets, but her green frock was of an artful shade to match her brassy hair. Her hat was new and jaunty and challenging.

" Tell you what," she said, turning from me, and seeming to wake up ; " tell you what I'd like to do to that old counsel. I'd like to——" And here she poured forth a string of suggestions so disgusting that I cannot even convey them by euphemism.

Her mouth was a sewer. The air about us stunk with her talk. When she had finished, my mate again leaned across me, and asked in a hollow whisper, like the friction of sand-paper—

" 'Ere—Luba—tell us. Why d'you go back on Billie, eh?"

Luba made an expressive gesture with her fingers in his face, and that was the only answer he received; for she suddenly noticed me again, and, without another word, she dipped her hand to her bosom and pulled out a naked knife of the bowie pattern and twisted it under my nose. With the nervous instinct of the moment, I dodged back; but it followed me.

"No monkey-tricks with me, dear! See? Else you'll know what. See?"

I was turning to my friend, in an appeal for intervention, when, quite as suddenly as the knife was drawn, it disappeared, for Luba overbalanced because of the gin that was in her, and slipped from the form. Between us, we picked her up, replaced her, and tucked the knife into its sheath. Whereupon she at once got up, and said she was off. For some reason she went through an obscure ritual of solemnly pulling my ear and slapping my face. Then she slithered across the room, fell up the stair into the passage, and disappeared into the caverns of gloom beyond the door. When she had gone, some one said, "Daddy—Luba's gone!"

Daddy leaped from the form, snarled something inarticulate, fell up the same stair, and went babbling and yelling after Luba. Some one came and shoved a fuzzy head through the door, asking lazily, "Whassup?" "Luba's gone." "Oh!"

I wondered vaguely if it was a nightmare; if I had gone mad; or if other people had gone mad. I don't know now what it all meant. I only know that the girl was the Crown's principal witness in a now notorious murder case. My ear still burns.

A CHARITABLE NIGHT
EAST, WEST, NORTH, SOUTH

POOR

*From jail he sought her, and he found
A darkened house, a darkened street,
A shrilly sky that screamed of sleet,
And from The Lane quick gusts of sound.*

*He mocked at life that men call sweet.
He went and wiped it out in beer—
"Well, dammit, why should I stick here,
By a dark house in a dark street?"*

*For he and his but serve defeat;
For kings they gather gems and gold,
And life for them, when all is told,
Is a dark house in a dark street.*

A CHARITABLE NIGHT

EAST, WEST, NORTH, SOUTH

CHARITY . . . the most nauseous of the virtues, the practice of which degrades both giver and receiver. The practice of Charity brings you into the limelight; it elevates you to friendship with the Almighty; you feel that you are a colleague of the Saviour. It springs from Pity, the most unclean of all human emotions. It is not akin to love; it is akin to contempt. To be pitied is to be in the last stages of spiritual degradation. You cannot pity anything on your own level, for Pity implies an assumption of superiority. You cannot be pitied by your friends and equals, only by your self-elected superiors. Let us see Pity at work in London. . . .

As I lounged some miles east of Aldgate Pump, an old song of love and lovers and human kindliness was softly ringing in my head, and it still haunted me as I slid like a phantom into that low-lit causeway that slinks from a crashing road to the dark wastes of waters beyond. At the far end a brutal black building broke the sky-line. A few windows were thinly lit by gas. I climbed the stone steps, hollowed by many feet, and stood in the entrance-hall.

Then, as it seemed from far away, I heard an insistent murmur, like the breaking of distant surf. I gazed around and speculated. In the bare brick wall was a narrow, high door. With the instinct of the journalist, I opened it. The puzzle was explained. It was the Dining Hall of the Metropolitan

Orphanage, and the children were at their seven o'clock supper. From the cathedral-like calm of the vestibule, I passed into an atmosphere billowing with the flutter of some five hundred small tongues. Under the pendant circles of gas-jets were ranged twelve long, narrow tables packed with children talking and eating with no sense of any speed-limit. On the one side were boys in cruelly ugly brown suits, and on the other side, little girls from seven to fifteen in frocks of some dark material with a thin froth of lace at neck and wrists and coarse, clean pinafores. Each table was attended by a matron, who served out the dry bread and hot milk to the prefects, who carried the basins up and down the tables as deftly as Mr. Paul Cinquevalli. Everywhere was a prospect of raw faces and figures, which Charity had deliberately made as uncomely as possible by clownish garb and simple toilet. The children ate hungrily, and the place was full of the spirit of childhood, an adulterated spirit. The noise leaped and swelled on all sides in an exultant joy of itself, but if here and there a jet of jolly laughter shot from the stream, there were glances from the matrons.

The hall was one of wide spaces, pierced at intervals by the mouths of bleak, stark corridors. The air of it was limp and heavy with the smell of food. Polished beams ran below the roof, pretending to uphold it, and massive columns of painted stone flung themselves aggressively here and there, and thought they were supporting a small gallery. Outside a full moon shone, but it filtered through the cheap, half-toned glass of the windows with a quality of pale lilac. Here and there a window of stained glass stabbed the brick wall with passionate colour. The moral atmosphere suggested nut-foods and proteid values.

At half-past seven a sharp bell rang, and with much rumbling and manœuvring of forms, the children stood stiffly up, faced round, and, as a shabby piano tinkled a melody, they sang grace, somewhat in this fashion :—

> To Go doo give sus dailyb read
> Dour thankful song we raise-se,
> Sand prayth at he who serd susf ood,
> Dwillf ill lour reart swithp raise, *Zaaaamen.*

Then a wave of young faces rolled upwards to the balcony, where stood a grey-headed, grey-bearded, spectacled figure. It was one of the honorary managers. The children stood to attention like birds before a snake. One almost expected to hear them sing " God bless the squire and his relations. . . ." The Gentleman was well-tailored, and apart from his habiliments there was, in every line of his figure, that which suggested solidity, responsibility, and the substantial virtues. I have seen him at Committee meetings of various charitable enterprises; himself, duplicated again and again. One charitable worker is always exactly like the other, allowing for differences of sex. They are of one type, with one manner, and—I feel sure—with one idea. I am certain that were you to ask twenty members of a Charity committee for opinions on aviation, Swedenborgism, the Royal Academy, and Little Tich, each would express the same views in the same words and with the same gestures.

This gentleman was of the City class ; he carried an air of sleekness. Clearly he was a worthy citizen, a man who had Got On, and had now abandoned himself to this most odious of vices. And there he stood, in a lilac light, splashed with voluptuous crimsons and purples, dispensing Charity to the little ones before him whose souls were of hills and the sea. He began to address them. It appeared that the Orphanage had received, that very morning, forty more children; and he wished to observe how unnecessary it was for him to say with what pleasure this had been done. Many thousands of children now holding exalted positions in banks and the Civil Service could look to them as to their father, in the eighty or more years of the School's life, and he was proud to feel that his efforts were producing such Fine Healthy Young Citizens.' The children knew—did they not?—that they had a Good Home, with loving guardians who would give them the most careful training suited to their position in life. They were clothed, maintained, and drilled, as concerned their bodies; and, as concerned their souls, they had the habits of Industry and Frugality inculcated into them, and they were guided in the paths of Religion and Virtue. They had good plain food, suited to their position in life, and healthy exercise in the way of Manly Sports and Ladylike Recreations. He quoted texts from the Scriptures, about the sight of the Widow touching those chords which vibrate sympathetically in all of us, and a lot of stuff about a Cup of Cold Water and These Little Ones. He exuded self-content.

He went on to remark that the hazardous occupations of Modern Industry had, by their many mischances, stripped innumerable families of their heads, and reduced them to a condition of the most deplorable. He desired to remind them that the class to which they belonged was not the Very Poor of the gutters, but the Respectable Poor who would not stoop to receive the aid doled out by the State. No; they were not Gutter Children, BUT, at the same time, the training they received was not such as to create any distaste among them for the humblest employments of Honest Industry, suitable to their position in life. He redeemed the objects interested in his exertions from the immoralities of the Very Poor, while teaching them to respect their virtues, and to do their duty in that station of life to which it had pleased God to call them.

(The little objects seemed to appreciate this, for they applauded with some spirit, on prompting from the matrons.)

He went on to suggest, with stodgy jocularity, that among them was possibly a Prime Minister of 1955—think of Pitt—and perhaps a Lord Kitchener. He spoke in terms of the richest enthusiasm of the fostering of the Manly Qualities and the military drill—such a Fine Thing for the Lads; and he urged them to figure to themselves that, even if they did not rise to great heights, they might still achieve greatness by doing their duty at office desk, or in factory, loom, or farmyard, and so adding to the lustre of their Native Land—a land, he would say, in which they had so great a part.

(Here the children cheered, seemingly with no intent of irony.) He added that, in his opinion, kind hearts were, if he might so put it, more than coronets.

The Gentleman smiled amiably. He nourished no tiny doubt that he was doing the right thing. He believed that Christ would be pleased with him for turning out boys and girls of fourteen, half-educated, mentally and socially, to spend their lives in dingy offices in dingy alleys of the City. There was no humbug here; impossible for a moment to doubt his sincerity. He had a childlike faith in his Great Work. He was, as he annually insisted, with painful poverty of epithet, engaged in Philanthropic Work, alleviating the Distresses of the Respectable Poor and ameliorating Social Conditions Generally. So he trained his children until he trained them into desk or farm machines; trained them so that their souls were starved, driven in on themselves, and there stifled, and at last eaten away by the canker of their murky routine.

I looked at those children as they stood before me. I looked at their bright, clear faces, their eyes wonder-wide, their clean brows alert for knowledge, hungry for life and its beauty. Despite their hideous clothes, they were the poetry of the world : all that is young and fresh and lovely. Then I thought of them five years hence, their minds larded with a Sound Commercial Education, tramping the streets of the City from nine o'clock in the morning until six o'clock in the evening, living in an atmosphere of intellectual vacuity, their ardent temperaments fled, their souls no longer desiring beauty. I felt a little sick.

But The Gentleman. . . . The Gentleman stood there in a lilac light, and took unction unto himself. He smiled benignly, a smile of sincere pleasure. Then he called the children to attention while he read to them a prayer of St. Chrysostom, which he thought most suitable to their position in life. A ring of gas-jets above his head hovered like an aureole.

. . . .

I do wish that something could somehow be done to restrain the Benevolent. We are so fond, as a nation, of patronizing that if we have nothing immediately at hand to patronize, we must needs go out into the highways and hedges and bring in anything we can find, any old thing, so long as we can patronize it. I have often thought of starting a League (I believe it would be immensely popular) for The Suppression of Social Service. The fussy, incompetent men and women who thrust themselves forward for that work are usually the last people who should rightly meddle with it. They either perform it from a sense of duty, or what they themselves call The Social Conscience (the most nauseous kind of benevolence), or they play with it because it is Something To Do. Always their work is discounted by personal vanity. I like the Fabians : they are funny without being vulgar. But these Social Servants and their Crusades for Pure and Holy Living Among Work-Girls are merely fatuous and vulgar when they are not deliberately insulting. Can you conceive a more bitter mind than that which calls a girl of the streets a Fallen Sister? Yet that is what these people have done; they have labelled a house with the device of The Midnight Crusade for the Reclamation of our Fallen Sisters; and they expect self-respecting girls of that profession to enter it. . . .

I once attended one of these shows in a North London slum. The people responsible for it have the impudence to send women-scouts to the West End thoroughfares at eleven o'clock every night, there to interfere with these girls, to thrust their attentions upon them, and, if possible, lure them away to a service of song—Brief, Bright, and Brotherly. It was a bitter place in a narrow street. The street was gay and loud with humanity, only at its centre was a dark and forbidding door, reticent and inhuman. There was no sign of good-fellowship here; no warm touch of the flesh. It was as brutal as justice; it seemed to have builded itself on that most horrible of all texts: *"Be just before you are generous."*

I went in at an early hour, about half-past ten, and only two victims had then been secured. The place stunk of *The Church Times* and practical Christianity. In the main room was a thin fire, as skimpy as though it had been lit by a spinster, as, I suppose, it had. There was a bare deal table. The seating accommodation was cane chairs, which I hate; they always remind me of the Band of Hope classes I was compelled to attend as a child. They suggest something stale and cheesy, something as squalid as the charity they serve. On a corner table was a battered urn and a number of earthenware cups, with many plates of thick, greasy bread-and-butter; just the right fare to offer a girl who has put away several benedictines and brandies. The room chilled me. Place, people, appointments, even the name—Midnight Crusade for the Reclamation of our Fallen Sisters —smacked of everything that is most ugly. Smugness and super-piety were in the place. The women —I mean, ladies—who manage the place, were the kind of women I have seen at the Palace when Gaby is on. (For you will note that Gaby does not attract the men; it is not they who pack the Palace nightly to see her powder her legs and bosom. They may be there, but most of them are at the bar. If you look at the circle and stalls, they are full of elderly, hard women, with dominant eyebrows, leering through the undressing process, and moistening their lips as Gaby appears in her semi-nakedness.)

The walls of the big bedroom were adorned with florid texts, tastefully framed. It was a room of many beds, each enclosed in a cubicle. The beds were hard, covered with coarse sheets. If I were a Fallen Brother, I hardly think they would have tempted me from a life of ease. And there were RULES.... Oh, how I loathe RULES! I loathed them as a child at school. I loathed drill, and I loathed compulsory games, and I loathed all laws that were made without purpose. There were long printed lists of Rules in this place, framed, and hung in each room. You can never believe how many things a Fallen Sister may not do. Certain rules are, of course, essential; but the pedagogic mind, once started on law-making, can never stop; and it is usually the pedagogic type of mind, with the lust for correction, that goes in for Charity. Why may not the girls talk in certain rooms? Why may they not read anything but the books provided? Why may they not talk in bed? Why must they fold their bed-clothes in such-and-such an exact way? Why must they not descend from the bedroom as and when they are dressed? Why must they let the Superior read their letters? And why, oh, why are these places run by white-faced men and elderly, hard women?

I have written, I fear, rather flippantly on this topic; but that is only because I dare not trust myself to be serious. I realize as much as any one that the life is a shameful life, and all that sort of thing; but I boil with indignation at the hundred shamefulnesses which these charity-mongers heap upon defenceless girls who, in a weak moment, have sought their protection. If you know anything about the matter, you will know that these girls have in their little souls an almost savage flame of self-respect which burns with splendour before the bleak, miserable flame of Organized Charity. If I spoke my mind on the subject, this page would blaze with fury . . . and you would smile.

. . . . .

But amid all this welter of misdirected endeavour, there is just one organized charity for which I should like to say a word; and that is The Salvation Army. I do not refer to its religious activities so much as to its social work as represented in the excellent Shelters which have been opened in various districts. There is one in Whitechapel Road, which is the identical building where General Booth first started a small weekly mission service which was afterwards known all over the world as The Salvation Army. There is one in Hoxton. There is one—a large one—in Blackfriars Road. And there are others wherever they may be most needed.

The doors open at five o'clock every evening. The Shelter, mark you, is not precisely a Charity. The men have to pay. Here is shown the excellent understanding of the psychology of the people which the University Socialist misses. You cannot get hold of people by offering them something for nothing; but you can get hold of them by tens of thousands by offering them something good at a low price. For a halfpenny the Salvation Army offers them tea, coffee, cocoa, or soup, with bread-and-butter, cake, or pudding. All this food is cooked and prepared at the Islington headquarters, and the great furnaces in the kitchens of the Shelters are roaring night and day for the purpose of warming-up the food, heating the Shelter, and serving the drying-rooms, where the men can hang their wet clothes.

A spotlessly clean bed is offered for threepence a night, which includes use of bathroom, lavatory, and washhouse. The washhouse is in very great demand on wet nights by those who have been working out of doors, and by those who wish to wash their underclothes, etc.

In addition to this, the men have the service of the Army orderlies, in attention at table and in " calling " in the morning. The staff is at work all night, either attending new-comers or going round with the various " calls," which, as some of the guests are market porters, are for unearthly hours, such as half-past three or four o'clock. The Shelters are patronized by many " regulars "—flower-sellers, pedlars, Covent Garden or Billingsgate odd men, etc.—who lodge with them by the week, sometimes by the year. Lights are officially out at half-past nine, but of course the orderly is on duty at the door until eight o'clock the following morning, and no stranger who wants food and bed is refused. He is asked for the threepence and for the halfpenny for his food, but if he cannot produce these he has but to ask for the Brigadier, and, if he is a genuine case, he is at once taken in.

Every Saturday night at half-past eleven certain of the orderlies, supplied with tickets, go out, and to any hungry, homeless wanderer they give a ticket with directions to the Shelter. These Saturday night tickets entitle him, if he chooses to accept them, to bath, breakfast, bed, and the Sunday service.

Further, the Shelter acts as employment agency, and, once having found their man, the first step towards helping him is to awaken in him the latent sense of responsibility. The quickest way is to find him work, and this they do ; and once their efforts show results, they never lose sight of him.

Many heartbreaking cases go by the orderly's box at the door, and I would like to set some of those young Oxford philanthropists who write pamphlets or articles in *The New Age* on social subjects by the door for a night. I think they would learn a lot of things they never knew before. Often, at two or three o'clock in the morning, the scouts will bring in a bundle of rain-sodden rags that hardly looks as if it could ever have been a man. How can you deal scientifically or religiously with that?

You can't. But the rank and file of The Salvation Army, with its almost uncanny knowledge of men, has found a better, happier way. I have spent many nights in various of their Shelters, and I should like to put on record the fine spirit which I have found prevailing there. It is a spirit of camaraderie. In other charitable institutions you will find timidity, the cowed manner, sometimes symptoms of actual fear. But never at the Salvation Army. There every new-comer is a pal, until he is proved to be unworthy of that name. There is no suspicion, no underhanded questioning, no brow-beating : things which I have never found absent from any other organized charity.

The Salvation Army method is food, warmth, mateyness; and their answer to their critics, and their reward, is the sturdy, respectable artisan who comes along a few months later to shake hands with them and give his own services in helping them in their work.

.   .   .   .   .

Far away West, through the exultant glamour of theatre and restaurant London, through the solid, melancholic greys of Bayswater, you find a little warm corner called Shepherd's Bush. You find also Notting Dale, where the bad burglars live, but we will talk of that in another chapter. Back of Shepherd's Bush is a glorious slum, madly lit, uncouth, and entirely wonderful.

To Shepherd's Bush I went one evening. I went to fairyland. I went to tell stories and to lead music-hall choruses. No; not at the Shepherd's Bush Empire, but at a dirty little corrugated hall in a locked byway. Some time ago, the usual charitably minded person, finding time hang heavy on her hands, or having some private grief which she desired to forget in bustle and activity, started a movement for giving children happy evenings. I have not been to one of the centres, and I am sure I should not like to go. I dislike seeing children disciplined in their play. Children do not need to be taught to play. Games which are not spontaneous are as much a task as enforced lessons. I have been a child myself. The people who run charities, I think, never have been. . . . However . . .

This Shepherd's Bush enterprise was an entirely private affair. The idea was based on the original inception, and much improved. At these organized meetings the children are forced to go through antics which, three hundred years ago, were a perfectly natural expression of the joy of life. These antics were called morris dances; they were mad, vulgar, joyous abandonment to the mood of the moment; just as the dances performed by little gutter-arabs and factory-girls around street organs are an abandonment to the mood of to-day's moment. But the elderly spinsters have found that what was vulgar three hundred years ago is artistic to-day; or if it isn't they will make it so. Why on earth a child should have to dance round a maypole just because children danced round a maypole centuries ago, I cannot understand. To-day, the morris dance is completely self-conscious, stiff, and ugly. The self-developed dance of the little girl at the organ is a thing of beauty, because it is a quite definite expression of something which the child feels; it follows no convention, it changes measure at fancy, it regards nothing but its own rapture. . . . The morris dance isn't.

So, at the hall to which I went, the children were allowed to play exactly as and when they liked. Any child could come from anywhere, and bring other children. There was a piano, and some one was always in attendance to play whatever might be required by the children. If they wanted " The Cubanola Glide," or " Down in Jungle-Town," or " In the Shadows," they got it, or anything else they might choose. Toys of all kinds were on hand —dolls, engines, railways, dolls'-houses, little cooking-stoves, brick puzzles, regiments of soldiers, picture-books, and, indeed, everything that a child could think of.

When I arrived I tripped over the threshold of the narrow entrance, and fell into a warmly lighted room, where the meetings of some local Committee were usually held. All chairs had been cleared to the wall, and the large central space was littered with troops of glad girls and toddlers from the stark streets around. Instead of teaching the children to play, the management here set the children to play by themselves and set elder children to attend them. Great was the fun. Great was the noise. On a little daïs at the end, coffee and sweet cakes were going, but there was no rush. When the kiddies wanted a cake they went up and asked for it; but for the most part they were immersed in that subdued, serious excitement which means that games are really being enjoyed. All of the attendants were girls of 12 or 13, of that sweet age between childhood and flapperhood, when girls are at their loveliest, with short frocks that dance at every delicate step, and with unconcealed glories of hair golden or dusky; all morning light and melody and fearlessness, not yet realizing that they are women. Many of them, shabby and underfed as they were, were really lovely girls, their beauty shining through their rags with an almost religious radiance, as to move you to prayer and tears. Their gentle ways with the baby-children were a joy to watch. One group was working a model railway. In another a little twelve-year-old girl was nursing two tinies, and had a cluster of others at her feet while she read "Jack and the Beanstalk" from a luridly illustrated rag-book. Another little girl was figuring certain steps of a dance of her own invention, each step being gravely followed by two youngsters who could scarcely walk.

Then the wonderful woman—a local woman, she bought a small shop years ago, and now owns a blazing rank of Stores—who financed the play-room went to the piano, crashed a few chords, and instantly every head, golden or brown or dark, was lifted to us. My hostess said something—a word of invitation—and, as though it were a signal, the crowd leaped up, and rushed, tumbled, or toddled towards us.

"What about a song?" cried the lady.

"Ooo-er . . . rather!"

"What'll we have, then?"

The shrill babel half-stunned me. No two called for the same thing. If my hearing were correct, they wanted every popular song of the last ten years. However, we compromised, for a start, on "Jungle-Town," and, though I felt extremely nervous of such an audience, I gave it them, and then invited them for the second chorus.

What a chorus! Even the babies, who knew

nothing of the words and could not have spoken them if they had, seemed to know the tune, and they let it out in every possible key. That song went with a bang, and I had no rest for at least half an hour. We managed to get them to write their favourites on slips of paper, and I took them in rotation, the symphony being in every case interrupted by long-drawn groans from the disappointed ones, and shrieks of glee from those who had chosen it. " On the Mississippi " was the winner of the evening; it was encored five times ; and a hot second was " I do Kinder Feel I'm in Love."

When their demands had been exhausted I had a rest, and some coffee, while Iris, a wicked little girl of eleven, told the story of Joan of Arc. Other girls followed her, each telling her own pet story. Their skill in this direction was a thing to marvel at. The audience was a joy, with half-raised heads, wide eyes, open mouths, every nerve of them hanging on the reciter's words. Indeed, I, too, found that one of the tale-tellers had " got " me with her story of Andersen's " Little Match Girl."

On their asking another song, I told them the " creepy-creepy " story of Mark Twain's—the one about " Who's got my Golden Arm," where, if you have worked it up properly, you get a shriek of horror on the last word. I got it. A shriek of horror? It nearly pierced the drums of the ear. Then they all huddled together in a big bunch, each embracing the other, and begged me to tell it again ; so, while they clung tightly together for safety, I told it again, but instead of a shriek I got a hysterical laugh which lasted for nearly a minute before they disentangled themselves. Then I gave them Charles Pond's recital about the dog-hospital, and the famous " Cohen at the Telephone."

At half-past nine they were collected into bunches, and dispatched home under the guidance of the bigger girls. They paused at the door to scream messages to me, to chant bits of the choruses we had sung, to dance with loud, defiant feet on the hollow floor, and one little girl gave me a pearl button from her pinafore as a keepsake, and hoped I would come again. Then she kissed me Good-Night, and ran off amid jeers from the boys.

At ten o'clock I helped my hostess in the clearing away of the cakes and coffee-cups, and, half an hour later we were out in the clamorous wilds of Shepherd's Bush.

A FRENCH NIGHT
OLD COMPTON STREET

OLD COMPTON STREET

Through London rain her people flow,
And Pleasure trafficks to and fro.
  A gemmy splendour fills the town,
  And robes her in a spangled gown
Through which no sorry wound may show.

But with the dusk my fancies go
To that grey street I used to know,
  Where Love once brought his heavy crown
    Through London rain.

And ever, when the day is low,
And stealthy clouds the night forethrow,
  I quest these ways of dear renown,
  And pray, while Hope in tears I drown,
That once again her face may glow,
    Through London rain!

A FRENCH NIGHT

OLD COMPTON STREET

STEP aside from the jostle and clamour of Oxford Street into Soho Square, and you are back in the eighteenth century and as lonely as a good man in Chicago. Cross the Square, cut through Greek Street or Dean Street, and you are in—Paris, amid the clang, the gesture, and the alert nonchalance of metropolitan France.

Soho—magic syllables ! For when the respectable Londoner wants to feel devilish he goes to Soho, where every street is a song. He walks through Old Compton Street, and, instinctively, he swaggers ; he is abroad; he is a dog. He comes up from Surbiton or Norwood or Golder's Green, and he dines cheaply at one of the hundred little restaurants, and returns home with the air and the sensation of one who has travelled, and has peeped into places that are not . . . Quite . . . you know.

Soho exists only to feed the drab suburban population of London on the spree. That artificial atmosphere of Montmartre, those little touches of a false Bohemia are all cunningly spread from the brains of the restaurateurs as a net to catch the young bank clerk and the young Fabian girl. Indeed, one establishment has overplayed the game to the extent of renaming itself " The Bohemia." The result is that one dare not go there for fear of dining amid the minor clergy and the Fabians and the girl-typists. It is a little pitiable to make a tour of the cafés and watch the Londoner trying to be Bohemian. There has been, of course, for the last few years, a growing disregard, among all classes, for the heavier conventionalities; but this determined Bohemianism is a mistake. The Englishman can no more be trifling and light-hearted in the Gallic manner than a Polar bear can dance the *maxixe brésilienne* in the jungle. If you have ever visited those melancholy places, the night clubs and cabarets, which had a boom a year or two ago, you will appreciate the immense effort that devilry demands from him. Those places were the last word in dullness. I have been at Hampstead tea-parties which gave you a little more of the joy of living. I have watched the nuts and the girls, and what have I seen? Boredom. Heavy eyes, nodding heads, a worn-out face, saying with determination, " I WILL be gay ! " Perhaps you have seen the pictures of those luxuriously upholstered and appointed establishments : music, gaiety, sparkle, fine dresses, costume songs, tangos, smart conversation and faces, and all the rest of it. But the real thing. . . . Imagine a lot of dishevelled girls pouring into a stuffy room after the theatre, looking already fatigued, but bracing themselves to dance and eat and drink and talk until—as I have seen them—they fall asleep over the tables, and hate the boy who brought them there.

Practically the sole purpose of the place was to fill some one's pockets, for, as the patrons were playing at being frightful dogs, the management knew that they could do as they liked with the tariff. The boys wouldn't go to night-clubs if they were not spendthrifts. Result : whisky-and-soda, seven-and-sixpence; cup of coffee, half a crown. And nobody ever had the pluck to ask for change out of a sovereign.

' Now, I love my Cockneys, heart and soul. And, just because I love them so much, I do wish to goodness they wouldn't be Bohemian; I do wish to goodness they would keep out of the Soho cafés. They only come in quest of a Bohemianism which isn't there. They can get much better food at home, or they can afford to get a really good meal at an English hotel. I wish they would leave Soho alone for the people like myself who feed there because it is cheap, and because the waiters will give us credit.

"Garcong," cried the diner whose food was underdone, "these sausages ne sont pas fait!"

If the Cockney goes on like this, he will spoil Soho, and he will lose his own delightful individuality and idiosyncrasy.

But, apart from the invasion of Soho by the girl-clerk and the book-keeper, one cannot but love it. I love it because, in my early days of scant feeding, it was the one spot in London where I could gorge to repletion for a shilling. There was a little place in Wardour Street, the Franco-Suisse—it is still there—whose shilling table d'hôte was a marvel. And I always had my bob's worth, I can assure you; for those were the days when one went hungry all day in order to buy concert tickets. Indeed, there were occasions when the bread-basket was removed from my table, so savage was the raid I made upon it.

There, one night a week, we feasted gloriously. We revelled. We read the *Gaulois* and *Gil Blas* and papers of a friskier tone. There still exists a Servian café where all manner of inflammatory organs of Nihilism may be read, and where heavy-bearded men—Anarchists, you hope, but piano-builders, you fear—would sit for three hours over their dinner Talking, *Talking*, TALKING. Then for another hour they would play backgammon, and at last roll out, blasphemously, to the darkened street, and so Home to those mysterious lodgings about Broad Street and Pulteney Street.

How the kitchens manage to do those shilling table d'hôtes is a mystery which I have never solved, though I have visited "below" on one or two occasions and talked with the chefs. There are about a dozen cafés now which, for the Homeric shilling, give you four courses, bread *ad lib*, and coffee to follow. And it is good; it is a refection for the gods—certain selected gods.

You stroll into the little gaslit room (enamelled in white and decorated with tables set in the simplest fashion, yet clean and sufficient) as though you are dropping in at the Savoy or Dieudonné's. It is rhomboidal in shape, with many angles, as though perspective had suddenly gone mad. Each table is set with a spoon, a knife, a fork, a serviette, a basket of French bread, and a jar of French mustard. If you are in spendthrift mood, you may send the boy for a bottle of *vin ordinaire*, which costs tenpence; on more sober occasions you send him for beer.

There is no menu on the table; the waiter or, more usually, in these smaller places, the waitress explains things to you as you go along. Each course carries two dishes, *au choix*. There are no *hors d'œuvres*; you dash gaily into the soup. The tureen is brought to the table, and you have as many goes as you please. Hot water, flavoured with potato and garnished with a yard of bread, makes an excellent lining for a hollow stomach. This is followed by omelette or fish. Of the two evils you choose the less, and cry "Omelette!" When the omelette is thrown in front of you it at once makes its presence felt. It recalls Bill Nye's beautiful story about an introspective egg laid by a morbid hen. However, if you smother the omelette in salt, red pepper, and mustard, you will be able to deal with it. I fear I cannot say as much for the fish. Then follows the inevitable chicken and salad, or perhaps Vienna steak, or *vol-au-vent*. The next item is Camembert or fruit, and coffee concludes the display.

Dining in these places is not a matter of subdued murmurs, of conversation in dulcet tones, or soft strains from the band. Rather you seem to dine in a menagerie. It is a bombardment more than a meal. The air buckles and cracks with noise. The first outbreak of hostilities comes from the counter at the entry of the first guest. The moment he is seated the waitress screams, " Un potage—un ! " The large Monsieur, the proprietor, at the counter, bellows down the tube, " Un POTAGE—Un ! " Away in subterranean regions an ear catches it, and a distant voice chants " *Potage!* " And then from the far reaches of the kitchen you hear a smothered tenor, as coming from the throat of one drowned in the soup-kettle, " P o t a g e ! " As the customers crowd in the din increases. Everywhere there is noise; as a result the customers must shout their conversation. As the volume of conversation increases the counter, finding itself hard-pressed, brings up its heavy artillery.

" Vol-au-vent ! " sings the waitress. " *Vol-au-vent!* " chants the counter in a bass as heavy and with as wide a range as Chaliapine's. " VOL-AU-VENT ! " roars the kitchen with the despair of tears in the voice; and " V o l-a u-v e n t ! " wails the lost soul beyond the Styx. By half-past seven it is no longer a restaurant : it is no longer a dinner that is being served. It is a grand opera that is in progress. The vocalists, " finding " themselves towards the end of the first act, warm up to the second, and each develops an individuality. I have often let my Vienna steak get cold while listening and trying to distinguish between the kitchen lift-man and the cook. Lift-man is usually a light and agreeable baritone, while the cook has mostly a falsetto, with a really exciting register. This grand opera idea affects, in turn, the waitresses. To the first-comers they are casual and chatty; but towards seven o'clock there is a subtle change. They become tragic. They are as the children of destiny. There is that Italianate sob in the voice as they demand *Poulet roti au salade!* as who should cry, "Ah, fors è lui!" or "In questa tomba...." They do not serve you. They assault you with soup or omelette. They make a grand pass above your head, and fling knife and fork before you. They collide with themselves and each other, and there are recriminations and reprisals. They quarrel, apparently, to the death, while M'sieu and Madame look on, passive spectators of the eternal drama. The air boils. The blood of the diners begins to boil, too, for they wave napkins and sticks of bread, and they bellow and scream defiance at one another. They draw the attention of the waitress to the fact that there is no salt on the table; what they seem to be telling her is that the destinies of France are in the balance, the enemy is at the gates, and that she must deliver herself as hostage or suffer dreadful deaths. Everything, in fact, boils, except the soup and the coffee; and at last, glad to escape, you toss your shilling on the table and tumble out, followed by a yearning cry of "Une salade—une!"

Even then your entertainment has not ceased with the passing of the shilling. For there are now numerous coffee-bars in Old Compton Street where for a penny you may lounge at the counter and get an excellent cup of black coffee, and listen to the electric piano, splurging its cheap gaiety on the night, or to the newsmen yelling "*Journaux de Paris!*" or "*Dernière Heure!*" There are "The Chat Noir," "The Café Leon," and "The Café Bar Conte"; also there is "The Suisse," where you may get "rekerky" liqueurs at threepence a time, and there is a Japanese café in Edward Street.

Of course there are numbers of places in Soho where you may dine more lavishly and expensively, and where you will find a band and a careful wine-list, such as Maxim's, The Coventry, The Florence, and Kettner's. Here you do not escape for a shilling, or anything like it. Maxim's does an excellent half-crown dinner, and so, too, does The Rendezvous. The others range from three shillings to five shillings ; and as the price of the meal increases so do the prices on the wine-lists increase, though you drink the same wine in each establishment.

The atmosphere of the cheaper places is, however, distinctly more companionable than that of these others. In the latter you have Surbiton and Streatham, anxious to display its small stock of evening frocks and dress suits ; very proper, very conscious of itself, very proud of having broken away from parental tradition. But in the smaller places, which are supported by a regular clientèle of the French clerks, workmen, and warehouse porters who are employed in and about Oxford Street, the sense of camaraderie and naturalness is very strong. These people are not doing anything extraordinary. They are just having dinner, and they are gay and *insouciant* about it, as they are about everything except frivolity. It is not exciting for them to dine on five courses instead of on roast mutton and vegetables and milk-pudding. It is a commonplace. For that is the curious thing about the foreigner : wherever he wanders he takes his country with him. Englishmen get into queer corners of the world, and adapt themselves to local customs, fit themselves into local landscapes. Not so the Continental. Let him go to London, New York, Chicago, San Francisco, and he will take France, or Germany, or Italy, or Russia with him. Here in this little square mile of London is France : French shops, French comestibles, French papers, French books, French pictures, French hardware, and French restaurants and manners. In Old Compton Street he is as much in France as if he were in the rue Chaussée d'Antin. I met some time since a grey little Frenchman who is first fiddle at a hall near Piccadilly Circus. He has never been out of France. Years and years ago he came from Paris, and went to friends in Wardour Street. There he worked for some time in a French music warehouse; and, when that failed, he was taken on in a small theatre near Shaftesbury Avenue. Thence, at fifty-two, he drifted into this music-hall orchestra, of which he is now leader. Yet during the whole time he has been with us he has never visited London. His London life has been limited to that square mile of short, brisk streets, Soho. If he crossed Piccadilly Circus, he would be lost, poor dear!

"Ah!" he sighs. "France . . . yes . . . Paris. Yes." For he lives only in dreams of the real Paris. He hopes soon to return there. He hoped soon to return there thirty years ago. He hates his work. He does not want to play the music of London, but the music of Paris. If he must play in London, he would choose to play in Covent Garden orchestra, where his fancy would have full freedom. When he says Music, he means Massenet, Gounod, Puccini, Mascagni, Leoncavallo. He plays Wagner with but little interest. He plays Viennese opera with a positive snort. Ragtime—well, I do not think he is conscious of playing it; he fiddles mechanically for that. But when, by a rare chance, the bill contains an excerpt from Pagliacci, La Bohème, or Butterfly, then he lives. He cares nothing for the twilight muse of your intellectual moderns — Debussy, Maurice Ravel, Scriabine, and such. For him music is melody, melody, melody—laughter, quick tears, and the graceful surface of things; movement and festal colour.

He seldom rises before noon—unless rehearsals

compel—and then, after a coffee, he wanders forth, smoking the cigarette of Algeria, and humming, always humming, the music that is being hummed in Paris. He is picturesque, in his own way—shabby, but artistically shabby. At one o'clock you will see him in "The Dieppe," taking their shilling table d'hôte *déjeuner*, with a half-bottle of *vin ordinaire* ; and he will sit over the coffee perhaps until three o'clock, murmuring the luscious, facile phrases of Massenet.

His great friend is the Irishman who plays the drum, for they have this in common : they are both exiles. They are both "saving up" to return home. They have both been "saving up" for the last twenty years. In each case there is a girl. . . . Or there was a girl twenty years ago. She is waiting for them—one in Paris, and the other in Wicklow. At least, so they believe. Sometimes, though, I think they must doubt ; for I have met them together in the Hotel Suisse putting absinthes away carelessly, hopelessly ; and a man does not play with absinthe when a girl is waiting for him.

AN ITALIAN NIGHT
CLERKENWELL

CLERKENWELL

Deep in the town a window smiles—
  You shall not find it, though you seek;
But over many bricky miles
  It draws me through the wearing week.
Its panes are dim, its curtains grey,
  It shows no heartsome shine at dusk;
For gas is dear, and factory pay
Makes small display:
On the small wage she earns she dare not be too gay!

A loud saloon flings golden light
  Athwart the wet and greasy way,
Where, every happy Sunday night,
  We meet in mood of holiday.
She wears a dress of claret glow
  That's thinly frothed with bead and lace.
She buys this lace in Jasmine Row,
A spot, you know,
Where luxuries of lace for a mere nothing go.

I love the shops that flare and lurk
  In the big street whose lamps are gems,
For there she stops when off to work
  To covet silks and diadems.
At evenings, too, the organ plays
  "My Hero" or in "Dixie Land";
And in the odoured purple haze,
Where naphthas blaze,
The grubby little girls the dust of dancing raise.

AN ITALIAN NIGHT

CLERKENWELL

FOR some obscure reason Saffron Hill is always associated in the public mind with Little Italy. Why, I do not know. It isn't and never was Italian. There is not a trace of anything the least Italian about it. There isn't a shop or a home in the whole length of it. It is just a segment of the City, E.C.—a straggling street of flat-faced warehouses and printing-works; high, impassive walls; gaunt, sombre, and dumb; not one sound or spark of life to be heard or seen anywhere. Yet that is what the unknowing think of when they think of the Italian quarter.

The true, warm heart of Italy in London is Eyre Street Hill, which slips shyly out of one of the romantic streets of London—Clerkenwell Road. There is something very taking about Clerkenwell Road, something snug and cheering. It is full, clustering, and alive. Here is the Italian Church. Here is St. John's Gate, where Goldsmith and Isaac Walton and a host of other delightful fellows lived. This gatehouse is now all that remains of the Priory of St. John of Jerusalem around which the little village of Clerkenwell developed. Very near, too, are Cloth Fair, Bartholomew's Close, Smithfield, and a hundred other echoes of past times. And here—most exciting of all—the redoubtable Mr. Heinz (famous for his 57 Varieties) has his warehouse.

There is a waywardness about Clerkenwell Road.

It never seems quite to know where it shall go. It drifts, winds, rises, drops, debouches. You climb its length, and, at the top, you see a wide open space, which is Mount Pleasant, and you think you have reached its end; but you haven't. There is much more to come. It doesn't stop until it reaches Gray's Inn Road, and then it stops sharply, unexpectedly. But the romance of the place lies not only in its past.; there is an immediate romance, for which you must turn into its byways. Here live all those bronzed street-merchants who carry delightful things to our doors—ice-cream, roast chestnuts, roast potatoes, chopped wood, and salt. In unsuspected warehouses here you may purchase wonderful toys that you never saw in any other shops. You may buy a barrow and a stove and a complete apparatus for roasting potatoes and chestnuts, including a natty little poker for raking out the cinders. You may buy a gaudily decorated barrow and freezing-plant for the manufacture and sale of ice-cream. Or—and as soon as I have the money this is what I am going to buy in Clerkenwell— you may buy a real street organ—a hundred of them, if you wish. While the main road and the side streets on the south are given up to the watch and clock-makers, the opposite side-streets are Italian soil. Here are large warehouses where the poor Italian may hire an organ for the day, or week, or month. A rehearsal at one of these show-rooms is a deafening affair; it is just like Naples on a Sunday morning. As the organs come over from Italy, they are "tried out," and any flaws are immediately detected by the expert ear. In the same way, a prospective hirer always tries his instrument before concluding the deal, running through the tunes to be sure that they are fairly up-to-date. When you get, say, six clients all rehearsing their organs at once in a small show-room . . .

This organ industry, by the way, is a very big

CLERKENWELL

thing; and the dealers make much more by hire than by sale. Sometimes a *padrone,* who has done very well, will buy an organ; later, he may buy another organ, and perhaps another. Then, with three organs, he sits down, and sends other men out with them. Street organs, under our fatherly County Council, are forbidden on Sundays; nevertheless, Sunday being the only day when millions of people have any chance of recreation, many organs go out. Whither do they go? East, my dears. There, in any ramshackle hall, or fit-up arch-way, or disused stables, the boys and girls, out for fun, may dance the golden hours away throughout Sunday afternoon and evening. Often the organs are hired for Eastern weddings and christenings and other ceremonials, and, by setting the musician to work, say, in the back parlour, the boys and girls can fling their little feet about the garden without interference from any one of the hundred authorities who have us at their mercy.

It is because of the organs, I think, that I chiefly loved Clerkenwell. Organs have been part of my life ever since I was old enough to sit up and take notice. Try to think of London without organs. Have they not added incalculably to the store of human happiness, and helped many thousands over the waste patches of the week? They have; and I heap smouldering curses upon the bland imbeciles of Bayswater who, some time ago, formed themselves into a society for, I think they called it, The Abatement of Street Noises, and stuck their loathly notices in squares and public streets forbidding street organs to practice there. Let house-agents take note that I and a dozen of my friends will never, never, never take a house in any area where organs or street vendors or street cries are prohibited. They are part of the very soul of London. Kill them, and you kill something lovely and desirable, without which the world will be the sadder. That any one should have the impudence to ask for money for the carrying out of such a project is merely another proof of the disease of the age. They might as well form a society and appeal for funds for suppressing children from laughing or playing in the streets. They might as well form a society for the strangulation of all babies. They might as well . . . But if I go on like this, I shall get angry. Thank Heaven, organs are not yet suppressed, though, after the curtailing of licensed hours, anything is possible. In that event, it really looks as if America were the only country in which to live, unless one could find some soft island in the Pacific, where one could do just as one jolly well pleased.

Let's all go down Eyre Street Hill, for there, you know, organs are still gurgling, and there are lazy laughter and spaghetti and *dolce far niente*, and cigarettes are six a penny. There are little restaurants here hardly bigger than a couple of telephone boxes. They contain but two tables, and some wooden benches, but about a dozen gloriously savage boys from Palermo and Naples are noisily supping after their day's tramp round London with whatever industry they affect. They have olive skins, black curly hair, flashing eyes, and fingers that dance with gemmy rings. A newcomer arrives, unhooking from his shoulders the wooden tray which holds the group of statuettes that he has been hawking round Streatham and Norwood. He salutes them in mellifluous tones, and sits down. He orders nothing; but a heaped-up dish of macaroni is put before him, and he attacks it with fork and finger. There are few women to be seen, but those few are gaudily arrayed in coloured handkerchiefs, their mournful eyes and purring voices touching the stern night to beauty. Of children there are dozens: furious boys and chattering girls. All the little girls, from four to fourteen, wear socks, and the narrow roadway flashes with the whirling of little white legs, so that the pedestrian must dodge his way along as one dancing a *schottische*. A few public-houses shed their dusty radiance, but these, too, are little better than dolls' houses. I have never seen village beer-shops so small. They are really about the size of the front room of a labourer's cottage, divided into two— Public Bar and Private Bar.

Such is the High Street of Italy, where one feeds. Most of the Italians, however, live in one of those huge blocks of tenements of which there are, I should think, a dozen in Clerkenwell. They seem to centre about the sounding viaducts that leap over Rosebery Avenue. Upon a time the place had a reputation for lawlessness, but that is now gone, with most of the colour of things. Occasionally there is an affray with knives, but it is always among themselves: a sort of vendetta; and nobody interferes so long as they refrain from bloodshed or from annoying peaceable people. The services in the Italian Church are very picturesque, and so, too, are their ceremonies at Christmas-time; while the procession of the children at First Communion is a thing of beauty. The little girls and boys walk together, the boys in black, the girls in white, with white wreaths gleaming in their dark curls. At Christmas-time there are great feasts, and every Italian baker and restaurant-keeper stocks his trays with Panetonnes, a kind of small loaf or bun, covered with sugar, which are distributed among the little ones of the Church.

An old friend of mine, named Luigi, who once kept a tiny wine-shop, lives in a little dirty room in Rosoman Street, and I sometimes spend an evening with him. But not in summer. I adjure you—do not visit an impoverished Italian who lives in one room in Clerkenwell, in the summer; unless, of course, you are a sanitary inspector. He is an entertaining old fellow, and speaks a delicious Italian-Cocknese, which no amount of trickery could render on the printed page. When I go, I usually take him a flask of Chianti and some Italian cigars, for which he very nearly kisses me.

But Luigi has a story. You will see that at once if you scan his face. There is something behind him—something he would like to forget. It happened about ten years ago, and I witnessed it. Ten years ago, Luigi did something—an act at once heroic, tragic, and idiotic. This was the way of it.

It was an April night, and we were lounging at that corner which was once called Poverty Point; the corner where Leather Lane crashes into Clerkenwell Road, and where, of a summer night, gather the splendid sons of Italy to discuss, to grin, to fight, and to invent new oaths. On this corner, moreover, they pivot in times of danger, and, once they can make the mazy circle of which it is the edge, safety from the pursuer is theirs. The place was alive with evening gladness. In the half-darkness, indolent groups lounged or strolled, filling their lungs with the heavily garlicked air of the place.

Then an organ pulled up at the public-house which smiles goldenly upon Mount Pleasant, and music broke upon us. Instantly, with the precision of a harlequinade, a stream of giggling girls poured from Eyre Street Hill and Back Hill. With the commencement of a rag-tag dance, the Point was whipped to frivolous life. The loungers grunted, and moved up to see. Clusters of children, little angels with dark eyes and language sufficiently seasoned to melt a glacier, slipped up from nowhere, and, one by one, the girls among them slid into the dance. One of them had a beribboned tambourine. Two others wanted it, and would snatch it away. Its owner said they were—something they could not possibly have been.

Stabs of light from the tenements pierced the dusk high and low. The night shone with recent rain, and in a shifting haze of grey and rose the dancers sank and glided, until the public-house lamp was turned on and a cornet joined the organ. In the warm yellow light, the revels broke bounds, and, to the hysterical appeal of "Hiawatha," the Point become a Babel. . . . When most of the dancers had danced themselves to exhaustion, two of the smaller maidens stood out and essayed a kind of can-can.

The crowd swooped in. It crowed with appreciation as they introduced all the piquant possibilities of the dance. It babbled its merriment at seeing little faces, which should show only the revel of April, bearing all the ravage of Autumn.

Comments and exhortations, spiced to taste, flew about the Point, ricochetted, and returned in boomerang fashion to their authors, who repolished them and shot them forth again. Heads bobbed back, forth, and up in the effort to see. In a prestissimo fire of joy, the novel exercise reached its finale, when . . .

"Hi-hi! *Hè. Eeeee!*" As though by signal, the whole Point was suddenly aspurt with spears of flame, leaping, meeting, and crossing. We looked round. The dance stopped, the organ gurgled away to rubbish, the crowd took open order, and stared at the narrow alley of Back Hill. Blankets of smoke moved from its mouth, pushing their suffocating way up the street. Twenty people hurt themselves in shrieking orders. Women screamed and ran. From an open window a tongue of flame was thrust derisively; it tickled a man's neck, and he swore. Then a lone woman had the sense to scream something intelligible.

We all ran. English, Italian, and profane clashed together. Three small boys strangled each other in a race for the fire-bell. In Back Hill, men, women, and children were hustling themselves through the ground-floor window of the doomed house. Thick, languid flames blocked the doorway, swaying idly, ready to fasten their fangs in anything that approached. Furniture crashed and bounded to the pavement. Mattresses were flung out to receive the indecent figures of their owners. The crowed swelled feverishly. Women screamed.

Gradually the crackle of burning wood and the ripple of falling glass gained voice above the outcry of the crowd. A shout of fear and admiration surged up, as a spout of flame darted through the roof, and quivered proudly to the sky. Luigi threw back his sweeping felt hat, loosened his yellow neck-cloth, tightened his scarlet waistband. "It is bad," he said. "It is a fire."

I said "Yes," having nothing else to say. A few Cockneys inquired resentfully why somebody didn't do something. Then the word went round that all were out but one. A woman was left at the top. A sick hush fell. Away in the upper regions a voice was wailing. The women turned pale, and one or two edged away. The men whistled silently, and looked serious. They had the air of waiting for something. It came. Luigi moved swiftly away from me, fought a way through the crowd, and stood by the door, his melodious head lashed by the fringe of the flames.

"I go up," he said operatically.

A dozen men dashed from him, crying things. "Wet blanket, there. Quick! Here's a bloke going up. Italiano's going up!"

At the back of the crowd, where I stood, a few fools cheered. They were English. "'Ray! 'Ray! 'Ray! Good iron! 'E's gotter nerve, 'e 'as. Wouldn't athought it o' them Italians."

The Italians were silent. From the house came long screams, terrible to hear in the London twilight. A Sicilian said something in his own language which cannot be set down ; the proprietor of the Ristorante del Commercio also grew profane. The children stared and giggled, wonderingly. Blankets and buckets of water were conjured from some obscure place of succour. In half a minute the blankets were soaked, and Luigi was ready.

A wispy man in a dented bowler danced with excitement. " Oh, he's gotter nerve, if yeh like. Going to risk his life, he is. Going to risk his blasted life." Fresh and keener screams went down the golden stairway. Luigi flung the wet folds about him, vaulted the low sill, and then the wild light danced evilly about him. Outside, we watched and waited. A lurid silence settled, and the far cries of one of the late dancers who was receiving correction for dancing indecent dances seemed entirely to fill space. The atmosphere was, as it were, about to crack and buckle, and I was feeling that Luigi was a heroic fool, when a passing navvy, not susceptible to influences, saved the situation by bursting into song :—

> "You're here and I'm here,
> So what do we care?"

The wispy man looked round, reprovingly. " Easy on, there ! " he implored.

" Whaffor ? "

" Well . . . chep's risking his life."

" Well . . . 'at don't make no difference. Be 'appy while yeh can, I say."

" No, but . . . chep's risking his life."

> "Yew maide me love yew,
> I didn't wanter do it !"

" Risking his life, and all ! "

Then the climax was reached. A scream sounded from above, then silence, then a confused rush of feet. The figure of Luigi filled the opening of the low window, and those nearest surged in to help and see. He was dragged through, head first, and set on his feet. The fire-engine raved and jangled in Clerkenwell Road, but there was no way for it. The firemen tried to clear the crowd, but it would not be denied its sight of the hero. It struggled in to admire. It roared and yelled in one and a hundred voices. The café proprietor gestured magnificently. Regard the hero ! How he was brave ! The wispy man nearly had a fit. He skipped. Risked his life, and all. For a blasted stranger.

Luigi dropped the bundle gently from his arms, and stood over it, a little bewildered at his reception. The firemen fought furiously, and at last they cleared a passage for their plant. Then, as they cleared, the wispy man danced again, and seemed likely to die. He sprang forward and capered before Luigi. I tried to get through to help Luigi out, but I was wedged like a fishbone in the throat of the gang.

It was then that horrid screams came again from the house, winding off in ragged ends. The wispy man spluttered.

" Yeh damn fool ! Look what yeh brought down. Look at it. Yeh damn fool ! "

Luigi looked still bewildered, and now I fought with sharp elbows, and managed to get to the front rank. The man's shaking finger pointed at Luigi's feet. " D'you know what you done, Italiano ? You made a mistake. A blasted mistake. Aw . . . yeh damn fool ! "

I looked too. There was no woman at Luigi's feet. There was a bundle of sheets, blanket, and carpet. A scream came from the house. Every window filled with flame. The roof fell inwards with a crash and a rain of sparks.

Clerkenwell has never forgiven Luigi. Luigi has never forgiven himself.

A BASHER'S NIGHT
HOXTON

LONDON JUNE

*Rank odours ride on every breeze;
Skyward a hundred towers loom;
And factories throb and workshops wheeze,
And children pine in secret gloom.
To squabbling birds the roofs declaim
Their little tale of misery;
And, smiling over murk and shame,
A wild rose blows by Bermondsey.*

*Where every traffic-thridden street
Is ribboned o'er with shade and shine,
And webbed with wire and choked with heat;
Where smokes with fouler smokes entwine;
And where, at evening, darkling lanes
Fume with a sickly ribaldry—
Above the squalors and the pains,
A wild rose blows by Bermondsey.*

*Somewhere beneath a nest of tiles
My little garret window squats,
Staring across the cruel miles,
And wondering of kindlier spots.
An organ, just across the way,
Sobs out its ragtime melody;
But in my heart it seems to play:
A Wild Rose blows by Bermondsey!*

*And dreams of happy morning hills
And woodlands laced with greenest boughs
Are mine to-day amid the ills
Of Tooley Street and wharfside sloughs,
Though Cherry Gardens reek and roar,
And engines gasp their horrid glee;
I mark their ugliness no more:
A wild rose blows by Bermondsey.*

A BASHER'S NIGHT

HOXTON

HOXTON is not merely virile; it is virulent. Life here hammers in the blood with something of the insistence of ragtime. The people—men, women, and children—are alive, spitefully alive. You feel that they are ready to do you damage, with or without reason. Here are antagonism and desire, stripped for battle. Little children, of three years old, have the spirit in them; for they lean from tenement landings that jut over the street, and, with becoming seriousness, spit upon the passing pedestrians, every hit scoring two to the marksman.

The colour of Hoxton Street is a tremendous purple. It springs upon you, as you turn from Old Street, and envelops you. There are high, black tenement houses. There are low cottages and fumbling passages. There are mellow fried-fish shops at every few yards. There are dirty beer-houses and a few public-houses. There are numerous cast-off clothing *salons*. And there are screeching Cockney women, raw and raffish, brutalized children, and men who would survive in the fiercest jungle. Also there is the Britannia Theatre and Hotel. The old Brit.! It stands, with Sadler's Wells and the Surrey, as one of the oldest homes of fustian drama. Sadler's Wells is now a picture palace, and the Surrey is a two-houses Variety show. The old Brit. held out longest, but even that is going now. Its annual pantomime was one of the events of the London Season for the good Bohemian. Then all the Gallery, First Nighters boys and girls would go down on the last night, which was Benefit Night for Mrs. Sara Lane, the proprietress. Not only were bouquets handed up, but the audience showered upon her tributes in more homely and substantial form. Here was a fine outlet for the originality of the crowd, and among the things that were passed over the orchestra-rails or lowered from boxes and circles were chests of drawers, pairs of corsets, stockings, pillow-cases, washhand jugs and basins, hip-baths, old boots, mince-pies, Christmas puddings, bottles of beer, and various items of lumber and rubbish which aroused healthy and Homeric laughter at the moment, but which, set down in print at a time when Falstaffian humour has departed from us, may arouse nothing but a curled lip and a rebuke. But it really was funny to see the stage littered with these tributes, which, as I say, included objects which are never exhibited in the light of day to a mixed company.

But the cream of Hoxton is its yobs. It is the toughest street in London. I don't mean that it is dangerous. But if you want danger, you have only to ask for it, and it is yours. It will not be offered you anywhere in London, but if you do ask for it, Hoxton is the one place where there is "no waiting," as the barbers say. The old Shoreditch Nile is near at hand, and you know what that was in the old days. Well, Hoxton to-day does its best to maintain the tradition of "The Nile."

Now once upon a time there was a baby-journalist named Simple Simon. He went down to Hoxton one evening, after dinner. It had been the good old English dinner of Simpson's, preceded by two vermuths, accompanied by a pint of claret, and covered in the retreat by four maraschinos. It was a picturesque night. A clammy fog blanketed the whole world. It swirled and swirled. Hoxton Street was a glorious dream, as enticingly indefinite as an opium-sleep. Simple Simon had an appointment here. The boys were to be out that night. Jimmie Flanagan, their leader, had passed the word to Simon that something would be doing, something worth being in. For that night was to witness the complete and enthusiastic bashing of Henry Wiggin, the copper's nark, the most loathed and spurned of all creeping things that creep upon the earth.

Simon walked like a lamb into the arms of trouble. He strolled along the main street, peering every yard of his way through the writhing gloom. Nobody was about. He reached Bell Yard, and turned into it. Then he heard something. Something that brought him to a sharp halt. Before he saw or heard anything more definite, he felt that he was surrounded. To place direction of sound was impossible. He heard, from every side, like the whisper of a load of dead leaves, the rush of rubber shoes. With some agility he leaped to what he thought was the clear side, only to take a tight arm like a rope across his chest and another about his knees.

"There's one fer yew, 'Enry!" cried a spirited voice as a spirited palm smote him on the nose.

"Hi! Hi! Easy!" Simon appealed. "I ain't 'Enry, dammit! You're bashing me—me—Simon!" He swore rather finely; but the fog, the general confusion, and, above all, the enthusiasm of bashing rendered identification by voice impracticable. Indeed, if any heard it, it had no effect; for, so they had some one to bash, they would bash. It didn't matter to them, just so it was a bash. Flanagan heard it quite clearly, but he knew the madness of attempting to stop eleven burly Hoxton yobs once they were well in. . . .

"I'm not 'Enry. I ain't the nark!" But he was turned face downward, and his mouth was over a gully-hole, so that his protests scared only the rats in the sewer. He set his teeth, and writhed and jerked and swung, and for some seconds no bashing could proceed, for he was of the stuff of which swordsmen are made—small, lithe, and light: useless in a stand-up fight with fists, but good for anything in a scrum. When, however, as at present, eleven happy lads were seeking each a grip on his person, it became difficult to defeat their purpose. But at last, as he was about to make a final wrench at the expense of his coat, the metal tips on his boots undid him. He dug his heels backward to get a purchase, he struck the slippery surface of the kerb instead of the yielding wood of the roadway, and in a moment he was down beyond all struggle. A foot landed feelingly against his ribs, another took him on the face; and for all that they were rubbered they stung horribly. Then, with two pairs of feet on his stomach, and two on his legs, he heard that wild whisper that may unnerve the stoutest—

"Orf wi' yer belts, boys!"

The bashing of the nark was about to begin. There was a quick jingle as many leather belts were loosed, followed by a whistle, and—*Zpt!* he received the accolade of narkhood. Again and again they came, and they stung and bit, and he could not move. They spat all about him. He swore crudely but sincerely, and if oaths have any potency his tormentors should have withered where they stood. Two and three at a time they came, for there were eleven of them—Flanagan having discreetly retired—and all were anxious to christen their nice new belts on the body of the hated nark; and they did so zealously, while Simon could only lie still and swear and pray for a happy moment that should free one of his hands. . . .

He knew it was a mistake, and he kept his temper so far as possible. But human nature came out with the weals and bruises. He didn't want to do the dirty on them, he didn't want to take extreme steps, but dammit, this was the frozen limit. He knew that when their mistake was pointed out they would offer lavish apologies and pots of four-'arf, but the flesh is only the flesh.

"Turn the blanker over!"

In that moment, as he was lifted round, his left hand was freed. In a flash it fumbled at his breast. Twisting his head aside, he got something between his teeth, and through the fetid fog went the shiver and whine of the Metropolitan Police Call. Three times he blew, with the correct inflection.

At the first call he was dropped like a hot coal. From other worlds came an answering call. He blew again. Then, like thin jets of water, whistles spurted from every direction. He heard the sound of scuttering feet as his enemies withdrew. He heard the sound of scuttering feet as they closed in again. But he was not waiting for trouble. He pulled his burning self together, and ran for the lights that stammered through the gloom at the Britannia. He whistled as he ran. Curses followed him.

At the Britannia he collided with a slow constable. He flung a story at him. The constable inspected him, and took notes. The lurking passages began to brighten with life, and where, a moment ago, was sick torpidity was now movement, clamour. Distant whistles still cried. The place tingled with nervous life.

Some cried "Whassup?" and some cried "Stanback, cancher!" They stared, bobbed, inquired, conjectured. The women were voluble. The men spat. A forest of faces grew up about Simple Simon. A hurricane of hands broke about his head. The constable took notes and whistled. A humorist appeared.

" 'Ullo, 'ullo, 'ullo! Back water there, some of yer. Stop yer shoving. Ain't nobody bin asking for me? Stop the fight. I forbid the bangs!"

But he was not popular. They jostled him.

" 'Ere," cried some one, " let some one else have a see, Fatty ! Other people wanter have a see, don't they ? "

" Stanback—stanback ! Why cancher stanback ! "

Fatty inquired if Someone wanted a smash over the snitch. Because, if so . . .

A woman held that Simple Simon had a rummy hat on. There were pauses, while the crowd waited and shuffled its feet, as between the acts.

Fatty asked why some one didn't do something. Alwis the way, though—them police. Stanback—git back on your mat, Toby.

And then . . . and then the swelling, clamorous, complaining crowd swooped in on itself with a sudden undeniable movement. Its centre flattened, wavered, broke, and the impelling force was brought face to face with Simple Simon and the constable. It was Flanagan and the boys.

Three pairs of arms collared the constable low. Simple Simon felt a jerk on his arm that nearly pulled it from its socket, and a crackling like sandpaper at his ear. " Bolt for it ! "

And he would have done so, but at that moment the answering whistles leaped to a sharper volume, and through the distorting fog came antic shapes of **blue,** helmeted. The lights of the Britannia rose up. Panic smote the crowd, and for a moment there was a fury of feet.

Women screamed. Others cried for help. Some one cried, " Hot stuff, boys—let 'em 'ave it where it 'urts most ! "

Fatty cried : " Git orf my foot ! If I find the blank blank blank what trod on my blank 'and, I'll——!! "

" Look out, boys ! ! Truncheons are out ! "

They ran, slipped, fell, rolled. A cold voice from a remote window, remarked, above the din, that whatever he'd done he'd got a rummy hat on. A young girl was pinioned against the wall by a struggling mass for whom there was no way. There was in the air an imminence of incident, acid and barbed. The girl screamed. She implored. Then, with a frantic movement, her free hand flew to her hat. She withdrew something horrid, and brought it down, horridly, three times. Three shrieks flitted from her corner like sparks from a funnel. But her passage was cleared.

Then some important fool pulled the fire-alarm.

" Stanback, Stinkpot, cancher? Gawd, if I cop that young 'un wi' the bashed 'elmet, I'll learn him hell ! "

" If I cop 'old of the blanker what trod on my 'and, I'll—— ! "

" No, but—'e 'ad a rummy 'at on. 'E 'ad."

Away distant, one heard the brazen voice of the fire-engine, clanging danger through the yellow maze of Hoxton streets. There was the jangle of harness and bells; the clop-clop of hoofs, rising to a clatter. There was the scamper of a thousand feet as the engine swung into the street with the lordliest flourish and address. Close behind it a long, lean red thing swayed to and fro, like some ancient dragon seeking its supper.

" Whichway, whichway, whichway? " it roared.

" Ever bin had? " cried the humorist. " There ain't no pleading fire ! This is a picnic, this is. 'Ave a banana? "

" WhichWAY? " screamed the engine. " Don't no one know which way? "

The humorist answered them by a gesture known in polite circles as a " raspberry." Then a constable, with fierce face, battered helmet, and torn tunic, and with an arm-lock on a perfectly innocent non-combatant, flung commands in rapid gusts—

" This way, Fire. King's name. Out hoses!! "

The fog rolled and rolled. The Britannia

gleamed on the scene with almost tragic solemnity. Agonized shapes rushed hither and thither. Women screamed. Then a rich Irish voice sang loud above all : " Weeny, boys ! "

As the firemen leaped from their perches on the engine to out hoses, so, mysteriously, did the combat cease. Constables found themselves, in a moment, wrestling with thick fog and nothing more. The boys were gone. Only women screamed.

Some one said : " If I cop a hold of the blankety blank blanker what trod on my blanking 'and, I'll just about—— ! "

On the word " Weeny " Simple Simon was once again jerked by the arm, and hustled furiously down passages, round corners, and through alleyways, finally to be flung into the misty radiance of Shoreditch High Street, with the terse farewell : " Now run—for the love of glory, run ! "

But he didn't. He stood still against a friendly wall, and suffered. He straightened his dress. He touched sore places with a tender solicitude. His head was racking. All his limbs ached and burned. He desired nothing but the cold sheets of his bed and a bottle of embrocation. He swore at the fog, with a fine relish for the colour of sounds. He swore at things that were in no way responsible for his misfortune. Somewhere, he conjectured, in warmth and safety, Henry Wiggin, the copper's nark, was peacefully enjoying his supper of fried fish and 'taters and stout.

And then, over the sad, yellow night, faint and sweet and far away, as the memory of childhood, came a still small voice—

" No, but 'e 'ad a rummy 'at on, eh ? "

A DOWN-STREAM NIGHT
BLACKWALL

WEST INDIA DOCK ROAD

Black man—white man—brown man—yellow man—
  All the lousy Orient loafing on the quay:
Hindoo, Dago, Jap, Malay, and Chinaman
  Dipping into London from the great green sea!

Black man—white man—brown man—yellow man—
  Pennyfields and Poplar and Chinatown for me!
Stately-moving cut-throats and many-coloured mysteries,
  Never were such lusty things for London lads to see!

On the evil twilight—rose and star and silver—
  Steals a song that long ago in Singapore they sang:
Fragrant of spices, of incense and opium,
  Cinnamon and aconite, the betel and the bhang.

Three miles straight lies lily-clad Belgravia,
  Thin-lipped ladies and padded men and pale.
But here are turbaned princes and velvet-glancing gentlemen,
  Tom-tom and sharp knife and salt-caked sail.

Then get you down to Limehouse, by rigging, wharf, and smoke-stack,
  Glamour, dirt, and perfume, and dusky men and gold;
For down in lurking Limehouse there's the blue moon of the Orient—
  Lamps for young Aladdins, and bowies for the bold!

A DOWN-STREAM NIGHT

BLACKWALL

TIDE was at flood, and below Limehouse Hole the waters thrashed the wharves with malice. The hour was late, but life ran high in those parts. Against the savage purple of the night a few wisps of rigging and some gruff funnels stood up in East and West India Docks.

Sheer above the walls of East India Dock rose the deck of the *Cawdor Castle*, as splendidly correct as a cathedral. The leaping lines of her seemed lost in the high skies, and she stood out sharply, almost ecstatically. Against such superb forces of man, the forces of Nature seemed dwarfed. It was a lyric in steel and iron. Men hurried from the landing-stage, up the plank, vanishing into the sly glooms of the huge port-holes. Chains rang and rattled. Lascars of every kind flashed here and there: Arabs, Chinkies, Japs, Malays, East Indians. Talk in every lingo was on the air. Some hurried from the dock, making for a lodging-house or for The Asiatics' Home. Some hurried into the dock, with that impassive swiftness which gives no impression of haste, but rather carries a touch of extreme languor. An old cargo tramp lay in a far berth, and one caught the sound of rushing blocks, and a monotonous voice wailing the Malayan chanty: "Love is kind to the least of men, EEEE-*ah*, EEEE-*ah*!" Boats were loading up. Others were unloading. Over all was the glare of arc-lights, and the flutter of honeyed tongues.

A few tugs were moored at the landing-stages. One or two men hung about them, smoking, spitting. The anger of the Blackwall streets came to them in throbbing blasts, for it was Saturday night, and closing time. Over the great plain of London went up a great cry. Outside the doors of every hostelry, in Piccadilly and Bermondsey, in Blackwall and Oxford Street, were gathered bundles of hilarity, lingering near the scenes of their recent splendours. A thousand sounds, now of revelry, now of complaint, disturbed the brooding calm of the sky. A thousand impromptu concerts were given, and a thousand insults grew precociously to blows. A thousand old friendships were shattered, and a thousand new vows of eternal comradeship and blood-brotherhood were registered. A thousand wives were waiting, sullen and heavy-eyed, for a thousand jovial or brutal mates; and a thousand beds received their occupants in full harness, booted and hatted, as though the enemy were at the gates. Everywhere strains of liquor-music surged up for the next thirty minutes, finally to die away piecemeal as different roads received different ·evellers.

In the hot, bilious dark of Blackwall, the tug swayed and jerked, and the voices of the men seemed almost to shatter the night. But high above them was the dirty main street, and there " The Galloping Horses " flared and fluttered and roared. There seemed to be trouble. . . . One heard a querulous voice : " I said TIME, din' I ? " And another : " Well, let 'im prove it. Let 'im 'it me, that's all ! " From the tug you could see the dust of the street rise in answering clouds to the assaults of many feet. Then, quite suddenly, the wide swing-doors of the bar flapped back. A golden gleam burst on the night and seemed to vomit a slithering mass of men which writhed and rolled like an octopus. Then you heard the collapsible gates run to their sockets with a glad clang, and the gas was switched off.

The fester of noise widened and widened, and at last burst into twenty minute pieces. And now a large voice commanded the silence of the night, and cried upon London : " What I said is what I say now : that fan-tan is fan-tan. And blasted miracles is blasted miracles."

I stood on the tug, with some of the boys, and in silence we watched the drama that was about to unfold itself. I had tramped there, unthinkingly, up the thunderous length of Rotherhithe Tunnel and down East India Dock Road and had fallen in with Chuck Lightfoot and some of his waterside cronies. We were lounging on the tug, so far as I remember, because we were lounging on the tug. For no other reason.

After the outcry of the Great Voice, there was a short silence. It was broken by a woman, who cried : " Ar-ferr ! "

" You go on 'ome ! " cried Arfer.

The woman replied that bad-word husbands who stayed out so bad-wordily late ought to be bad-wordily bad-worded. The next moment Arfer had gone down to a blow from the Great Voice.

Things began to happen. There was a loud scratch as a hundred feet scuttered backward. The victim sprang up. For a moment astonishment seemed to hold him, as he bleared ; then he seemed about to burst with wrath , then he became a cold sportsman. The lady screamed for aid. He spat on his hands. He hitched his trousers. Hands down, chin protruded, he advanced on his opponent with the slow, insidious movement of the street fighter. The other man dashed in, beat him off with the left, and followed it with three to the face with the right. He pressed his man. He ducked a lumbering right swing, and sent a one-two to the body. The lady had lashed herself to a whirlwind of profanity. She spat words at the crowd, and oaths fell like toads from her lips. We below heard the crowd and the lady; but we saw only the principals of the combat until . . . until the lady, disregarding the ethics of the game, flew in with screwed face, caught the coming arm of the big man, and pinioned it beneath her own.

"'Elp, 'elp, some of yeh!" she cried. Her husband fastened on to his enemy, tore at his collar with wild fingers, opened his mouth, and tried to bite. The big man struggled with both. The bulky form of the lady was swung back and forth by his cunning arm; and one heard the crowd stand by, press in, rush back, in rhythm to the movements of the battlers. A moment later the lady was down and out. A sudden blow at the breast from the great elbow. I heard her fall . . . I heard the gasp of the crowd.

Here and there the blank street was suddenly struck to life. Warm blinds began to wink. One heard the creak of opening windows, and voices: "Why doncher separate 'em? Why cancher shut that plurry row?" With the new light one saw the crowd against a ground of chocolate hue. Here and there a cigarette picked out a face, glowing like an evil eye. All else was dank darkness.

Round and round the combatants went. Two well-set youngsters made a dash upon them, only to be swung from their feet into the crowd. They kicked, twisted, jerked, panted, now staggered a few paces, now stood still, straining silently. Now they were down, now up. Another woman's voice wailed across the unhappy water in the mournful accent of Belfast: "Fr-r-rank, Fr-rank, where arrre ye? Oh, Fr-rank, Fr-rank—ye br-reak me hear-r-t!"

Then Chuck Lightfoot, known also as The Panther, The Croucher, and The Prize Packet, shifted from my side. I looked at him. "Fed up on this, I am. Wait here." He vaulted from the deck of the tug to the landing-stage, strode up the gang-plank, and was lost in the long shaft of darkness.

From above one heard a noise—a nasty noise: the sound of a man's head being banged on the pavement. Frank's wife screamed: "Separate 'em! He's killin' 'im! Why don't some one do somethin'?"

Another woman cried: "I'll be sick. Stop 'em! I daresn't look."

Then everything stopped. We heard a low hum, swelling swiftly to a definite cry. The word "dead—dead—dead" flitted from mouth to mouth. Some turned away. Others approached as near as they dared, retreating fearfully when a push from behind drove them forward. . . .

But nobody was dead. Into the centre light had dashed Chuck Lightfoot. Chuck Lightfoot was a pugilistic manager. He was a lot of other things besides. He was the straightest boy I have ever met in that line. He had every high animal quality that a man should have. And he had a cold nerve that made men twice his size afraid of him.

The fight was stopped. Two blows from Chuck had stopped it. The crowd gathered round and gave first aid to both combatants, while Chuck faced them, and waited for assaults. We climbed up and stood with him, but nothing happened. Tragedy is so often imminent in this region, and so often trickles away to rubbish. The crowd was vociferous and gestic. It swooped about us, and inquired, conjectured, disapproved, condemned.

Then came several blue helmets and swift dispersal.

The affair was over.

AN ART NIGHT
CHELSEA

A LONDON MOMENT

Often have I, in my desolate years,
   Flogged a jaded heart in loud saloons;
Often have I fled myself with tears,
   Wandering under pallid, passionate moons.

Often have I slunk through pleasured rites,
   Lonely in the tumult of decay;
Often marked the hectic London nights
   Flowing from the violet-lidded day.

Yet, because of you, the world has been
   Kindlier. Oh, little heart-o'-rose,
I have glimpsed a beauty seldom seen
   In this labyrinthine mist of woes.

Beauty smiles at me from common things,
   All the way from Fleet Street to the Strand;
Even in the song the barmaid sings
   I have found a fresh enchanted land.

Pass me by, you little vagrant joy.
   Brush me from your delicate mimic world.
Nothing of you now can e'er annoy,
   Since your beauty has my heart empearled.

Pass me by; and only let me say:
   Glad I am for pain of loving you,
Glad—for, in the tumult of decay,
   Life is nobler than I ever knew.

AN ART NIGHT

CHELSEA

"THE choicest bit of London!" That is William Dean Howells' impression of Chelsea. And, if you would perceive rightly the soul of Chelsea, you must view it through the pearl-grey haze of just such a temperament as that of the suave American novelist. If you have not that temperament, then Chelsea is not for you ; try Hampstead or Streatham or Bayswater.

Of all suburbs it is the most subtle. It has more soul in one short street than you will find in the whole mass of Oxford Street and Piccadilly. There is something curiously feminine and intoxicating in the quality of its charm, something that evokes the silver-pensive mood. One visions it as a graceful spinster—watered silks, ruffles, corkscrew curls, you know, with lily fingers caressing the keys of her harpischord. Pass down Cheyne Walk at whatever time you will, and you are never alone ; little companies of delicate fancy join you at every step. The gasworks may gloom at you from the far side. The L.C.C. cars may hum and clang. But fancy sweeps them away. It is like sitting amid the barbarities of a Hyde Park drawing-room, in the emerald dusk, listening to the pathetic wheezing of a musical-box, ridiculously sweet :—

> Oh, don't you remember the days when we roamed,
> Sweet Phyllis, by lane and by lea?

Whatever you want in Chelsea—that you will find, assuming, of course, the possession of the Chelsea temperament. Whistler discovered her silvern beauty when he first saw her reclining by the river, beautifying that which beautifies her. All about Chelsea the colours seem to chime with their backgrounds as though they loved them; and when the lamps are lighted, flinging soft shadows on sixteenth and seventeenth-century gables and doorways and passages, then she becomes a place of wonder, a Bagdad, a treasure-ground for the artist.

And the artists have discovered her. Chelsea has much to show. Hampstead, Kensington, Mayfair—these be rich in gilt-trapping names, but no part of England can produce such a shining array of names, whose greatness owes nothing to time, place, or social circumstance: the names of those whose greatness is of the soul, and who have shaken the world with the beauty they have revealed to us. But Art has now taken possession of her, and it is as the studio of the artist that Chelsea is known to-day. Step this way, if you please. We draw the curtain. *Vie de Bohème!* But not, mark you, the *vie de Bohème* of Murger. True, Rodolphe and Marcel are here, and Mimi and Musette. But the studio is not the squalid garret that we know. We have changed all that. Rodolphe writes light verse for the "largest circulations." Mimi draws fashion plates, and dresses like the Duchess of the novelettes. Marcel—well, Marcel of Chelsea may be poor, but his is only a relative poverty. He is poor in so far as he dines for two shillings instead of five. The Marcel of to-day who is accustomed to skipping a meal by stress of circumstances doesn't live in Chelsea. He simply couldn't do it; look at the rents. He lives in Walworth Road or Kentish Town. No; there is a *vie de Bohème* at Chelsea, but it is a Bohemia of coffee liqueurs and Turkish cigarettes.

The beginnings of the delectable suburb are obscure. It seems to have assumed importance on the day when Henry VIII "acquired" its manor, which led to the building of numerous sycophantic houses. The Duchess of Monmouth had a residence here, with the delightful John Gay as secretary. Can one imagine a modern Duchess with a modern poet as secretary? The same house was later occupied by the gouty dyspeptic Smollett, who wrote all his books at the top of his bad temper. Then came—but one could fill an entire volume with nothing but a list of the goodly fellowship of Chelsea.

The book about Chelsea has yet to be written. Such a book should disclose to us the soul of the place, with its eternal youth and eternal antiquity. It should introduce us to its charming ghosts—it is difficult to name one disagreeable person in this pageant; even the cantankerous Smollett was soothed when he came under its spell. It should enable us to touch finger-tips, perhaps make closer acquaintance, with Sir Thomas More, Erasmus, Hans Holbein, Thomas Shadwell (forgotten laureate), Carlyle, Whistler, Edwin Abbey, George Meredith, Swinburne, Holman Hunt, William Morris, Ford Madox Brown, Oscar and Willie Wilde, Count d'Orsay, George Eliot, and a host of lesser but equally adorable personalities whose names must come "among those present." It should show us its famous places. It should afford us peep-holes into the studios of famous artists—Augustus John's studio is a revelation in careful disarrangement; it should take us round a 'Show Sunday"; it should reconstruct the naïve gaieties of Cremorne; and, finally, it should recreate and illumine all the large, forgotten moments in the lives of those apostles of beauty whose ruminations and dreams the soul of Chelsea has fused with more of herself than men may know; ending, perhaps, with a disquisition on the effects of environment on the labours of genius.

Such a book must be done by a stranger, an observer, one with a gracious pen, a delicate, entirely human mind. There is one man above all who is divinely appointed for the task.

Please, Mr. W. D. Howells, will you write it for us?

· · · · ·

I was strolling in philosophic mood down the never-ending King's Road, one November night, debating whether I should drop in at the Chelsea Palace, or have just one more at the "Bells," when I ran into the R.B.A. He is a large man, and running into him rather upsets one's train of thought. When I had smoothed my nose and dusted my trousers, I said: "Well, what about it?" He said: "Well, what about it?"

So we turned into the "Six Bells," the evening haunt of every good artist. He said he hadn't much money, so what about it? We decided on a Guinness to begin with, and then he ordered some Welsh Rarebits, while I inspected the walls of the saloon, which are decorated with nothing but originals, many of them bearing resounding names. In the billiard-room he introduced me to Augustus John and three other famous men who might not like it known that they drink beer in public-houses. When the Welsh Rarebits were announced, we went upstairs to the cosy dining-room and feasted gorgeously, watching, from the window, the many-coloured life of Chelsea. . . .

When every scrap of food on our plates was gone, we had another Guinness, and I went back to his studio, a beautiful room with oak panelling and electric light, which he rented from a travelling pal for the ridiculous sum of three shillings a week. It stood next to the reconstructed Crosby Hall, and looked out on a wide prospect of sloping roofs, peppered with sharp light.

He sat down and showed me his day's work. He showed me etchings, oils, pastels. He told me stories. He showed me caricatures of the famous people with whom he had *bohèmed*. Then, at about

ten o'clock, he said it was rather dull; and what
about it? He knew a place, quite near, where some
of the boys were sure to be; what about it?
 So we descended the lone staircase, and came out
to the windy embankment, where self-important little
tugs were raking the water with the beams of their
headlights. Thence we made many turnings, and
stopped at a house near the Models' Club. At this
club, which was formed only in 1913, the artists
may go at any time to secure a model—which is a
distinct boon. The old way was for the model
to call on the artist, the result being that the un-
fortunate man was pestered with dozens of girls for
whom he had no use, while the one model he really
wanted never appeared. The club combines the
advantages of club, employment bureau, and hotel.
There is no smoking-room; every room is a
smoking-room, for there are two things which are
essential to the comfort of the girl-model, and they
are cigarettes and sweets. These are their only
indulgences, for, obviously, if you are depending
for your livelihood on your personal figure, self-
denial and an abstemious life are compulsory.
 If you want to know what is doing in the art
world, who is painting what, and why, then get yourself invited to tea—China tea only. The gathering is
picturesque, for the model has, of course, the knack
of the effective pose, not only professionally but
socially. It is a beautiful club, and it is one more
answer to the eternal question Why Girls Don't
Marry. With a Models' Club, the Four Arts Club,
the Mary Curzon Hotel, and the Lyceum Club, why,
on earth should they?
 The R.B.A. pulled up short and said there we
were, and what about it? We knocked at the door,
and were admitted by an anarchist. At least, I
think he was an anarchist, because he was just like
the pictures. I have met only eighteen real anarchists, two of whom had thrown a bomb; but I

could never really believe in them; they wore morning coats and bowler hats and were clean-shaven.

"Where are they?" asked the R.B.A.

"They're awa' oopstairs, laddie," said the anarchist. "Taak heed ye dinna stoomble; the carrrpet's a wee bit loose."

We crossed the tiny hall and ascended the shabby stairs. From an open door trickled the tones of a cheap piano and the mellow, philosophic chant of the 'cello. They were playing Elgar's "Salut d'Amour." The room was dark save for one candle at the piano and the dancing firelight. In the dusk it looked just like Balestieri's picture of "Beethoven" which adorns every suburban drawing-room with a leaning towards the Artistic. People were sprawled here and there, but to distinguish them was impossible. I fell over some one's foot, and a light treble gurgled at me, "Sorry, old boy!" I caught a whisk of curls as the thin gleam of the candle fell that way. The R.B.A. crossed the room as one who was familiar with its topography, and settled himself in a far chair. The anarchist took my arm, and said:—

"Do ye sit down whurr ye can, laddie. And ye'll ha 'a drink?"

I fell over some more feet and collapsed on a low settee. I found myself by the side of a lady in solemn crimson. Her raven hair was hanging down her back. Her arms were bare. She smoked a Virginia cigarette vindictively. Sometimes she leaned forward, addressed the piano, and said: "Shut that row, Mollie, can't you. We want to talk."

The anarchist brought me a Scotch-and-soda, and then she became aware of my presence. She looked at me; she looked at the drink. She said to the anarchist: "Where's mine?" He said: "What is it?" "Cremdermont!" she snapped

Out of the smoky glooms of the room came light laughter and merry voices. One saw dimly, as in a dream, graceful forms reclining gracefully, attended by carelessly dressed but distinguished young men. Some of these raised their voices, and one heard the self-proud accent of Oxford. The music stopped, and the girls sprawled themselves more and more negligently, nestling to the rough coats of the boys. The haze of smoke thickened. I prepared for a boring evening.

One of the Oxford boys said he knew an awfully good story, but it was rather risky, you know. I pricked up my ears. Did we know the story—story about a fellah—fellah who had an aunt, you know? And fellah's aunt was most frightfully keen on dogs and all that, you know. . . . After three minutes of it I lost interest in the story. It concerned Old George and Herbert and young Helen, and various other people who seemed familiar to everybody but myself.

I never heard the finish of it. I became rather interested in a scene near the window, where a boy of about my own age was furiously kissing a girl somewhat younger. Then the lady at my side stretched a long arm towards me, and languished, and making the best of a bad job, I languished, too. When the funny story and the fellah's aunt had been disposed of, some one else went to the piano and played Debussy, and the anarchist brought me another drink; and the whole thing was such painfully manufactured Bohemianism that it made me a little tired. The room, the appointments, the absence of light, Debussy, the drinks, and the girls' costumes were so obviously part of an elaborate make-up, an arrangement of life. The only spontaneous note was that which was being struck near the window. I decided to slip away, and fell down the ragged stairs into Chelsea, and looked upon the shadow-fretted streets, where the arc-lamps, falling through the trees, dappled the pavements with light.

The skies were dashed with stars and a sick moon. It was trying to snow. I tripped down the steps from the door, and ran lightly into a girl who stood at the gate, looking up at the room I had just left. The cheek that was turned toward me was clumsily daubed with carmine and rouge. Snowflakes fell dejectedly about her narrow shoulders. She just glanced at me, and then back at the window. I looked up, too. The piano was at it again, and some one was singing. The thread of light just showed you the crimson curtains and the heavy oak beams. The pianist broke into Delilah's song, and the voice swam after it. It was a clear, warm voice, typical of the fifth-rate concert platform. But the girl, her face uplifted, dropped her lips in a half-whispered exclamation of wonder, " Cuh ! " I should have said that she was, for the first time, touching finger-tips with beauty. It moved her as something comic should have done. Her face lit to a smile, and then a chuckle of delight ran from her.

The voice was doing its best. It sank to despair, it leaped to lyric passion, it caressed a low note of ecstatic pain, and then, like a dew-delighted bird, it fled up and hovered on a timid note of appeal. The girl giggled. As the voice died on a long, soft note, she laughed aloud, and swallowed. She looked around and caught my eye. It seemed that she had something about which she must talk.

. . . " Not bad, eh ? " she said.

" No," I answered. " Not so dusty."

" Makes you feel . . . kind of rummy, you know, don't it ? Wonder what it feels like to sing like that, eh ? Makes me . . . sort of . . . 'fyou understand . . . funny like. Makes me want to . . ."

From the window came one of the Oxford voices. "*No* EARTHLY, dear old girl. You'll *never* sing. Your *values*, you know, and *all that* are . . ."

A RUSSIAN NIGHT
SPITALFIELDS AND STEPNEY

STEPNEY CAUSEWAY

Beyond the pleading lip, the reaching hand,
  Laughter and tear;
Beyond the grief that none would understand;
  Beyond all fear.
Dreams ended, beauty broken,
Deeds done, and last words spoken,
  Quiet she lies.

Far, far from our delirious dark and light,
  She finds her sleep.
No more the noisy silences of night
  Shall hear her weep.
The blossomed boughs break over
Her holy breast to cover
  From any eyes.
Till the stark dawn shall drink the latest star,
  So let her be.
O Love and Beauty! She has wandered far
  And now comes home to thee.

A RUSSIAN NIGHT

SPITALFIELDS AND STEPNEY

THE Russian quarter always saddens me. For one thing, it has associations which scratch my heart regularly every month when my affairs take me into those parts. Forgetting is the most wearisome of all pains to which we humans are subject; and for some of us there is so much to forget. For some of us there is Beatrice to forget, and Dora, and Christina, and the devastating loveliness of Isabel. For another thing, its atmosphere is so depressingly Slavonic. It is as dismal and as overdone as Rachmaninoff's Prelude in C sharp minor. How shall I give you the sharp flavour of it, or catch the temper of its streets?

It seems impossible that one should ensnare its elusive spirit. Words may come, but they are words, hard and stiff-necked and pedestrian. One needs symbols and butterflies.

.   .   .   .   .

Beauty is a strange bird. Hither and thither she flies, and settles where she will; and men will say that she is found here and there—sometimes in Perugia, sometimes in Mayfair, sometimes in the Himalaya. I have known men who found her in the dark melancholy of Little Russia, and I can understand them. For beauty appears, too, in various guise; and some men adore her in silks and some in rags. There are girls in this quarter who will smite the heart out of you, whose beauty will cry itself into your very blood. White's Row and the fastnesses of Stepney do not produce many choice blooms ; there are no lilies in these gardens of weeds. The girls are not romantic to regard or to talk with. They are not even clean. The secrets of their toilet are not known to me, but I doubt if soap and water ever appear in large quantities. And yet . . . They walk or lounge, languorous and heavy-lidded, yet with a curious suggestion of smouldering fire in their drowsy gaze. Rich, olive-skinned faces they have, and hair either gloomy or brassy, and caressing voices with the lisp of Bethnal Green. You may see them about the streets which they have made their own, carrying loads of as enchanting curls as Murger's Mimi.

But don't run away with the idea that they are wistful, or luscious, or romantic ; they are not. Go and mix with them if you nurse that illusion. Wistfulness and romance are in the atmosphere, but the people are practical . . . more practical and much less romantic that Mr. John Jenkinson of Golder's Green.

You may meet them in the restaurants of Little Montagu Street, Osborn Street, and the byways off Brick Lane. The girls are mostly cigarette-makers, employed at one of the innumerable tobacco factories in the district. Cigarette-maker recalls " Carmen " and Marion Crawford's story ; but here are only the squalid and the beastly. Brick Lane and the immediate neighbourhood hold many factories, each with a fine odour—bed-flock, fur, human hair, and the slaughter-house. Mingle these with sheep-skins warm from the carcass, and the decaying refuse in every gutter, and you will understand why I always smoke cigars in Spitalfields. In these cafés I have met on occasion those serio-comics, Louise Michel, Emma Goldmann, and Chicago May. Beilis, the hero of the blood-ritual trial, was here some months ago ; and Enrico Malatesta has visited, too. Among the men—fuzzy-bearded, shifty-eyed fellows—there are those who have been to Siberia and back. But do not ask them about Siberia, nor question how they got back. There are some things too disgusting even to talk about. Siberia is not exciting ; it is filthy. But you may sit among them, the men and the dark, gazelle-eyed girls ; and you may take caviare, tea-and-lemon, and black bread ; and conversation will bring you a proffered cigarette.

It was in these streets that I first met that giant of letters, Mr. W. G. Waters, better known to the newspaper public as " Spring Onions," but unfortunately I did not meet him in his gay days, but in his second period, his regeneracy. He was introduced to me as a fearsome rival in the subtle art of Poesy. I stood him a cup of cocoa—for you know, if you read your newspaper, that Spring was a teetotaller. He signed the pledge, at the request of Sir John Dickinson, then magistrate at Thames Police Court, in 1898, and it was his proud boast that he had kept it ever since. He was then seventy-nine. His father died of drink at thirty-seven, and Dean Farrar once told Spring that his case was excusable, since it was hereditary. But, although Spring went to prison at the age of thirteen for drunkenness, and has " been in " thirty-nine times, he didn't die at thirty-seven. I wonder what the moral is? His happiest days, he assured me, were spent in old Clerkenwell Prison, now Clerkenwell Post Office, and on one occasion, as he was the only prisoner who could read, he was permitted to entertain his companions by extracts from *Good Words*, without much effect, he added, as most of them are in and out even now. One important factor in the making of his grand resolution was that a girl he knew in Stepney, who was so far gone that even the Court missionary had given her up, came to him one Christmastime. She was in the depths of misery and hunger.

"Spring," she said, "give me a job!"

So Spring gave her the job of cleaning out his one room, for which she was to receive half a crown. She obeyed him; and when he returned, and looked under the floor where he stored his savings from the sale of his poems (nearly seven pounds) they also had been cleaned.

That settled it. Spring decided to cut all his acquaintances, but he could only do that successfully by some very public step. So he went to Sir John Dickinson and signed the pledge in his presence. Said he—

"And now, I find that after fifteen years of teetotalism, I write better poetry. Every time I feel I want a drink, I say to myself: 'Spring—sit down and write a poem!'"

He was then messenger at Thames Police Court, enjoying the friendship and interest of all. He read me about a dozen of his lighter lyrics. Here is one of the finer gems:—

> How many a poet would like to have
> Letters from royalty—prince, king, and queen;
> But, like some insignificant ocean wave,
> They are passed over, mayhap never seen.
> But when I myself address good Royals,
> And send them verses from my fertile brain,
> See how they thank me very much for my flowing strain!

In proof of which he would dig out letters from King Edward, Queen Alexandra, and Queen Mary.

One of these days I am going to do a book about those London characters without reference to whom our daily newspapers are incomplete. I mean people like the late lamented Craig, the poet of the Oval Cricket Ground, Captain Hunnable, of Ilford, Mr. Algernon Ashton, Spiv. Bagster, of Westminster, that gay farceur, "D. S. Windell,"

Stewart Gray, the Nature enthusiast. But first and foremost must come—Spring Onions.

On the southern side of the quarter is Sidney Street, of sinister memory. You remember the siege of Sidney Street? A great time for Little Russia. You may remember how the police surrounded that little Fort Chabrol. You may remember how the deadly aim of Peter the Painter and his fellow-conspirators got home on the force again and again. You remember how the police, in their helplessness against such fatalistic defiance of their authority, appealed to Government, and how Government sent down a detachment of the Irish Guards. There was a real Cabinet Minister in it, too; he came down in his motor-car to superintend manœuvres and compliment gallant officers on their strategy. And yet, in that great contest of four men versus the Rest of England, it was the Rest of England that went down; for Fort Chabrol stood its ground and quietly laughed. They were never beaten, they never surrendered. When they had had enough, they just burnt the house over themselves, and . . . hara-kiri. . . . Of course, it was all very wicked; it is impossible to justify them in any way. In Bayswater and all other haunts of unbridled chastity they were tortured, burnt alive, stewed in oil, and submitted to every conceivable penalty for their saucy effrontery. Yet, somehow, there was a touch about it, this spectacle of four men defying the law and order of the greatest country in the world, which thrilled every man with any devil in him. Peter the Painter is a hero to this day.

· · · · ·

I had known the quarter for many years before it interested me. It was not until I was prowling around on a Fleet Street assignment that I learnt to hate it. A murder had been committed over a café in Lupin Street : a popular murder, fruity, cleverly done, and with a sex interest. Of course every newspaper and agency developed a virtuous anxiety to track the culprit, and all resources were directed to that end. Journalism is perhaps the only profession in which so fine a public spirit may be found. So it was that the North Country paper of which I was a hanger-on flung every available man into the fighting line, and the editor told me that I might, in place of the casual paragraphs for the London Letter, do something good on the Vassiloff murder.

It was a night of cold rain, and the pavements were dashed with smears of light from the shop windows. Through the streaming streets my hansom leaped ; and as I looked from the window, and noted the despondent biliousness of Bethnal Green, I realized that the grass withereth, the flower fadeth.

I dismissed the cab at Brick Lane, and, continuing the tradition which had been instilled into me by my predecessor on the London Letter, I turned into one of the hostelries and had a vodka to keep the cold out. Little Russia was shutting up. The old shawled women, who sit at every corner with huge baskets of black bread and sweet cakes, were departing beneath umbrellas. The stalls of Osborn Street, usually dressed with foreign-looking confectionery, were also retiring. Indeed, everybody seemed to be slinking away, and as I sipped my vodka, and felt it burn me with raw fire, I cursed news editors and all publics which desired to read about murders. I was perfectly sure that I shouldn't do the least good ; so I had another, and gazed through the kaleidoscopic window, rushing with rain, at the cheerful world that held me.

Oh, so sad it is, this quarter ! By day the streets are a depression, with their frowzy doss-houses and their vapour-baths. Grey and sickly is the light.

Grey and sickly, too, are the leering shops, and grey and sickly are the people and the children. Everything has followed the grass and the flower. Childhood has no place; for above the roofs you may see the sharp points of a Council School. Such games as happen are played but listlessly, and each little face is smirched. The gaunt warehouses hardly support their lopping heads, and the low, beetling, gabled houses of the alleys seem for ever to brood on nights of bitter adventure. Fit objects for contempt by day they may be, but when night creeps upon London, the hideous darkness that can almost be touched, then their faces become very powers of terror, and the cautious soul, wandered from the comfort of the main streets, walks and walks in a frenzy, seeking outlet and finding none. Sometimes a hoarse laugh will break sharp on his ear. Then he runs.

Well, I finished my second, and then sauntered out. As I was passing a cruel-looking passage, a gang of lads and girls stepped forward. One of the girls looked at me. Her face had the melancholy of Russia, but her voice was as the voice of Cockaigne. For she spoke and said—

"Funny-looking little guy, ain't you?"

I suppose I was. So I smiled and said that we were as God made us.

She giggled. . . .

I said I felt sure I should do no good on the Vassiloff murder. I didn't. For just then the other four marched ahead, crying, "Come on!" And, surprised, yet knowing of no good reason for being surprised, I felt the girl's arm slip into mine, and we joined the main column.

That is one of London's greatest charms: it is always ready to toss you little encounters of this sort, if you are out for them.

Across the road we went, through mire and puddle, and down a long, winding court. At about midway our friends disappeared, and, suddenly drawn to the right, I was pushed from behind up a steep, fusty stair. Then I knew where we were going. We were going to the tenements where most of the Russians meet of an evening. The atmosphere in these places is a little more cheerful than that of the cafés—if you can imagine a Russian ever rising to cheerfulness. Most of the girls lodge over the milliners' shops, and thither their friends resort. Every establishment here has a piano, for music, with them, is a sombre passion rather than a diversion. You will not hear comic opera, but if you want to climb the lost heights of melody, stand in Bell Yard, and listen to a piano, lost in the high glooms, wailing the heart of Chopin or Rubinstein or Glazounoff through the fingers of pale, moist girls, while the ghost of Peter the Painter parades the naphthaed highways.

At the top of the stair I was pushed into a dark, fusty room, and guided to a low, fusty sofa or bed. Then some one struck a match, and a lamp was lit and set on the mantelshelf. It flung a soft, caressing radiance on its shabby home, and on its mistress, and on the other girls and boys. The boys were tough youngsters of the district, evidently very much at home, smoking Russian cigarettes and settling themselves on the bed in a manner that seemed curiously continental in Cockney toughs. I doubt if you would have admired the girls at that moment.

The girl who had collared me disappeared for a moment, and then brought a tray of Russian tea. "Help 'selves, boys!" We did so, and, watching the others, I discovered that it was the correct thing to lemon the ladies' tea for them and stir it well and light their cigarettes.

The room, on which the wallpaper hung in dank strips, contained a full-sized bed and a chair bedstead, a washstand, a samovar, a pot-pourri of a carpet, and certain mysteries of feminine toilet. A rickety three-legged table stood by the window, and Katarina's robes hung in a dainty riot of frill and colour behind the door, which only shut when you thrust a peg of wood through a wired catch.

One of the girls went to the piano and began to play. You would not understand, I suppose, the intellectual emotion of the situation. It is more than curious to sit in these rooms, in the filthiest spot in London, and listen to Mozskowsky, Tchaikowsky, and Sibelius, played by a factory girl. It is . . . something indefinable. I had visited similar places in Stepney before, but then I had not had a couple of vodkas, and I had not been taken in tow by an unknown gang. They play and play, while tea and cigarettes, and sometimes vodka or whisky go round ; and as the room gets warmer, so does one's sense of smell get sharper ; so do the pale faces get moister ; and so does one long more and more for a breath of cold air from the Ural Mountains. The best you can do is to ascend to the flat roof, and take a deep breath of Spitalfields ozone. Then back to the room for more tea and more music.

Sanya played. . . . Despite the unventilated room, the greasy appointments, and other details that would have turned the stomach of Kensington, that girl at the piano, playing, as no one would have dreamed she could play, the finer intensities of Wieniawski and Moussorgsky, shook all sense of responsibility from me. The burdens of life vanished. News editors and their assignments be damned. Enjoy yourself, was what the cold, insidious music said.

Devilish little fingers they were, Sanya's. Her technique was not perhaps all that it might have been ; she might not have won the Gold Medal of our white-shirted academies, but she had enough temperament to make half a dozen Steinway Hall virtuosi. From valse to nocturne, from sonata to prelude, her fancy ran. With crashing chords she dropped from "L'Automne Bacchanale" to the Nocturne in E flat; scarcely murmured of that, then tripped elvishly into Moszkowsky's Waltz, and from that she dropped to a song of Tchaikowsky, almost heartbreaking in its childish beauty, and then to the austere music of the second act of "Tristan." Mazurka, polonaise, and nocturne wailed in the stuffy chamber; her little hands lit up the enchanted gloom of the place with bright thrills.

But suddenly there came a whisper of soft feet on the landing, and a secret tap at the door. Some one opened it, and slipped out. One heard the lazy hum of voices in busy conversation. Then silence; and some one entered the room and shut the door. One of the boys asked casually, "What's up?" His question was not answered, but the girl who had gone to the door snapped something in a sharp tone which might have been either Russian or Yiddish. The other girls sat up and spat angry phrases about. I called to one of the boys—"What's the joke? Anything wrong?" and received reply—

"Owshdiknow? Ain't a ruddy Russian, am I?"

The girl at the door spoke in a hoarse whisper: "'Ere—you better go—you first?"

"Whaflor?" asked the boys.

"'Cos I say so."

"No, but——"

Again there came a stealthy tap at the door, again the whispering of slippered feet. More words were exchanged. Then Sanya grabbed the boys by arms, and they and the girls disappeared.

I was alone.

I got up, and moved to the door. I heard nothing. I stood by the window, my thoughts dancing a ragtime. I wondered what to do, and how, and whether. I wondered what was up exactly. I wondered . . . well, I just wondered.

My thoughts got into a tangle, sank, and swam, and sank again. Then there was a sudden struggle and spurt from the lamp, and it went black out. From a room across the landing a clock ticked menacingly. I saw, by the thin light from the window, the smoke of a discarded cigarette curling up and up to the ceiling like a snake.

I went again to the door, peered down the steep stair and over the crazy balustrade. Nobody was about; no voices. I slipped swiftly down the five flights, met nobody. I stood in the slobbered vestibule. From afar I heard the sluck of the waters against the staples of the wharves, and the wicked hoot of the tugs.

It was then that a sudden nameless fear seized me; it was that simple terror that comes from nothing but ourselves. I am not usually afraid of any man or thing. I am normally nervous, and there are three or four things that have the power to terrify me. But I am not, I think, afraid. At that moment, however, I was afraid of everything: of the room I had left, of the house, of the people, of the inviting lights of the warehouses and the threatening shoals of the alleys.

I stood a moment longer. Then I raced into Brick Lane, and out into the brilliance of Commercial Street.

A SCANDINAVIAN NIGHT
SHADWELL

AT SHADWELL

He was a bad, glad sailor-man,
  Tan-ta-ta-ran-tan-tare-o!
You never could find a haler man,
  Tan-ta-ta-ran-tan-tare!
All human wickedness he knew,
From Millwall Docks to Pi-chi-lu;
He loved all things that make us gay,
He'd spit his juice ten yards away,
  And roundly he'd declare—oh!
" It isn't so much that I want the beer
  As the bloody good company,
      Whow!
  Bloody good company!"

He loved all creatures—black, brown, white,
  Tan-ta-ta-ran-tan-tare-o!
And never a word he'd speak in spite,
  Tan-ta-ta-ran-tan-tare!
He knew that we were mortal men
Who sinned and laughed and sinned again;
And never a cruel thing he'd do
At Millwall Docks or Pi-chi-lu;
If you were down he'd make you gay:
He'd spit his juice ten yards away,
  And roundly he'd declare—oh!
" It isn't so much that I want yer beer
  As yer bloody good company,
      Whow!
  Bloody good company!"

A SCANDINAVIAN NIGHT

SHADWELL

ONE night, when I was ten years old, I was taken by a boy who was old enough to have known better into the ashy darkness of Shadwell and St. George's. Along that perilous mile we slipped, with drumming hearts. Then a warm window greeted us . . . voices . . . gruff feet . . . bits of strange song . . . and then an open door and a sharp slab of mellow light. With a sense of high adventure we peeped in. Some one beckoned. We entered. The room was sawdusted as to the floor, littered with wooden tables and benches. All was sloppy with rings and pools of spent cocoa. The air was a conflict : the frivolous odour of fried sausage coyly flirted with the solemn smell of dead smoke, and between them they bore a bastard perfume of stale grease. Coffee-urns screamed and belched. Cakes made the counter gay.

We stood for a moment, gazing, wondering. Then the blond-bearded giant who had beckoned repeated his invitation ; indeed, he reached a huge arm, seized me, and set me on his knee. I lost all sense of ownership of my face in the tangles of his beard. He hiccuped. He coughed. He rattled. He sneezed. His forearms and fingers flew, as though repelling multitudinous attacks. His face curled, and crinkled, and slipped, and jumped suddenly straight again, and then vanished in infinite corrugations. He seemed to be in the agony of a lost soul which seeks to cleanse the stuffed bosom of that perilous stuff. . . . Arms and lips lashed the air about them, and at last the very lines of his body seemed expressive of the state of a man who has explained himself forty-five times, and is then politely asked to explain himself. For half an hour, I suppose, I sat on his knee while he sneezed and roared and played games with his vocal chords.

It was not until next morning that I learnt that he had been speaking Norwegian and trying to ask me to have a cake. When I knew that I had been in the lair of the Scandinavian seamen, I thrilled. When I learnt that I had lost a cake, I felt sad.

It is a curious quarter, this Shadwell and St. George's: a street of mission-halls for foreign sailors and of temperance restaurants, such as that described, mostly for the Scandinavians, though there are many shops catering for them still farther East. Sometimes you may hear a long, savage roar, but there is no cause for alarm. It is only that the great Mr. Jamrach, London's leading dealer in wild animals, has his menagerie in this street.

The shop-fronts are lettered in Danish, Norwegian, and Swedish. Strange provisions are found in the "general" shops, and quaintly carved goods and long wooden pipes in other windows. Marine stores jostle one another, shoulder to shoulder, and there is a rich smell of tar, bilge-water, and the hold of a cargo tramp. Almost you expect to hear the rattle of the windlass, as you stand in the badly lighted establishment of Johann Dvensk, surrounded by ropes, old ship's iron, bloodthirsty blades, canvas, blocks, and pulleys. Something in this narrow space seizes you, and you feel that you must " Luff her ! " or " Starrrrrb'd yer Hellllllm ! " or " Ease 'er ! " or " Man the tops'l ! " or whatever they do and say on Scandinavian boats. You may see these boats in the Pool any night; timber boats they are, for the most part ; squat, low-lying affairs, but curiously picturesque when massed close with other shipping, steam or sail. One of our London songsters has recorded that "there's always something doing by the seaside"; and that is equally true of down Thames-side. London River is always alive with beauty, splendid with stress and the sweat of human hands. There is something infinitely saddening in watching the casual, business-like departure of one of these big boats. As she swings away and drops downstream, her crew, idling, lean over the side, and spit, smoking their long Swedish pipes, and looking curiously unearthly as the dock lights fall, now on one, now on the other. I always want to plunge into the water and follow them through that infinitude of travel which is suggested by the dim outline of Greenwich.

The lamps in Shadwell High Street and what was once Ratcliff Highway are few and very pale ; and each one, welcome as it is, flings shapes of fear across your path as you leave its radius and step into darkness more utter. The quality of the darkness is nasty. That is the only word for it. It is indefinite, leering. It says nothing to you. It is reticent with the reticence of Evil. It is not black and frightful, like the darkness of Hoxton or Spitalfields. It is not pleasant, like the darkness of Chinatown. It is not matey, like the darkness of Hackney Marshes. It is . . . nasty. At every ten paces there is the black mouth of an alley with just space enough for the passage of one person. Within the jaws of each alley is a lounging figure— man, woman, or child, Londoner or foreigner, you cannot discern. But it is there, silent, watchful, expectant. And if you choose to venture, you may examine more closely. You may note that the faces that peer at you are faces such as one only sees elsewhere in the pictures of Felicien Rops. Sometimes it is a curl-sweet little girl who greets you with a smile strangely cold. Sometimes the mouth of the alley will appear to open and will spit at you, apparently by chance. If it hits you, the alley swears at you: a deep, frightfully foreign oath. Sudden doors flap, and gusts of brutal jollity sweep up the street.

In the old days, Shadwell embraced the Oriental quarter, and times, in the 'seventies, long before I was thought of, seem to have been really frolicsome, or so I gather from James Greenwood. The chief inhabitants of to-day are those little girls just mentioned. Walk here at any time of the day or night, and you will find in every doorway and at those corners which are illuminated, clusters of little girls, all of the same age, all of the same height, their glances knowing so much more than their little fresh lips imply. They seem all to be born at that age, and they never grow up. For every boy and woman that you pass in that dusty mile you will find dozens of pale little girls. There is a reason for this local product, about which I have written more seriously elsewhere, and if you saunter here, beware of sympathy with crying children. I could tell things; curious things. But if I did you would not believe them; and if you believed them you would be sick.

I have mentioned the peculiar darkness. It is provocative and insistent. It possesses you. For you know that in this street, or rather, back of it, there are the homes of the worst vices of the sea-going foreigner. It is the haunt of the dissolute and the indigent; not only of the normal brute, but also of the satyr. You know that behind those heights of houses, stretching over the street with dumb, blank faces, there are strangely lighted rooms, where unpleasant rites are celebrated.

I can never understand why artists and moralists paint Temptation invariably in gaudy scarlet and jewels, tinted cheeks, and laughing hair. If she were always like that, morality would be gloriously triumphant ; for she would attract nobody. The true Temptation of this world and flesh wears grey rags, dishevelled hair, and an ashen cheek. Any expert will prove that. I can never believe that any one would be lured to destruction by those birds of paradise whom one has met in the stuffy, over-gilded, and, happily, abortive night-clubs and cabarets. If a consensus were taken, I think it would be found that wickedness gaily apparelled is seldom successful. It is the subtle and the sinister, the dark and half-known, that make the big appeal. Lace and scent and champagne and the shaded glamour of Western establishments leave most men cold, I know. But dirt and gloom and secrecy. . . . We needs must love the lowest when we see it.

As far back as I can remember the Eastern parishes have been, to me, the home of Romance. My romance was not in the things of glitter and chocolate-box gaiety, but rather in the dolours and silences of the East. Long before I had adventured there, its very street-names—Whitechapel High Street, Ratcliff Highway, Folly Wall, Stepney Causeway, Pennyfields—had thrilled me as I believe other children thrill to the names of The Arabian Nights.

That is why I come sometimes to Shadwell, and sit in its tiny beershops, and listen to the roaring of Jamrach's lions, and talk with the blond fellows whose conversation is mostly limited to the universalities of intercourse. I was there on one occasion, in one of the houses which are, in the majority of cases, only licensed for beer, and I made the acquaintance of a quite excellent fellow, and spent the whole evening with him. He talked Swedish, I talked English ; and we understood one another perfectly. We did a "pub-crawl" in Commercial Road and East India Dock Road, and finished up at the Queen's Theatre in Poplar High Street. A jolly evening ended, much too early for me, at one o'clock in the morning, when he insisted on entering a lodging-house in Gill Street because he was sure that it was his. I tried to make him understand, by diagrams on the pavement, that he was some half-mile from St. George's. But no; he loomed above me, in his blond strength, and when he tried to follow the diagram, he toppled over. I spent five minutes in lifting six foot three and about twelve stone of Swedish manhood to its feet.

He looked solemn, and insisted: "I ban gude Swede."

I told him again that he must not enter the lodging-house, but must let me see him safe to his right quarters. But he thrust me aside: "I ban gude Swede!" he said, resentfully this time, with hauteur. I pulled his coat-tails, and tried to lead him back to Shadwell; but it was useless.

"I ban gude Swede!"

There I left him, trying to climb the six steps leading to the lodging-house entrance. I looked back at the corner. He turned, to wave his hand in valediction, and, floating across the night, came a proud declaration—

"I ban gude Swede!"

This is one of the few occasions when I have been gay in Shadwell. Mostly you cannot be gay; the place simply won't let you be gay. You cannot laugh there spontaneously. You may hear bursts of filthy laughter from this or that low-lit window; but it is not spontaneous. You only laugh like that when you have nine or ten inside you. The spirit of the place does not, in the ordinary way, move you to cheer. Its mist, and its dust-heaps, and its coal-wharves, and the reek of the river sink into you, and disturb your peace of mind.

Most holy night descends never upon Shadwell. The night life of any dockside is as vociferant as the day. They slumber not, nor sleep in this region.

They bathe not, neither do they swim; and Cerberus in all his hideousness was not arrayed like some of these. If you want to make your child good by terror, show him a picture of a Swede or a Malay, pickled in brown sweat after a stoking-up job.

Of course, the seamen of St. George's do not view it from this angle. Shadwell is only fearful and gloomy to those who have fearful and gloomy minds. Seamen haven't. They have only fearful and gloomy habits. Probably, when the evening has lit the world to slow beauty, and a quart or so has stung your skin to a galloping sense of life, Shadwell High Street and its grey girls are a garden of pure pleasure. I shouldn't wonder.

There are those among them who love Shadwell. A hefty seafaring Dane whom I once met told me he loved the times when his boat brought him to London—by which, of course, he meant Shadwell. He liked the life and the people and the beer. And, indeed, for those who do love any part of London, it is all-sufficient. I suppose there are a few people living here who long to escape from it when the calendar calls Spring; to kiss their faces to the grass; to lose their tired souls in tangles of green shade. But they are hardly to be met with. Those rather futile fields and songs of birds and bud-spangled trees are all very well, if you have the narrow mind of the Nature-lover; but how much sweeter are the things of the hands, the darling friendliness of the streets! The maidenly month of April makes little difference to us here. We know, by the calendar and by our physical selves, that it is the season of song and quickening blood. Beyond London, amid the spray of orchard foam, bird and bee may make their carnival; lusty spring may rustle in the hedgerows; golden-tasselled summer may move along the shadow-fretted meadows; but what does it say to us? Nothing. . . . Here we still gamble, and worship the robustious things that come our way, and wait to find a boat. We have no seasons. We have no means of marking the delicate pomp of the year's procession. We have not even the divisions of day and night, for, as I have said, boats must sail at all hours of the day and night, and their swarthy crews are ever about. In Shadwell we have only more seamen or less seamen. Summer is a spell of stickiness and Winter a time of fog. Season of flower and awakening be blowed ! I'll have the same again !

This is a book of adventures in and about London : not a sociological pamphlet ; but I do seriously feel that if I am writing on the subject at all, I may as well write the complete truth. I have heard, often, in this macabre street, the most piercing of all sounds that the London night can hold : a child's scream. The sound of a voice in pain or terror is horrible enough anywhere at night ; it is twenty times worse in this district, when the voice is a child's. I want, very badly, to tell the story I refrained from telling. I want to tell it because it is true, because it ought to be told, and because it might shake you into some kind of action, which newspaper reports would never do. Yet I know perfectly well that if I did tell it, this book would be condemned as unclean, and I as a pornographist, if not something worse. So let our fatuous charity-mongers continue to supply Flannel Underclothing for the Daughters of Christian Stevedores ; let them continue to provide Good Wholesome Meals for the Wives of God-Fearing Draymen, and let them connive by silence at those other unspeakable things.

The University men and the excellent virgins who carry out this kind of patronage might do well to drop it for a while, and tell the plain truth about the things which they must see in the course of their labours. If you stand in Leicester Square, in the gayest quarter of the gayest city in the world, after nightfall, indeed, long after theatres, bars, and music-halls are closed, and their saucy lights extinguished, you will see, on the south side, a single lamp glowing through the green of the branches. That lamp is shining the whole night through. The door that it lights is never closed day or night; it dare not close. Through the leafy gloom of the Square it shines—a watchful eye regarding the foulest blot on the civilization of England. It is the lamp of the office of the National Society for the Prevention of Cruelty to Children. This Society keeps five hundred workers incessantly busy, day and night, preventing cruelty to little English children. Go in, and listen to some of the stories that the inspectors can tell you. They can tell you of appalling sufferings inflicted on children, of bruised bodies and lacerated limbs and poisoned minds, not only in the submerged quarters but in comfortable houses by English people of education and position. Buy a few numbers of the Society's official organ, *The Child's Guardian*, and read of the hundreds of cases which they attack every month, and of the bestialities to which children are submitted, and you will then see that light as the beacon-light of England's disgrace. I once showed it to a Spanish friend, and he looked at me with polite disgust. "And your countrymen, my friend," he said, "speak of the Spaniards as cruel. Your countrymen, who gather themselves in dozens, protected by horses and dogs, to hunt a timid fox, call us cruel because we fight the bull—because our toreadors risk their lives every moment that they are in the ring, fighting a savage, maddened animal five times larger and stronger than themselves. You call us cruel—you, who have to found a Society in order to stop cruelty to your little children. My friend, there is no Society like that in Spain, for no society like that is necessary. The most depraved Spaniard, town or countryman, would never dream of raising his hand against a child. And your countrymen, in face of that building, which is open day and night, and supports a staff of five hundred, call the Spaniards cruel! My friend, yours surely must be the cruellest people on earth."

And I had no answer for him, because I knew. I knew what Mr. Robert Parr had told me: and I knew why little girls of twelve and thirteen are about the dripping mouths of the Shadwell alleys at all queer hours. You will understand why some men, fathers of little girls, suddenly have money for beer when a foreign boat is berthed. You will appreciate what it is that twists its atmosphere into something anomalous. You remember the gracious or jolly fellows you have met, the sweet, rich sea-chanties you have heard; and then you remember other things, and the people suddenly seem monstrous, the spirit of the place bites deep, and the dreadful laughter of it shocks.

A SUNDAY NIGHT ANYWHERE

SUNDAY TEA-TIME

There is a noise of winkles on the air,
Muffins and winkles rattle down the road,
The sluggish road, whose hundred houses stare
One on another in after-dinner gloom.
    "Peace, perfect Peace!" *wails an accordion,*
    "Ginger, you're barmy!" *snarls a gramophone.*

A most unhappy place, this leafless Grove
  In the near suburbs; not a place for tears
Nor for light laughter, for all life is chilled
  With the unpurposed toil of many years.
But once—ah, once!—the accordion's wheezy strains
Led my poor heart to April-smelling lanes.

A SUNDAY NIGHT

ANYWHERE

THERE is something almost freakish in the thoughtful calm of the London Sunday. During the night the town seems to have cleaned and preened itself, and the creamy, shadow-fretted streets of the Sabbath belong more to some Southern region than to Battersea or Barnsbury. The very houses have a detached, folded manner, like volumes of abstruse theological tracts. From every church tower sparks of sound leap out on the expectant air, mingling and clashing with a thousand others; and the purple spires fling themselves to heaven with the joy of a perfect thought. In the streets there is an atmosphere of best clothes and best manners. There is a flutter of bright frocks. Father, in his black coat and silk hat, walks seriously, as befits one with responsibilities, what time mother at home is preparing the feast. The children, poor darlings, do not skip or jump or laugh. They walk sedately, in their starchy attire, holding father's arm and trying to realize that it really is Sunday, and therefore very sinful to fling oneself about. The people taking their appetite stroll before midday dinner look all so sleek and complacent that one would like to borrow money from them. The 'buses rumble with a cheeriness that belongs not to weekdays; their handrails gleam with a new brightness, and the High Street, with shops shuttered and barred, bears not the faintest resemblance to the High Street you know so well, even as policemen, with helmets and tunics, look surprisingly unlike human beings. The water-carts seem to work with cleaner, lighter water, and as the sun catches the sprayed stream it whips it into a thousand drops of white fire. It is Sunday. The roads are blazing white ribbons under the noon sun. A stillness broods over all, a stillness only accentuated by the brazen voice of the Salvation Army band and the miserable music of winkles rattling on dinner-plates. The colours of the little girls' dresses slash the grey backgrounds of the pavement with rich streaks. Spears of sunshine, darting through the sparse plane-trees, play all about them, and ring them with radiance; and they look so fresh and happy that you want to kiss them. It is Sunday.

Yes, it is Sunday, and you will realize that as the day wears on. These pleasant people are walking about the streets for a very definite reason. What is that? It is that there is nothing else to do. That is the tragedy of the London Sunday; there is nothing else to do. Why does the submerged man get drunk on Sunday? There is nothing else to do. Why does the horse-faced lady, with nice clothes, go to church on Sunday? There is nothing else to do. Why do people overeat themselves on Sunday? There is nothing else to do. Why do parents make themselves stiff and uncomfortable in new clothes, and why do they get irritable and smack their children if they rouse them from their after-dinner sleep? Because there is nothing else to do. Why does the young clerk hang round the West End bars, and get into trouble with doubtful ladies? Because there is nothing else to do.

And in the evening you feel this more terribly. If it is summer, you may listen to blatant bands in our very urban parks, which have been thoughtfully and artistically " arranged " by stout gentlemen on the London County Council, whose motto seems to be: " Let's have something we *all* know! " or you may go for a 'bus-ride to Richmond, Hampton Court, St.

Albans, or Uxbridge, or Epping Forest. If you want to know, merely for information, to what depths London can sink in the way of amusing itself on Sundays, then I recommend the bands in the parks. Otherwise there is something to be said for the 'bus-ride. You cannot enjoy yourself in London on the Lord's Day, but you can take London with you into some lonely spot and there re-create it. Jump on the Chingford 'bus any Sunday evening, and let yourself go with the crowd. Out in the glades of the Forest things are happening. The dappled shades of the wood flash with colour and noise, and, if you are human, you will soon have succumbed to the contagion of the carnival. Voices of all varieties, shrill, hoarse, and rich, rise in the heavy August air, outside "The Jolly Wagoners," and the jingle of glasses and the popping of corks compete with the professional hilarity of the vendors of novelties. Here and there bunches of confetti shoot up, whirling and glimmering ; elsewhere a group of girls execute the cake-walk or the can-can, their van sustaining fusillade after fusillade of the forbidden squirters, their rear echoing to " chi-ikes," cat-calls, and other appreciations, until an approaching motor-'bus scatters them in squealing confusion. By the bridge, the blithe, well-bitten Bacchanalians offer to fight one another, and then decide to kiss. The babble of talk and laughter becomes a fury ; the radiant maidens and the bold boys become the eternal tragedy. Sometimes there is a dance, and the empurpled girls are " taken round " by their masterful squires, the steps of the dance involving much swirling of green, violet, pink, and azure petticoats.

But afar in the Forest there is Sabbath peace, the sound of far bells, the cry of the thrush, the holy pattering of leaves. The beeches, meeting aloft and entwining, fling the light and the spirit of the cathedral to the mossy floors. Here is purity and humanity. The air beats freshly on the face. Away in the soft blue distance is a shadowy suggestion of rolling country, the near fields shimmering under the sweet, hot sky of twilight, and the distant uplands telling of calm and deep peace in other places. Truly a court of love, and truly loved by those who, for an hour or so, dwell in it. Tread lightly, you that pass. It may move you to mirth, but there is nothing mirthful here; only the eternal sorrow and the eternal joy. Perchance you do not make love in this way; but love is love. . . . Under every brooding oak recline the rapt couples, snatching their moments in this velvety green. Drowsy fragrance is everywhere. The quiet breeze disorders stray ringlets, and sometimes light laughter is carried sleepily to sleepy ears Love, says an old Malayan chanty which I learned at West India Dock—Love is kind to the least of men. God will it so!

But if it be winter, then the Londoner is badly hit on Sundays. The cafés and bars are miserable, deserted by their habitués and full only of stragglers from the lost parts, who have wandered here unknowingly. The waiters are off their form. They know their Sunday evening clientèle and they despise it: it is not the real thing. The band is off its form. The kitchen is off its form. It is Sunday.

There are no shows of any kind, unless it be some "private performance" of the Stage Society, for which tickets have to be purchased in the week. Certainly there are, in some of the West End and most of the suburban halls, the concerts of the National Sunday League, but the orchestras and the singers are really not of a kind to attract the musical temperament. The orchestras play those hackneyed bits of Wagner and Tchaikowsky and Rossini of which all the world must be everlastingly sick, and the singers sing those tiresome songs which so satisfy the musical taste of Bayswater—baritone songs about the Army and the Navy and their rollicking ways, and about old English country life; tenor songs about

Grey Eyes and Roses and Waiting and Parting and Coming Back; soprano songs about Calling and Wondering and Last Night's Dance and Remembering and Forgetting—foolish words, foolish melodies, and clumsy orchestration. But they seem to please the well-dressed crowd that comes to listen to them, so I suppose it is justified. I suppose it really interprets their attitude toward human passion. I don't know. . . . Anyway, it is sorry stuff.

If you don't go to these shows, then there is nothing to do but walk about. I think the most pathetic sight to be seen in London is the Strand on a Sunday night. The whole place is shut up, almost one might say, hermetically sealed, except that Mooney's and Ward's and Romano's are open. Along its splendid length parade crowds and crowds of Jew couples and other wanderers from the far regions. They look lost. They look like a Cup Tie crowd from the North. They don't walk; they drift. They look helpless; they have an air expressive of: "Well, what the devil shall we do *now*?" I have a grim notion that members of the London County Council, observing them—if, that is, members of the London County Council ever do penance by walking down the Strand on Sunday—take to themselves unction. "Ah!" they gurgle in their hearts, "ah! —beautiful. Nice, orderly crowd; all walking about nice and orderly; enjoying themselves in the right way. Ah! Yes. We *like* to see the people enjoy themselves."

And, in their Christian way, they pat themselves on the back (if not too stout) and go home to their cigars and liqueurs and whatever else they may want in the way of worldly indulgence. It is Sunday.

Some years ago there was a delightful song that devastated New York. It was a patriotic song, and it was called: "The sun is always shining on Broadway." At the time, I translated this into English, for rendering at a private show, the refrain being that the sun is always shining in the Strand. So it is. Dull as the day may be elsewhere, there is always light of some kind in the Strand. It is the gayest, most Londonish street in London. It is jammed with Life, for it is the High Street of the world. Men of every country and clime have walked down the Strand. Whatever is to be found in other streets in other parts of the world is to be found in the Strand. It is the homeliest, mateyest street in the world. Let's all go down it !

But not—not, my dears, on Sundays. For a wise County Council has decreed that whatsoever things are gay, whatsoever things are true, whatsoever things are human and lovely—these things shall not be thought upon on Sundays.

. . . . .

The English Sunday at home is in many cases even worse than the Sunday out. Of course it has considerably improved since the hideous eighties, but there are still survivals of the old Sabbath, not so much among the mass of the people as among the wealthy. The new kindly Sabbath has arisen with the new attitude of children towards parents. The children of the £300-a-year parents are possessed of a natural pluck which is lacking in the children of the £3,000-a-year. They know what they want and they usually see that they get it.

Among the kindlier folk, in the suburbs, Sunday is the only day when Father is really at home with the children, and it is made the most of. It is the children's day. Morning, afternoon, and evening are given up to them. In the summer there is the great treat of tea in the garden. In the winter tea is taken in the room that is sometimes called the " drawing-room " by Mother and the " reception-room " by the house-agent ; and there are all manner of delicate cakes and, perhaps, muffins, which the youngsters are allowed to toast themselves.

After tea, Father romps with them, or reads to them from one of their own books or magazines ; or perhaps they roast chestnuts on the hearth, or sing or recite to the " company." Too, they are allowed to sit up an hour or so later, and in this last hour every kind of pagan amusement is set going for their delight, so that they tumble at last to bed flushed with laughter, and longing for the six days to pass so that Sunday shall come again.

That is one domestic Sunday. But there are others. I like to think that there are only about three others, but unfortunately I know that there are over two thousand Sundays just like the one which 1 describe below.

Here Father and Mother are very successful, so successful that they live in a big house near Queen's Gate, and keep five servants as well as a motor-car. Sunday is a little different here from week-days, in that the children are allowed to spend the day outside the nursery, with their parents. They go to church in the morning with Mother and Father. They dine at midday with Mother and Father. In the afternoon they go to The Children's Service. They have tea in the drawing-room with Mother and Father. Father and Mother are Calvinists.

In the evening, Father and Mother sit, one on either side of the hearth ; Father reading a weekly religious paper devoted to the creed of Calvin ; Mother reading another religious paper devoted to the creed of Calvin. Throughout the day the children are never allowed to sing or hum any tune that may be called profane. They are never allowed to hop, skip, or jump. They are told that Jesus will not be pleased with them if they do. They are not allowed to read secular books or look at pagan pictures. In the afternoon, they are given Doré's Bible and an illustrated " Paradise Lost " or " Pilgrim's Progress." In the evening, after tea (which carries with it one piece of seed-cake as a special treat), they are seated, with injunctions to silence, at the table, away from the fire, and set to finding Bible texts from one given key-word. The one who finds most texts gets a cake to go to bed with; the other gets nothing.

So Ethel and Johnnie are at work, from six in the evening until nine o'clock, scratching through a small-type Bible for flavourless aphorisms. Ethel is set to find six texts, and finds four of them, when she perceives something funny in one of them. She shows it to Johnnie, and they both giggle. Father looks up severely, and warns her. Then Johnnie, not to be outdone, remembers something he has heard about at school, and hunts through the Book of Kings to find it. He finds it. It is funnier still; and he shows it to Ethel. She giggles again. Father looks up reprovingly at her. She tries to maintain composure of face, but just then Johnnie pinches her knee, so that she squeals with long-pent-up laughter.

Father and Mother get up. Her Bible is taken from her. Her pencil and paper are taken from her. She is made to stand on the hearthrug, with her hands behind her, while Mother and Father lecture her on Blasphemy. The bell is then rung, and Nurse is sent for. She is handed over to Nurse, with pitiless instructions. Nurse then takes her to her room, where she is undressed, put to bed, and severely slapped.

It is Sunday. . . . Over her little bed is a text in letters of flame: "*Thou God seest me!*" After burning with indignation and humiliation for some time, she falls at last to sleep, with an unspoken prayer of thanksgiving to her Heavenly Father that to-morrow is Monday.

AT RANDOM

TWO IN A TAXI

From Gloucester Square to Golder's Green,
  We flash through misty fields of light.
Oh, many lovely things are seen
From Gloucester Square to Golder's Green!
We reign together, king and queen,
  Over the lilied London night.
From Gloucester Square to Golder's Green,
  We flash through misty fields of light.

So, driver, drive your taxi well
  To Golder's Green from Gloucester Square.
This dreaming night may cast a spell;
So, driver, drive your taxi well.
I have a wondrous tale to tell:
  Immortal Love is now your fare!
So, driver, drive your taxi well
  To Golder's Green from Gloucester Squars!

AT RANDOM

I ORIGINALLY planned this chapter to cover A German Night amid the two German colonies of Great Charlotte Street and Highbury; but I have a notion that the public has read all that it wants to read about Germans in London. Anyway, neither spot is lovable. I have never been able to determine whether the Germans went to Highbury and the Fitzroy regions because they found their atmosphere ready-made, or whether the districts have acquired their atmosphere from the German settlers. Certainly they have everything that is most Germanically oppressive: mist, large women, lager and leberwurst, and a moral atmosphere of the week before last that conveys to the mind the physical sensations of undigested cold sausage. So I was leaving Great Charlotte Street, and its Kaiser, its *kolossal* and its *kultur*, to hop on the first motor-'bus that passed, and let it take me where it would—a favourite trick of mine—when I ran into Georgie.

I have mentioned Georgie before. Georgie is one of London's echoes—one of those sturdy Bohemians who stopped living when Sala died. If you frequent the Strand or Fleet Street or Oxford Street you probably know him by sight. He is short. He wears a frock-coat, buttoned at the waist and soup-splashed at the lapels. His boots are battered, his trousers threadbare. He carries jaunty eye-glasses, a jaunty silk hat, and shaves once a week. He walks with both hands in trousers pockets and feet out-splayed. The poor laddie is sadly outmoded, but he doesn't know it. He still lunches on a glass of stout and biscuit-and-cheese at " The Bun Shop " in the Strand. He still drinks whisky at ten o'clock in the morning. He still clings to the drama of the sixties, and he still addresses every one as Laddie or My Dear.

He hailed me in Oxford Street, and cried: " Where now, laddie, where now ? "

" I don't know," I said. " Anywhere."

" Then I'll come with you."

So we wandered. It was half-past seven. The night was purple, and through a gracious mist the lights glittered with subdued brilliance. London was in song. Cabs and 'buses and the evening crowd made its music. I heard it calling me. So did Georgie. With tacit sympathy we linked arms and strolled westwards, and dropped in at one of the big bars, and talked.

We talked of the old days—before I was born. Georgie told me of the crowd that decorated the place in the nineties : that company of feverish, foolish verbal confectioners who set themselves Byronically to ruin their healths and to write self-pitiful songs about the ruins. Half a dozen elegant Sadies and Mamies were at the American end of the bar, with their escorts, drinking Horse's Necks, Maiden's Prayers, Mother's Milks, Manhattans, and Scotch Highballs. Elsewhere the Cockney revellers were drinking their eternal whisky-and-sodas or beers, and their salutations led Georgie to a disquisition on the changing toasts of the last twenty years. To-day it is something short and sharp : either " Hooray ! " or " Here's fun ! " or " Cheero ! " or a non-commital " Wow-wow ! " Ten years back it was : " Well, laddie, here's doing it again ! " or " Good health, old boy, and may we get all we ask for ! " And ten years before that it was something even more grandiloquent.

From drink we drifted to talking about food ; and I have already told you how wide is Georgie's knowledge of the business of feeding in London. We both hate the dreary, many-dished dinners of the hotels, and we both love the cosy little chop-houses, of which a few only now remain : one or two in Fleet Street, and perhaps half a dozen in the little alleys off Cornhill and Lombard Street. I agree, too, with Georgie in deploring the passing of the public-house mid-day ordinary. From his recollections, I learn that the sixties and seventies were the halcyon days for feeding—indeed, the only time when Londoners really lived ; and an elderly uncle of mine, who, at that time, went everywhere and knew everybody in the true hard-up Bohemia, tells me that there were then twenty or thirty taverns within fifty yards of Ludgate Circus, where the shilling ordinary was a feast for an Emperor, and whose interiors answered to that enthusiastic description of Disraeli's in *Coningsby*— perhaps the finest eulogy of the English inn ever written.

Unhappily, they are gone to make way for garish, reeking hotels and restaurants for which one has to dress. Those that remain are mere drinking-places; you can, if you wish, get a dusty sandwich, but the barmaid regards you as an idiot if you ask for one. But there are exceptions.

" The Cock," immortalized by Tennyson, is one of the few survivals of the simple, and its waiters are among the best in London. As a rule, the English waiter is bad and the foreign waiter is good. But when you get a good English waiter you get the very best waiter in the world. There is Albert—no end of a good fellow. He shares with all English waiters a fine disregard for form ; yet he has that indefinable majesty which no Continental has ever yet assimilated ; and he has, too, a nice sense of the needs of those who work in Fleet Street. You can go to Albert (that isn't his true name) and say,—

"Albert, I haven't much money to-day. What's good and what do I get most of for tenpence?" Or "Albert—I've had a cheque to-day. What's best—and damn the expense?" And Albert advises you in each emergency, and whether you tip him twopence or a shilling you receive the same polite "Much obliged, sir!"

Georgie and I began to remember feeds we had had in London—real feeds, I mean; not "dinners," but the kind of food you yearn for when you are hungry, and have, perhaps, only eleven pennies in your pocket. At these times you are not interested in Rumpelmayer's for tea, or Romano's for lunch, or the Savoy for dinner. Nix. It's Lockhart's, The A B C., cook-shops, coffee-stalls, cab-shelters, and the hundred other what-not feeding-bins of London. I talked of the Welsh rarebits at "The Old Bell," the theatrical house in Wellington Street, and of the Friday night tripe-and-onion suppers at "The Plough," Clapham. Georgie thought that his fourpenny feed in the cab-shelter at Duncannon Street was an easy first, until I asked him if he knew the eating-houses of the South London Road, and his hard face cracked to a smile. I was telling him how, when I first had a definite commission from a tremendous editor, I had touched a friend for two shillings, and, walking home, had stopped in the London Road and had ordered dishes which were billed on the menu as *Pudding, boiled and carli.* FOLLOW *Golden Roll;* and this, capped by a pint of hot tea, for sevenpence, when he burst into my words with—

"The South London Road, laddie? You ask *me* if *I* know the South London Road? Come again, boy, come again; I don't get you." He lay back in his chair, and recited, with a half-smile: "The —South—London—Road! God, what sights for the hungry! Let's see—how do they go? Good Pull Up For Carmen on the right. Far Famed

Eel Pie and Tripe House opposite. Palace Restaurant, Noted For Sausages, next. Then The Poor Man's Friend. Then Bingo's Fish Bar. Coffee Caravanserai farther up. And—Lord !—S. P. and O. everywhere for threepence-halfpenny. What a sight, boy ! Ever walked down it at the end of a day without a meal and without a penny? I should say so. And nearly flung bricks through the windows—what? Sausages swimming in bubbling gravy. Or tucked in, all snug and comfy, with a blanket of mashed. Tomatoes frying themselves, and whining for the fun of it. Onions singing. Saveloys entrenched in pease-pudding. Jellied eels and stewed tripe and eel-pies at twopence, threepence, and sixpence. Irish stew at sevenpence on the Come-Again style—as many follows as you want for the same money. *Do* I know the South London Road? Does a duck know the water ? "

We talked of other streets in London which are filled with shop-windows glamorous of prospect for the gourmet ; and not only for the gourmet, but for all simple-minded folk. Georgie talked of the toy-shops of Holborn. He made gestures expressive of paradisaical delight. He is one of the few people I know who can sympathize with my own childishness. He never snubs my enthusiasms or my discoveries. Other friends sit heavily upon me when I display emotion over things like shops, taxicabs, dinners, drinks, railway journeys, music-halls, and cry, " Tommy—for the Lord's sake, *shut up!* " But Georgie understands. He understands why I cackle with delight when the new Stores Catalogue arrives. (By the way, if ever I made a list of the Hundred Best Books, number one would be an Illustrated Stores Catalogue. What a wonderful bedside book it is ! There is surely nothing so provocative to the sluggish imagination. Open it where you will, it fires an unending train of dreams.

It is so full of thousands of things which you simply must have and for which you have no use at all, that you finally put it down and write a philosophic essay on The Vanity of Human Wishes, and thereby earn three guineas. Personally, I have found over a dozen short-story plots in the pages of the Civil Service Stores List.)

When we tired of talking, Georgie inquired what we should do *now*. I put it: suppose we took a stroll along Bankside to London Bridge, and turned off to Bermondsey to take a taste of the dolours of the Irish colony, and then follow the river to Cherry Gardens and cross to Wapping by the Rotherhithe Tunnel; but he said No, and gave as his reason that the little girls of the Irish and foreign quarters were too distractingly lovely for him, as he is one of those unfortunates who want every pretty thing they see and are miserable for a week if they can't get it. His idea was to run over to Homerton. Did I know old Jumbo? Fat old Jumbo. Jumbo, who kept Jumbo's, under the arches, where you got cut from the joint, two veg., buggy-bolster, and cheese-roll. I did. So to Jumbo's we went by the Stoke Newington 'bus, whose conductor shouted imperatively throughout the journey: "Aw fez pliz!" though we were the only passengers; and on the way I made a little, soft song, the burden of which was: "I do love my table d'hôte, but O you Good Pull Up For Carmen!"

Jumbo received us with that slow good-humour which has made his business what it is. He and his assistant, Dusty, a youngster of sixty-two who cuts about like a newsboy, have worked together for so many years that Dusty frequently tells his chief not to be such a Censored fool. Jumbo's joints are good, and so are his steak-toad, sprouts, and baked, but his steak-and-kidney puddings at fourpence are better. I had one of these, garnished with "boiled and tops." Georgie had "leg, well done, chips, and batter." I never knew a man who could do the commonplace with so much natural dignity. He gave his order with the air of a viveur planning a ten-course arrangement at Claridge's. He shouted for a half-of-bitter with the solemnity of one who commands that two bottles of dry Monopole be put on the ice. He is, too, the only man I know who salutes his food. I have been at dinners in Wesleyan quarters like St. John's Wood where heads of families have mumbled what they call Grace or "asking a blessing"; but I have seen nothing so simply beautiful as Georgie's obeisance to his filled plate. He bows to Irish stew as others dip to the altar.

While Dusty stalked a clean fork through a forest of dirty ones, Georgie fired at him questions in which I had no part. Did Dusty remember the show at Willie's about—how many was it?—twenty years ago? What a NIGHT! Did he remember how Phil May had squirted the syphon down poor old Pitcher's neck? And Clarence . . . Clarence was fairly all out that night—what? And next morning—when they met Jimmy coming down the steps of the Garrick Club—*what?*"

To all of which Dusty replied: "Ah, yes, sir. I should say so. That's the idea, sir. Those was the days!" Then the dinner came along, and we started on it. I prefer to be attended by Jumbo. Dusty's service of steak-pudding is rather in the nature of a spar. Jumbo, on the other hand, places your plate before you with the air of one doing something sacramental.

While we ate we looked out on the sad lights of Homerton, and the shadowy arches and cringing houses. A queer place, whose flavour I have never rightly been able to catch. It is nondescript, but full of suggestion. Some day, probably, its message will burst upon me, and I expect it will be something quite obvious. The shadow of history hangs over it all. Six hundred years ago, in the velvet dusk of a summer night, Sir John Froissart galloped this way, by plaguey bad roads, and he beguiled the tedium of his journey by making an excellent new pastourelle. But you will hear no echo of this delicious song to-day : that lies buried for ever in the yellow mists of the MS. Room at the British Museum. Motor-'buses will snatch you from St. James's Palace, dash you through the City, and land you, within twenty minutes, breathless and bewildered, in the very spot where Sir John climbed from his steed. There is little now that is naughty and light-hearted. There is much that is sombrely wicked, and there are numbers of unsweetened ladies attached to the churches ; and if it should chance to be one of your bad days, you may hear, as you stand musing upon the fringe of the Downs, in place of Sir John's insouciant numbers, " Mein liebe Schwann . . ." and other trifles rendered by gramophone at an opposite villa. But if ever it had any charms, they are gone. We may read in our histories that about these parts kings and princes, soldiers and wits, counselled, carolled, and caroused ; but you would never think it. Too soon, I fancy, the music and the wine were done, the last word said, and the guests sent their several ways into the night. For nothing remains—nothing of that atmosphere which grows around every spot where people have loved, and suffered, and hated, and died ; only Jumbo and a nameless spirit remain.

It is one of the few places in town where the street-merchant survives in all his glory. Everywhere in London, of course, we have the coffeestall, the cockle, whelk, and escallop stall, the oyster bar (8d. per doz.), the baked potato and chestnut man, and (an innovation of 1914) the man in the white dress with a portable tin, selling *pommes frites* in grease-proof bags at a penny a time. But in Homerton, in addition to these, you have the man with the white-metal stand, selling a saveloy and a dab of pease-pudding for a penny, or boiled pig's trotters, or many kinds of heavy, hot cakes.

After our orgy, we bought a sweet cake, and Georgie took me to what looked like a dirty little beerhouse that hid itself under one of the passages that lead to the perilous Marshes of Hackney. We slipped into a little bar with room for about four persons, and Georgie swung to the counter, peremptorily smashed a glass on it, and demanded: " Crumdy munt—two ! " I was expecting a new drink, but the barman seemed to understand, for he brought us two tiny glasses of green liqueur, looked at Georgie, casually, then again, sharply, and said, in mild surprise, " God . . . it's old Georgie ! " and then went to attend the four-ale bar. When he came back we exchanged courtesies, and bought, for ourselves and for him, some of the sixpenny cigars of the house. We lingered over our drink in silence, and, for a time, nothing could be heard except the crackling of the saltpetre in the Sunday-Afternoon Splendidos. Then Georgie inquired what was doing at my end, and told me of what he was writing and of how he was amusing himself, and I told him equally interesting things.

.   .   .   .   .

It was half-past eight before Georgie and I were tired of Homerton ; and he then demanded what we should do *now*. I said : Return ; and it was carried. We went westwards, and called at Rule's for a chat with Harry, and then dropped in at The Alhambra, just in time to catch Phyllis Monkman at her Peruvian Pom-Pom dance in a costume that is surely one of the inspirations of modern ballet. We remained only long enough to pay homage to the young danseuse, and then drifted to those parts of the Square where, from evening until midnight, the beasts of pleasure pace their cells. I have often remarked to various people on the dearth of decent music in our lounges and cafés. I once discussed the matter with the *chef d'orchestre* of the Café de l'Europe, but he confessed his inability to reform matters. Why can't we have one place in London where one can get drinks, or coffee if desired, and listen to really good music? There is a mass of the best work that is suitable for quartet or quintet, or has been adapted for small orchestra; why is it never heard? Mr. Jacobs says that Londoners don't want it. I don't believe him. "If I play," he says, "anything of Mozart or Bach or Handel or Ravel or Chopin, they are impatient. They talk—ever so loud. And when it is finished, they rush up and say: ' Play "Hitchy Koo." ' ' Play "The Girl in the Taxi." ' " But I believe there is really a big public for a fully licensed café with a good band which shall have a definite programme of the best music every evening, and stick to that programme regardless of " special requests."

At the café where Georgie and I were lounging, the band was kept hard at work by these Requests. They were " La Bohème " selection, " That Midnight Choo-choo," " Tipperary," " Tales of Hoffman " Barcarolle, " All Aboard for Dixie," " In my Harem," and " The Ragtime Navvy." At the first bars of the Navvy we drifted out, and fell into the arms of The Tattoo Artist, who was taking an evening off.

The tattoo artist is a person of some consequence. He has a knowledge of London that makes most Londoners sick, and his acquaintance with queer and casual characters is illimitable. He was swollen with good food and drink, and as he extended a strong right arm to greet us, he positively shed a lustre of success and power. The state of business in all trades and professions may be heartbreakingly bad, but there is one profession in which there are no bad seasons—one that will survive and flourish until the world ceases to play the quaint comedy of love. All the world loves a lover, and none more so than the tattoo artist, or, to give him his professional name, Professor Sylvanus Ruffino, the world's champion, whose studio is in Commercial Road. When a young man of that district has been bitten by the serpent of love, what does he do? He goes to Sylvanus, and has the name of the lady, garnished with a heart or a floral cupid, engraved on his hands, arms, or chest. His " studio " is a tiny shop, with a gaudy chintz curtain for door, the window decorated with prints of the tattooed bodies of his clients. Elsewhere about the exterior are coloured designs of Chinese dragons, floral emblems, cupids, anchors, flags, and other devices with which your skin may be beautified at trifling cost—anything from sixpence to five shillings.

The professor works every evening from seven to ten o'clock, in his shirt-sleeves. In the corner of the studio is the operating-table, littered with small basins of liquid inks of various hues, and a sterilizing-vessel, which receives the electric needle after each client has been punctured. Winter, he tells me, contradicting the poet, is his best time. He finds that in Shadwell and the neighbourhood the young man's fancy turns more definitely to love in the dark evenings than in the spring. As soon as October sets in his studio is crowded with boys who desire the imprinting of beautiful names on their thick skins. He calculates that he must have tattooed the legend " Mizpah " some eight thousand times since he started in the business. Girls, too, sometimes visit him, and demonstrate their love for their boy in a chosen masculine way.

To-night he had snatched a few hours in the

West, and was just returning home. It being then well past twelve, we sauntered a little way with him, and called at a coffee-stall for a cup of the leathery tea which is the speciality of the London coffee-stall. Most stalls have their " regulars," especially those that are so fortunate as to pitch near a Works of any kind. The stall we visited was on the outskirts of Soho, and near a large colour-printing house which was then working day and night. I wonder, by the way, why printers always drink tea and stout in preference to other beverages. I wonder, too, why policemen prefer hard-boiled eggs above all other food.

It is a curious crowd that gathers about the stalls. In the course of a night you may meet there every type of Londoner. You may meet policemen, chauffeurs, printers, toughs, the boy and girl who have been to a gallery and want to finish the night in proper style, and—the cadgers. At about the middle of the night there is a curious break in the company: the tone changes. Up to four o'clock it's the stay-up-all-nights; after that hour it's the get-up-earlys. One minute there would be a would-be viveur, in sleek dress clothes; then along comes a cadger; then along comes a warrior from the battlefield. Then, with drowsy clatter, up comes a gang of roadmen, scavengers, railway workers, and so on. A little later comes the cheerful one who has made a night of it, and, somehow, managed to elude the police. He takes a cup of strong tea, demonstrates the graceful dancing of Mr. Malcolm Scott, and smashes two cups in doing it. Then up comes the sport, with a cert. for the big race to-day. Then up comes six o'clock, and the keeper packs up, and shoves his stall to its yard.

After a long exchange of reminiscences, we parted with the tattoo artist, and I walked home with Georgie, the outmoded, who lives in Vauxhall Bridge Road. I have often told him that the stiff, crinoline atmosphere of the place is the right touch for him, but he does not understand. It is a poor faded thing, this district ; not glamorously old ; just ridiculously out of fashion. Shops and houses are all echoes of the terrible seventies, and you seem to hear the painful wheezing of a barrel-organ, to catch a glimpse of side-whiskers and bustles, and to be encompassed by all the little shamefaced emotions of that period which died so long ago and only haunt us now in this street and in the provinces.

There, on the steps of one of the silly little houses, I parted from Georgie and this book.

www.ingramcontent.com/pod-product-compliance
Lightning Source LLC
Chambersburg PA
CBHW020325170426
43200CB00006B/280

PEARLS OF THE FAITH

OR

Islam's Rosary

BEING

THE NINETY-NINE BEAUTIFUL NAMES OF ALLAH

(ASMÂ-EL-HUSNÂ)

With Comments in Verse from various Oriental Sources
(AS MADE BY AN INDIAN MUSSULMAN)

BY

EDWIN ARNOLD, C.S.I.

AUTHOR OF "THE LIGHT OF ASIA"; "THE INDIAN
SONG OF SONGS"; ETC.

"Allah hath most excellent names, therefore call upon Him by the same." *Korân*, ch. vii. "*Al Aarâf*"

Copyright © 2011 Read Books Ltd.
This book is copyright and may not be
reproduced or copied in any way without
the express permission of the publisher in writing

British Library Cataloguing-in-Publication Data
A catalogue record for this book is available from
the British Library